T0291190

Lecture Notes in
Risk Management

World Scientific Lecture Notes in Finance

ISSN: 2424-9939

Series Editors: Professor Alexander Lipton and Professor Itzhak Venezia

This series provides high quality lecture note-type texts in all areas of finance, for courses at all levels: undergraduate, MBA and PhD. These accessible and affordable lecture notes are better aligned with today's classrooms and are written by expert professors in their field with extensive teaching experience. Students will find these books less formal, less expensive and also more enjoyable than many textbooks. Instructors will find all the material that they need, thus significantly reducing their class preparation time. Authors can prepare their volumes with ease, as they would be based on already existing, and actively used, lecture notes. With these features, this book series will make a significant contribution to improving the teaching of finance worldwide.

Published:

More information on this series can also be found at https://www.worldscientific.com/series/wslnf

World Scientific Lecture Notes in Finance – **Vol. 7**

Lecture Notes in Risk Management

Yevgeny Mugerman

Bar-Ilan University, Israel

Yoel Hecht

College of Management Academic Studies, Israel

World Scientific

NEW JERSEY · LONDON · SINGAPORE · BEIJING · SHANGHAI · HONG KONG · TAIPEI · CHENNAI · TOKYO

Published by

World Scientific Publishing Co. Pte. Ltd.

5 Toh Tuck Link, Singapore 596224

USA office: 27 Warren Street, Suite 401-402, Hackensack, NJ 07601

UK office: 57 Shelton Street, Covent Garden, London WC2H 9HE

Library of Congress Cataloging-in-Publication Data

Names: Mugerman, Yevgeny, author. | Hecht, Yoel, author.
Title: Lecture notes in risk management / Yevgeny Mugerman, Bar-Ilan University, Israel,
    Yoel Hecht, College of Management Academic Studies, Israel.
Description: New Jersey : World Scientific, [2023] | Series: World Scientific lecture notes in finance,
    2424-9939 ; Vol. 7 | Includes bibliographical references and index.
Identifiers: LCCN 2023000236 | ISBN 9789811271946 (hardcover) |
    ISBN 9789811271953 (ebook) | ISBN 9789811271960 (ebook other)
Subjects: LCSH: Risk management.
Classification: LCC HD61 .M767 2023 | DDC 658.15/5--dc23/eng/20230106
LC record available at https://lccn.loc.gov/2023000236

British Library Cataloguing-in-Publication Data
A catalogue record for this book is available from the British Library.

For any available supplementary material, please visit
https://www.worldscientific.com/worldscibooks/10.1142/13297#t=suppl

Desk Editors: Aanand Jayaraman/Lai Ann

Typeset by Stallion Press
Email: enquiries@stallionpress.com

To Marina, Rephael, Roni, Fany, Lior, Inbar and Roei, you are the pillars of strength and the driving force behind our work. This dedication serves as a token of our deep appreciation for your love, support and unwavering belief in our endeavors.

Preface

You started managing risk the moment you laid eyes on the cover of this book. Would the book be useful, or at the very least interesting?

We learn how to deal with risks from the moment we are born. Our parents teach us about the dangers present in the world and tell us that we must be careful. Schools teach us what happens to those who do not study hard enough. All too often, we learn that it is better to stay put and do nothing.

The goal of risk management is, in fact, the very opposite of inaction. Managing risk means doing things correctly, doing more.

In Formula One racing, a key element is the braking ability of the car. Vehicle manufacturers dedicate large amounts of money and resources to improving the braking capacity of the cars they produce. They invest in heat management systems for the tires, install additional systems that manage the g-forces applied to the wheels and modify the shock absorbers to tolerate stronger braking. These companies allocate a significant portion of their financial and intellectual resources to the issue of braking.

Why do they do this? Racing cars are supposed to go as fast as possible, so why do manufacturers dedicate so much time and money to the braking capacity of their cars?

Racing drivers, much like regular drivers, have to slow down before a curve in the road. With inferior brakes, they are forced to press down the brake pedal well before the curve, requiring a longer stretch of road to slow their car down. With better brakes, slowing down only requires a short segment immediately before the curve, giving the driver a few additional fractions of a second at every curve. These precious moments could mean the difference between winning and losing a race.

Thus, surprisingly enough, the motivation for investing in a better braking system is, in fact, to allow the car to go faster overall!

This is the essence of risk management. Companies that invest in their metaphorical brakes — i.e., identify the risks they face, quantify them, initiate procedures to reduce them, add controls to existing procedures and allocate a budget reserve to facilitate recovery in case of a failure event — in short, manage risks — not only manage to avoid potential damages and losses but are also able to take greater risks and increase their profits.

This book is aimed at lecturers, students and anyone else who has an interest in risk management. This book is the fruit of the authors' long years of work in the field of risk management, serving as a risk management advisor and teaching an MBA-level academic course on the topic for economics and business administration students.

This book is accompanied by PowerPoint presentations which serve as instructional aides to the book itself. The presentations are made available to instructors who adopt this book for their courses. The file name of each presentation begins with the relevant chapter number. Each chapter should be allotted 3–4 academic hours, according to the desired level of study.

About the Authors

Yevgeny Mugerman is a senior lecturer of finance at the Bar-Ilan Graduate School of Business Administration. Also, he is a visiting fellow at the Federmann Center for the Study of Rationality. His main research interests are in behavioral and corporate finance. He has been particularly interested in understanding the empirical determinants and implications of the importance of the influence of behavioral factors considering financial decisions. As an independent (self-employed) adviser, his areas of concentration include damage assessment, causation analysis, valuation reports, market efficiency analysis, and expert witness testimony.

Yoel Hecht is a lecturer of financial risk at the College of Management Academic Studies — School of Economics master's degree program. He is an economist specializing in risk management, macroeconomics, and econometrics. He has worked at the Central Bank of Israel for many years during which he published position papers and articles in the field of FX markets, financial risks, banking and monetary policy. He served as the director of the risk department at the Statistical Analysis System (SAS), Israel. He is an entrepreneur and partner in a FinTech company that supplies a Web platform for managing loans, a risk manager at wealth management investment house, and a data analyst at commercial banks.

Acknowledgments

We gratefully acknowledge and extend our sincerest gratitude to all those who have contributed to the development and publication of this book.

First and foremost, we would like to express our heartfelt appreciation to the esteemed scholars, researchers, and industry experts who have generously shared their profound insights and expertise as contributors to this book. It is through your unwavering dedication and commitment to advancing the field of financial risk management that this book has been shaped into a valuable resource.

We would also like to convey our deepest gratitude to the diligent reviewers who meticulously assessed the chapters, providing invaluable feedback and suggestions that greatly enhanced the quality and coherence of this book. Your expertise and meticulous attention to detail have played a pivotal role in ensuring its academic rigor and relevance.

Our thanks are extended to the academic and research institutions that have supported our endeavors. Your continuous encouragement and provision of resources have been indispensable in facilitating our research and enabling the successful publication of this book.

Furthermore, we wish to express our profound appreciation to the exceptional editorial and production teams involved in the publication process. Your professionalism, expertise and unwavering dedication have been instrumental in ensuring the seamless execution of this project and the timely publication of this book.

Lastly, we are deeply grateful to our families, friends and colleagues for their unwavering support and understanding throughout the journey of producing this book. Your encouragement and belief in our work have served as a constant source of inspiration.

Once again, we extend our deepest appreciation to all who have contributed to this book. It is through your collective efforts that this publication has come to fruition, and we sincerely hope that it will serve as an invaluable resource for researchers, practitioners, lecturers and students in the field.

Contents

Chapter 1

Introduction

Accompanying presentation: 1. Risk Management — Introduction

1.1. Historical Milestones in Financial Risk Management[1]

Financial risk management as an academic discipline only came into existence in the years following the Second World War,[2] and the first academic books on the subject[3] were not published until the 1960s.

Since then, the field has seen rapid growth, accumulating extensive knowledge and expertise and becoming an integral component of business administration, public administration and international regulation.

Risk Management

- Academic study of risk management began after the Second World War.
  Source: Georges Dionne (2013).

- The years 1955–1964 mark the beginning of modern risk management.
  Source: Crockford (1982), Harrington and Neihaus (2003), Williams and Heins (1995).

- The first two academic books on the subject of risk management were published in 1963–1964.
  Source: Mehr and Hedges (1963) and Williams and Heins (1964).

---

[1]See also Georges Dionne (2013). Risk Management: History, Definition and Critique. *Risk Management and Insurance Review*, 16(2), 147–166.

[2]Georges Dionne (2013). According to Crockford (1982), Harrington and Neihaus (2003), Williams and Heins (1995), financial risk management in its modern form can trace its origins to the years 1955–1964.

[3]Mehr and Hedges (1963) and Williams and Heins (1964).

In this chapter, we shall present in chronological order some of the most significant milestones in the history of financial risk management and explain how they have influenced the development of the field from its infancy and up to the present day:

The first milestone in the history of risk management is the subject of an entertaining debate. Some would point to the Biblical story of the contract between Jacob and Laban. The vagueness of the contract's terms resulted in the materialization of legal risk — although the contract was supposed to grant Jacob the right to marry Rachel, Laban's youngest daughter, Jacob instead ended up marrying Leah, the eldest daughter, and had to work for seven more years before Laban would finally allow him to marry Rachel.

Others would put that first milestone at an even earlier point in the same story, arguing that Laban, in the business of financial derivatives pricing, sold Jacob an option granting him the right to marry Rachel for the premium of seven years of labor.

Others would go still further, all the way back to the Garden of Eden. According to this argument, the conduct of Adam and Eve surrounding the forbidden fruit was an example of failed risk management. This brought about a severe crisis, the consequences of which humanity continues to suffer to this very day.

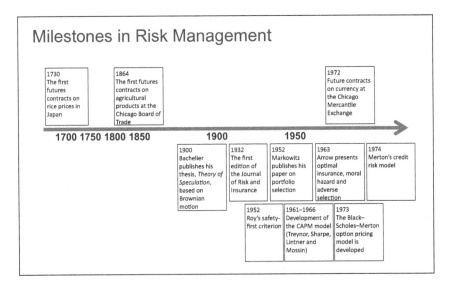

1730: We begin this historical overview with the first milestone of financial risk management in modern history. In 1730, the Dōjima Rice Exchange in Osaka, Japan, began trading in futures contracts. In those days, samurai would receive their wages in rice. The amount of rice was fixed, but its monetary value would vary depending on the abundance and quality of the season's harvest. Futures contracts made it possible to assign a fixed value to samurai wages, independent of fluctuations in rice prices. This milestone marked the first time that futures contracts were used as a tool to facilitate risk management, mitigating the market risks which had affected routine business activity since then. This was the starting point of an **era in which business needs play a key role in risk management**, an era which continues to our time.

1864: More than 130 years after futures contracts were introduced in Japan, the Chicago Board of Trade (CBOT) began conducting trade in agricultural commodity futures. This made it possible to plan business activity based on mutually agreed-upon commodity prices. CBOT continues to operate until our time and now conducts trade in thousands of futures contracts, as well as other types of derivatives that have developed over the years. This milestone saw regular business activity spark a development of additional tools for managing market risk.

1900: In 1900, French mathematician Louis Bachelier published his theoretical work, *Théorie de la speculation* (*The Theory of Speculation*), in which he conducted an analysis of the French stock market. This was considered a groundbreaking thesis: Bachelier, for the first time, made use of the model of Brownian motion to describe the development of financial asset prices analytically.

This was the first time market prices had ever received in-depth academic care and as such was a significant milestone in academic research.[4] Bachelier's thesis marks the start of the **academic era of risk**

---

[4] Some interesting facts…

A few interesting facts about the progression of scientific research into Brownian motion are as follows:

- Brownian motion was discovered in 1827 by Scottish botanist Robert Brown, who was researching the random movement of pollen in water.
- Not until 1880 did Danish astronomer Thorvald Nicolai Thiele outline the mathematical foundation of Brownian motion in an article on the method of least squares.

management, which has greatly contributed to our knowledge and understanding of various areas — definition and classification of risks, assessment and measurement of market risk and other types of risks, risk pricing, the invention of new tools to reduce and hedge risk and of course spreading all this new knowledge.

1932: This year marked the founding of the American Risk and Insurance Association. The Association began publishing the *Journal of Insurance*, which contained the first academic articles dedicated to risk management, primarily on the topic of insurance. Later on, the Association issued two publications: the *Journal of Risk and Insurance* and *Risk Management and Insurance Review*.

Many other risk management journals have sprung up since then, facilitating academic discussion of the ever-growing field and furthering its expansion.

1952: In March 1952, *The Journal of Finance* published an article on portfolio selection by Nobel laureate Harry Max Markowitz. What set this article apart from those that had come before was the integration of return and risk into the decision-making process, resulting in a portfolio composition based on the optimal distribution of assets.

1952: In July of the same year, *Econometrica* published an article by Arthur Roy presenting **Roy's safety-first criterion** for choosing between portfolios according to the principles of risk management. Roy's proposed innovation was to compare only the expected losses of the various portfolios, in order to select the portfolio with the lowest probability of significant losses.

- The mathematical development of Brownian motion was further advanced by Nobel-winning physicists, such as Albert Einstein and Norbert Wiener. Wiener's progress in the field proved to be particularly valuable to subsequent research.
- In 1973, Fischer Black and Myron Scholes published an article in which they presented the options pricing formula which came to be known as the Black–Scholes formula (which is included in the following as a milestone in its own right). Although they did not quote Bachelier directly in their article, his theory provided the groundwork for the description of the development of financial asset prices upon which they based their pricing model.

1961–1966: Treynor, Sharpe, Lintner and Mossin developed the Capital Asset Pricing Model (CAPM) and calculated the additional yield required to compensate for the risk of loss. This model is considered a milestone in financial risk management as it made it possible to assign a monetary value to risk, what is today referred to as a **risk premium**.

1963: Research into risk management continued with the publication of an article by Kenneth Arrow, who would later win the Nobel Prize in Economics, in 1972. The article, titled *Uncertainty and the Welfare Economics of Medical Care*, introduced two new concepts into the field of risk management: **moral hazard** and **adverse selection**. It would be ten years from the publication of Arrow's article until the next breakthrough in the field.

1972: Having abandoned the Bretton Woods system in favor of a U.S. Dollar exchange rate based on market forces, the Chicago Mercantile Exchange (CME) began trading in currency futures. This development meant that additional tools were now available to assist in the management of currency risk. Nevertheless, the academic study of risk management up to that point played no significant role in the development of this system.

1973: Fischer Black and Myron Scholes published an article in which they presented a formula for options pricing, which subsequently became known as the Black–Scholes formula. This was the first time an academic breakthrough in risk management has had such a substantial impact on the market.[5]

---

[5] Some interesting facts…

A few interesting facts on the article by Black and Scholes are as follows:

- Economist and Nobel laureate Robert C. Merton was the first to publish a mathematical model for options pricing. He had already made most of the theoretical progress in the development of the model before Black and Scholes published their work. It was the latter pair, however, who ultimately won the Nobel Prize for their work in the field, for proposing a method to implement Merton's model, using a simple formula which contained the assumption that the distribution of asset prices was a normal distribution, as well as a number of other simplifying assumptions. This was the formula adopted in the market, which remains at the base of options pricing since then until our time.

1974: Robert C. Merton published a model for calculating a company's credit risk, utilizing an expanded version of Bachelier's Brownian motion coupled with a number of simplifying assumptions. His article proposed innovative methods for quantifying credit risk, and it managed to find its way out of academic circles and into the world of finance. Private businesses and banks have since made extensive use of the ideas presented in Merton's article.

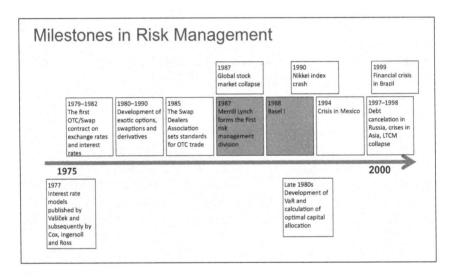

1975: Academic research into risk management continues, with the work of Cox, Ingersoll and Ross outlining a model for the evolution of interest rates. This model made use of an extended version of Brownian motion, as well as another extended mathematical model published by Vašíček describing the evolution of interest. Their work made it possible to implement a pricing system for interest rate derivatives.

- Merton himself coined the term "Black–Scholes options pricing model" in an article he published later in 1973.
- Most academic financial journals refused to publish Black and Scholes's article, claiming it was too revolutionary.
- Their article was eventually printed in the *Journal of Political Economy*, which was in fact an economic journal rather than a financial one.
- Until our time, the Black–Scholes model remains the most widely-used risk pricing model for derivatives markets around the world.

1979–1982: The first swaps are traded over the counter (OTC). These contracts make it possible to exchange the cash flow from one financial asset for the cash flow from another. One of the earliest and best-known swap deals was signed between IBM and the World Bank. IBM required its cash flow in U.S. Dollars, while the World Bank sought German Marks and Swiss Francs.

Swaps are among the most extensively traded financial assets world-wide, with trillions of U.S. Dollars in swaps traded every day — several times the entire gross world product for an entire year!

1980–1990: During these years, the area of exotic options trading saw significant development. Exotic options are options with complex features, such as multiple triggers. For example, the option to purchase Euros for U.S. Dollars at an exchange rate higher than EUR 1.2 per U.S. Dollar will only come into effect if the EUR/USD exchange rate rises above 1.3 at least once during the option's lifetime and various calculations of base asset price (e.g., monthly price average). In a later section of this book, we will expand on the different types of exotic options. It is important to note that despite their exotic name and the speculative nature, it would seem to imply, exotic options do, in fact, serve to reduce and hedge risk.

1985: The Swap Dealers Association established a set of standards for OTC trade. These standards ensured uniformity in business specifications and simplified trade between various financial institutions across the world.

1987: The financial crisis known as Black Monday occurred on October 19, 1987. Stock markets worldwide plummeted by tens of percentage points. Although we will not describe crisis in great depth, the reasons for its occurrence, the contagion effect which caused the crisis to spread across the world, from Hong Kong, through Western Europe and all the way to the United States, Australia and New Zealand (where it became known as Black Tuesday due to the differing time zones), its analysis and its consequences are fascinating in and of themselves.

Nevertheless, as we shall see, the crisis had some far-reaching implications for risk management. In the wake of the crisis, two years after its occurrence, regulators[6] began conducting risk management with a global outlook.

1987: The global financial crisis caused American investment broker Merrill Lynch to form a risk management division. This was the first time risk management had been recognized by a business firm as an independent field, requiring the constant attention of professionals in order to effectively reduce the market risk to which the company is exposed.

1988: As a consequence of Merrill Lynch's decision, the first of the Basel Accords was drafted. The Accord, which subsequently became known as Basel I, would be adopted by regulators in several countries, primarily in Europe. It contained banking management rules which were designed to reduce the scope of market and credit risks faced by banks in those countries that chose to implement its recommendations. These standards were so widely adopted that banks which would not comply with them were either prohibited from conducting business altogether or forced to pay a substantial fine in order to continue operations.

In 1988, regulation gained an international aspect for the first time, due to the understanding that a financial crisis in one country could soon lead to crises in neighboring countries. Basel I marks the beginning of **the era of international regulation**.

Late 1980s: A new measurement approach was developed, bearing the name Value at Risk (VaR). This will be discussed in depth later on. This method quantifies the risk in the event of an extreme crisis, of the sort that occurred on Black Monday. Bankers Trust was the first organization to make use of this method in its business activity, and virtually all banks have since followed suit. This method calculates the capital required to preserve the financial well-being of a banking institution. Several years later, regulators in many countries adopted this system, requiring all banks under their jurisdiction to allocate capital accordingly.

1990: Yet another crisis struck financial markets, this time with the collapse of the Nikkei index. This crisis marked the end of a financial bubble

---

[6]Bank and currency regulators, securities authorities, etc.

which had formed in the Japanese market, leading to a severe economic crisis in Japan and two decades of stunted growth in the country.

1994: Mexico found itself in an economic crisis, despite seemingly favorable macroeconomic conditions — a successful monetary policy had reduced annual inflation from 160% to just 7%, the budget was balanced, external and internal debt had been reduced, capital flows liberalized, free-market economic reform implemented, administrative distortions eliminated and the North American Free Trade Agreement (NAFTA) had been signed with Canada and the United States.

At that time, boundaries on the exchange rate ("Target Zone") had been implemented for the currency. In March 1994, in the aftermath of the assassination of the ruling party's candidate in the presidential elections, the value of peso dropped sharply, sticking to the upper limit of the target zone. In an attempt to protect its exchange rate, Mexico lost approximately USD 19 billion, leaving it with foreign exchange reserves of just USD 6 billion. At this point, Mexico chose to abandon the controlled exchange rate system and adopted a floating exchange rate, and the currency devalued by almost 90%. The collapse of the peso destabilized the entire financial system in the country. In an effort to prevent Mexico's impending bankruptcy and avert the crisis, the United States and the International Monetary Fund (IMF) put together an assistance package of USD 52 billion.

The Mexican crisis raised many doubts about the ability of a state to artificially stabilize its currency, particularly in times of financial pressure which would otherwise lead to currency devaluation.

Nevertheless, a number of other countries would experience currency crises of their own, losing significant portions of their foreign exchange reserves, before learning Mexico's lesson.

1997–1998: A further series of financial crises occurred. In 1997, Thailand lost billions of U.S. Dollars in an attempt to protect its currency. Giving in to market pressures, ending government intervention in the foreign exchange market and transitioning to a floating exchange rate caused the Thai baht to experience a 55% devaluation.

The local currencies of Malaysia and South Korea also dropped by 55%, and in Indonesia by 80%. The IMF pumped tens of billions of U.S.

Dollars in loans into these economies in order to assist in the recovery process.

These crises affected national production, employment and investment rates in these countries and led to mass protests by citizens, concerned about the lack of basic goods and the inability to repay the IMF loans.

The economic crises in East Asia were an important milestone which underlined the connection between negative developments in financial markets and economic crises affecting every citizen, and in particular disadvantaged sectors far removed from the financial market.

In August 1998, the wave of crises spread to Russia. The Russian government, with Boris Yeltsin at its head, announced that it would be unable to repay its debts and would initiate a process of debt relief.

Russia's debt relief led to a default on large debt payments to the Long-Term Capital Management (LTCM) hedge fund.[7] This hedge fund was unique by virtue of its use of mathematical formulas to create allegedly risk-free arbitrage profits and because Nobel laureates Black and Scholes were members of the fund's board of directors. LTCM's collapse became a significant milestone for two reasons:

First, since then until our time, the fund's collapse is given as an example of the enormous risk potential of financial markets.

Second, the fund's collapse served as a "proof" by contradiction for the argument against the use of mathematical models in policy and business-related decision-making, due to the inability of such models to take into account the human element involved. As a result, the analytical models were more carefully examined in order to reduce the model risks.

---

[7]Some interesting facts...

A few interesting facts on LTCM are as follows:
- LCTM's specialization was in using arbitrage gaps in bond pricing.
- The fund saw phenomenal returns — double-digit percentages every year between 1994 and 1997.
- The preeminent group involved with the fund was doctors and professors who were leaders in the field — among them were Nobel laureates Black and Scholes.
- Before the crisis, the fund's exposure reached a trillion U.S. Dollars, the equivalent of the GDP of a mid-sized country.

1999 — Crisis strikes Brazil: Having lost about half of its USD 70 billion of foreign exchange reserves, which were supposed to protect the exchange rate, Brazil learned the same lesson Mexico had learned five years previously.

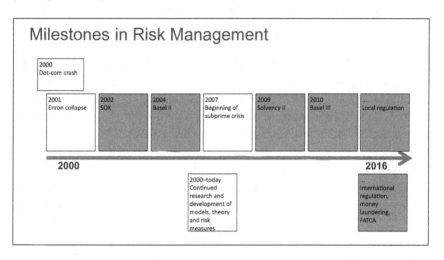

2000 — The dot-com crash: Internet companies had become modern-day "gold mines", and stock indices soared upwards for several years. NASDAQ doubled within a year from 2,500 to 5,000 points. This rapid rise in stock indices, however, represented a bubble which did not accurately reflect the actual growth of the traded companies. It was only a matter of time before investors realized that stock prices were significantly higher than the actual company values and started selling their shares. In the year 2000, many stock indices collapsed, with NASDAQ plummeting to below 2000 points. This was called the "dot-com crash".

2001 — The Enron scandal: Enron was a U.S.-based energy company which specialized primarily in electricity and natural gas. At its peak, the company employed 21,000 people. Enron filed for bankruptcy in 2001 after it was revealed that the company had falsified its balance sheets. Investors lost more than USD 60 billion as a result of this scam, and Enron's employees lost billions more in pension funds.

2002 — The Sarbanes–Oxley (SOX) Act: After the collapse of Enron, U.S. Senator Paul Sarbanes and U.S. Representative Michael G. Oxley sponsored the Sarbanes–Oxley Act, which stipulated that senior executives of public companies would be required to declare that the accounting reports published by their firm were an accurate reflection of the company's financial status. This law was a milestone for the implementation of organizational regulations and increasing the liability of corporate officers.

2004 — Basel II: The second Basel Accord was published, with over 100 signatory nations. The Accord, which dealt with the subject of banking risk management, extended the mitigation of market risks and credit risks, and, for the first time, specified regulations pertaining to operational risk management, which would be applied to all regulated banks.

2000 — Present day: Economic research into risk management continues, and the use of various risk indices has become widespread throughout the market. An empirical and theoretical breakthrough in decision-making under risk conditions earned its proponents, Daniel Kahneman and Amos Tversky, the Nobel Prize in Economics.[8] In a series of empirical experiments, the pair demonstrated that people do not always make rational decisions. Although this claim might seem obvious, the two managed to formulate a mathematical model for irrational decision-making and provided empirical evidence.

This model explains why people purchase lottery tickets, hoping to win against almost impossible odds, or, to give an example where the opposite occurs, why people choose not to apply for a job despite favorable odds, out of fear of failure.

2007 — The subprime crisis: In 2007, financial institutions began to collapse after borrowers, unable to repay their debts, defaulted on their mortgages. The price of apartments, which had been used as collateral, began to drop due to falling demand and the rising of supply, which was

---

[8] Some interesting facts…

Prof. Daniel Kahneman alone won the Nobel Prize in Economics in 2002, his partner Amos Tversky having passed away in 1996. The award had been granted, however, for an article written jointly by the two men. Shortly after winning the Nobel Prize, Daniel Kahneman stated: "I feel it is a joint prize. We were twinned for more than a decade." Since then, both men are mentioned together whenever the prize is mentioned.

the result of an attempt by financial institutions to realize the collateral. The collapse of the real estate market might have remained within the confines of the borders of the United States, but a part of the debt has been leveraged abroad. In practice, the real estate crisis triggered a general drop in U.S. stock indices, began snowballing and by early 2008 had reached global proportions.

One of the measures adopted by the U.S. Federal Reserve (the Fed) in an attempt to avoid a credit crunch was the lowering of interest rates to extremely low levels. By the end of 2008, the Fed's interest rate stood at just 0.25%.

This was an important milestone as, since the end of the subprime crisis, interest risk has changed dramatically. First of all, the crisis ushered an era of extremely low (sometimes even negative) interest rates worldwide. Second, fluctuations in interest rates were greatly reduced. Third, hopes of interest rates returning have been dashed time and time again, reducing the weight assigned to statistical risk indices and greatly increasing the importance of scenario-based risk management. Fourth, the use of central bank interest rates as a policy tool for managing market purchasing power was greatly limited — interest rates may still be raised, and so they remain an effective tool for times of increased inflation; however, as they cannot be lowered too much any further, they are no longer effective in case of price drops.

2009 — The Solvency II Directive: In the spirit of Basel II's recommendations on banking risk, insurance companies came out with their own set of directives for measuring insurance risks. The allocation of capital required to maintain the stability of insurance companies even in times of crisis was determined through risk aggregation. Despite the extensive experience gained implementing regulations in capital markets, it has taken years for insurance companies to implement these recommendations, and the process continues.

2010 — Basel III: Additional recommendations for the banking sector were turned into active regulation in many countries. The novelty of these recommendations was their mitigation of liquidity risk and asset liability management. According to the new regulations, banks are now required to perform heavy analytical calculations. For instance, in addition to disclosing future payments and obligations in great detail, they must perform dynamic simulations featuring the reactions of lenders and borrowers to various changes. Thus, for example, in addition to the standard tests, which are sensitive to upward and downward changes in interest rates, they must also take into account the changes in supply and demand which may be expected in response to these changed interest rates.

Local regulation: Local regulations remain in effect, with country-specific directives and instructions in place. To give an example, there has been growing concern regarding the issue of cybersecurity, and each country is adopting its own independent measures to tackle the issue.

International regulation (money laundering and the Foreign Account Tax Compliance Act (FATCA)): As part of its effort to combat tax evasion, the United States now demands reports on the financial status of U.S. citizens living abroad. The U.S. requires that foreign banks deliver reports on their citizens and prohibits business relations with any non-compliant institution. Many other countries have responded in kind, requesting reports on their citizens living in the United States as well as in other countries. Thus, financial institutions must report not only to the local regulator but also to the authorities of foreign nations.

As part of the international war against money laundering, financial institutions are required to track cash flows actively and verify the legitimacy and legality of funds originating from foreign financial institutions.

It must be said that the implementation of international regulation is far from simple.[9] In the European Union, for instance, every directive must be published in multiple languages, and the particulars of a directive may vary from one translation to the next.

1.1.1. *Conclusion*

The various milestones of risk management may be divided into three categories:

1. **Developments in risk management due to business needs:** From the early futures trading of 1730 and all the way to the present day,

---

[9]Mugerman, Y., Hecht, Y., & Wiener, Z. (2019). On the failure of mutual fund industry regulation. *Emerging Markets Review*, 38, 51–72.

numerous milestones across almost three centuries have underlined the need for risk management in markets in order to maintain regular business activity even in the event of failure.

2. **Academic research into risk management:** A series of milestones, mostly in the middle of the 20th century, have led to a number of breakthroughs in our ability to measure and understand risks. Toward the end of the 20th century, academic research and business requirements formed a bond of mutual correspondence and influence. Academic knowledge rapidly found its way into financial markets and corporate boardrooms worldwide.

3. **International regulation:** Every state has long possessed its own methods for regulating financial institutions. However, with the growing understanding that risks in one country could spread to other countries, regulators began to seek international regulation which would reduce the risk of financial crises spreading from one country to another. This is a relatively recent development of the past three decades or so, but extraordinary progress has been made during this short time.

In academic terms, risk management is a relatively new field of study, compared to such traditional fields as philosophy, astronomy, mathematics or physics. This is a growing field which offers many opportunities for pure research and for research and development (R&D) of both new tools for risk trading and advanced regulation methods.

1.2. Basic Concepts: Certainty, Uncertainty, Risk and Exposure

As in every profession, risk management also possesses its own jargon, and some key concepts must be defined before we can continue. While some of these terms are used in everyday conversation, in the field of risk management, they have acquired a very precise and specific meaning. The following are the most fundamental concepts of risk management:

Uncertainty vs. Risk

- Certainty
  - A given scenario effectively has a single possible outcome
    - It is a basic working assumption in risk management that the possibility of alternative outcomes always exists, however miniscule it may be.
- Risk
  - A given scenario has multiple possible outcomes
  - The probability of each outcome occurring is known
- Uncertainty
  - A given scenario has multiple possible outcomes
  - The probability of each outcome occurring is *not* known

- **Certainty**

A given situation has only a single possible outcome.[10]

Despite the prevalent skepticism surrounding the human capacity for prediction and prophecy, it is indeed possible to assume with certainty that some things will occur. For instance, a person swimming in the sea will get wet and therefore would be wise to bring along a towel.

As demonstrated by this example, there is room for risk assessment even in cases where certainty exists. This is typically a relatively simple process in such instances.

- **Risk**

A given situation has several possible outcomes, and the probability of each of these outcomes is known.

For example, the exchange rate of the U.S. Dollar against the Euro could go either up or go down tomorrow. The likelihood of each eventuality occurring is 50%.

As its name implies, the risk management process is intended for such risk scenarios. The tools that risk management provides for measuring and reducing risk and for maintaining business continuity ensure that risk scenarios are dealt with in the most effective manner possible.

---

[10]Nevertheless, it is a fundamental working assumption in risk management that even at the highest levels of certainty, other eventualities are still possible, however improbable they may be.

- **Uncertainty**

A given situation has several possible outcomes, but these outcomes are unknown (naturally, the probability of each outcome occurring is also unknown).

Geopolitical developments in Europe or China, or the effects of technological progress on the economy over the next two years are examples of uncertainty.

Situations involving uncertainty are the most complex type of situation to manage. Dealing with the unknown is also difficult from a psychological perspective. Decision makers, however, often have a tendency to define the situations they are faced with as situations of uncertainty, even when the situation is in fact one of risk and therefore easier to manage.

Furthermore, through effective risk management, it is often possible to reduce the extent of uncertainty by studying the situation in detail and remolding it into a risk situation, or, alternatively, reducing exposure to situations of uncertainty.

Now that we have defined these concepts, we shall give the following pair of examples:

Example 1: A commercial bank is looking to appoint a new risk manager

---

Example

A commercial bank is searching for a new CRO

- Certainty
  - The bank will pick a new CRO.
  - The probability that the bank will withdraw the tender and leave the position vacant is extremely small.

  Decision:
  I am interested in the job and would like to find out further details.

The chief risk officer (CRO) at a commercial bank has been reassigned and the bank is looking for a replacement to fill the position. It is certain that the bank will select a CRO, as the position is mandated by regulations which stipulate that banks must appoint a CRO.

I decide I am interested in the position and proceed to seek further details.

Example

A commercial bank is searching for a new CRO

- Uncertainty
  - I do not know who else has applied for the position, how many other candidates there are or how high my odds of getting the job are.

  <u>Decision:</u>
  I apply for the position.

I don't know how many other people are applying for the job or what my odds of success are. This is an example of the uncertainty that many people, lacking crucial information, face when looking for a job.

Example

A commercial bank is searching for a new CRO

- Risk
  - It turns out two other people are applying for the position.
  - The odds against me getting the job are 2/3, and the odds in favor 1/3.

  <u>Question:</u>
  - Should I withdraw my application to avoid the potential embarrassment of failure?

After a while, it turns out two other people have applied for the job. Both candidates have the same odds of acceptance as I do. This means that the probability that I will get the job is one-third, and the probability that I will not get it is two-thirds. The uncertainty turns to risk.

Still, this is a difficult dilemma, particularly for employees working for large organizations (e.g., banks), where an unsuccessful job application could tarnish their reputation and have an adverse impact on future job applications.

Every time we have students to vote on the question of whether or not to withdraw the application, the vote was inconclusive. In this risk situation, where both the outcomes themselves and the probability of their occurrence are known, different people make different choices. Some students assign greater weight to the potential damage and choose to withdraw their application, whereas others assign lesser weight to the damage and choose to proceed. This decision-making phenomenon was aptly described by Nobel laureates Daniel Kahneman and Amos Tversky, whose work was described in greater detail in the previous section, at the milestone for the year 2000.

Example 2: Buying a car

Example 2

I have bought a car

- Certainty
  - If I have an accident. I will not be able to afford to pay for the repairs and compensations.

I have a low-salary job but I have decided to buy a car. I can say with certainty that, in the event of an accident, I would not have enough money to afford to pay for any repairs or compensations.

Example 2

I have bought a car

■ Uncertainty
  · I myself may be a cautious driver, but I do not know how careful the
    other drivers on the road are.

  Decision:
  I buy insurance.

Although I can significantly reduce the probability of an accident occurring by driving carefully and only when traffic is light, I do not know how
cautious the other drivers are or at what time reckless drivers take to the
road. In this situation, I do not have information about every single possible accident eventuality or about the other drivers on the road, and
therefore I decide to purchase an insurance policy.

Example 2

The insurance company

■ Risk
  · A driver has approached us seeking to purchase insurance. We can
    measure the probability that the driver will be involved in an accident in
    the coming year.
  · We can also calculate the risk premium.

  Outcome:
  · The insurance company sells me a policy.
    Note the contrast between my uncertainty and the risk as seen by the insurance company.

From the perspective of the insurance company I approach, the eventuality of an accident occurring is not one of uncertainty but one of risk. The
insurance company gathers information on every driver and analyzes it in
order to estimate the probability of my involvement in an accident in the
next year. The insurance company also calculates the cost of this risk and
thus determines my insurance premium.

I buy the insurance.

In this example, a situation, which for me is one of uncertainty, is one of risk for the insurance company.

- **Exposure**

Risk exposure is the damage potential due to the occurrence of some sort of failure. This damage may be measured in various ways, such as money, loss of life and reputation.

Risk Exposure

- The potential loss which could be caused due to the occurrence of some event.

A company whose entire operation is conducted in U.S. Dollars, but which owns assets in Euros, faces potential financial losses if the value of the Euro depreciates.

The risk management process depends on identifying the exposure and risk factors which could result in a failure and estimating the potential damage from such a failure.

An example of exposure is as follows:

Example

Exporter
- Income — 1,000,000 GBP
- Expenses — 1,300,000 USD
  - This includes salaries, raw materials, electricity, water, office expenses, etc.
- The GBP/USD exchange rate is 1.3
  - 1,000K*1.3–1,300K $\cong 0$
  - The exporter breaks even

An exporter from the U.S. has an income of one million British pounds from exporting goods to the U.K. By contrast, this exporter must pay USD 1.3 million in salaries, raw materials, electricity, water, office expenses, etc.

The exporter breaks even when the GBP/USD exchange rate stands at 1.3.

Example

Exporter
- What is the risk to which the exporter is exposed?
- What possible event could cause the exporter to suffer a loss?
- What is the extent of the exporter's exposure to this risk?

Example

Exporter
- Income – 1,000,000 GBP
- Expenses – 1,300,000 USD
  - This includes salaries, raw materials, electricity, water, office expenses, etc.
- The GBP/USD exchange rate is 1.3
  - 1,000K*1.3-1,300K ≅ 0
  - The exporter breaks even

The previous image is visible at the bottom right corner of the current image as a reference.

- The risk to which the exporter is exposed is exchange rate risk.
- More specifically, the exporter is exposed to U.S. Dollar appreciation. If this happens, the GBP/USD exchange rate will drop below 1.3, and the value of the income will be lower than that of the expenses. For instance, an exchange rate of 1.2 would mean a loss of $100,000 ($1,000K \times 1.2 - 1,300K = -100K$).
- The scope of the exposure in this example is the entire sum of one million Pounds sterling (or USD 1.3 million). Such a risk will only materialize if the expression "risk potential" signifies in the context of determining exposure with no relation to the probability it will happen (though the probability that this will occur is more than 0 but very small).

1.3. Identifying Risks

The first step of the risk management process is the identification and classification of risks.

Risk Identification

- A systematic process for defining and recording the obstacles to reaching business goals
  - Market risk (stocks, exchange rates and interest rates)
  - Credit risk
  - Liquidity risk
  - Operational risk (embezzlement, fraud, physical damage and system failure)
  - Insurance risk (life, health and general insurance)
  - Reputational risk
  - Others (regulatory risk, country risk, geographic risk, etc.)

Some risk management consulting firms maintain lists detailing hundreds or even thousands of different risks. However, risks are typically classified according to a number of categories, which will be examined in detail in the following chapters.

- **Market risk**

Market risk pertains to changes in market prices, e.g., share prices, exchange rates and interest rates. These price changes affect the value of the assets (and debts) we own.

- **Credit risk**

The risk that a loan will not be repaid. Banks are often considered to be the type of financial entity most vulnerable to credit risks, but in fact, bondholders, who hold government or public debt in expectation of receiving an interest-bearing cash flow, are equally at credit risk.

- **Liquidity risk**

The risk of not having enough cash to conduct business activity or repay debts on time.

- **Operational risk**

The risk of embezzlement, fraud, physical damage, system failure, etc.

- **Insurance risk**

Insurance risks are typically subdivided into life, health and general insurance risks. For an example, one of the risks of life insurance is the longevity of the insured. From virtually any other standpoint, longevity would be seen as a positive event. Insurers, however, consider it risk as it means they must continue to pay the insured according to obsolete calculations formulated many years before, back when life expectancy was significantly lower.

- **Reputational risk**

This is the risk of potential damage due to loss of trust. In recent years, as the saying that "there is no such thing as bad publicity" has gained in popularity, the question of reputational risk has become an extremely interesting one, in particular how it is to be measured. Although accounting reports may include a section on reputational value, it is almost impossible to find proper estimates of reputational risk.

- **Others**

Other, heretofore unmentioned risks include the following: regulatory risk, which affects companies when they are forced to allocate resources to ensure compliance with a new regulation; country risk, the risk of a country experiencing a crisis or even going bankrupt; geographic risk, which stems from the location of an asset in an area prone to natural disasters, geological changes, wars, etc.

Example — Risk Identification

Name	Quantity	Price	Currency	Security type	Indexed	Ranking	Industry Sector	
BAIDU	100	150	CNY	Stocks			Pharmaceuticals	
Coca-Cola	80	608	USD	Stocks			Banks	**Types of exposure:**
Italy Generic Govt 10Y	1500	0.147	EUR	Bonds	Yes	A+	Government	Exchange rate
Apple Inc.	40	510	USD	Stocks			Electronics	Security type Indexation Credit
Spain Generic Govt 10Y	30	104	EUR	Bonds	No	AA+	Government	Industry sector

The example of risk identification in the above table shows a portfolio containing five different types of securities. Try to identify the different risk types in the portfolio. The purpose of this table is merely to classify the types of risk; at this stage, there is no need to quantify them.

In the same way that a disease must be accurately diagnosed in order to guarantee that the patient will receive the appropriate medical treatment, so too is proper risk identification an essential prerequisite to selecting the appropriate hedging tools. For instance, derivatives (forwards, options, swaps, etc.) may be used to hedge market risks, whereas the appropriate tool for dealing with liquidity risks would be a reserve of cash or other liquid assets.

1.4. Measuring Risk

Different risks are measured in different ways: financial risk is measured in terms of money, disease risk is measured in percentage, environmental risk is measured by the amount of pollutants, legal risk is measured by the odds of not winning, etc.

Assessment and Measurement of Risk

- Financial risk is measured in terms of money
- Disease risk is measured in percentage
- Environmental risk is measured by the amount of pollutants
- Legal risk is measured by the probability of not winning
- How is reputational risk measured?

The measurement of risk plays a crucial role in determining the priorities for risk mitigation as well as the scope of mitigation required.

Assessment and Measurement of Financial Risk

Examples of financial measures

What do we measure?	How do we measure it?	Which risks is it used for?
Fluctuation	σ, Var	Market risk
Maximum loss	Max DD VaR, Conditional VaR	Market risk Market and operational risk
Loss frequency	Frequency	Market and operational risk
Loss severity	Severity	Operational risk
Probability of loss	PD Ranking Rating	Credit risk
Loss in various scenarios	What if Scenario Stress	Market, credit and operational risk

The above table shows which elements we measure and which types of risk they may be used for.

Just as, during a medical evaluation, the doctor takes the patient's temperature, pulse, blood pressure and other physiological measures in order to better assess the patient's condition, so too in risk management do we use several measurement methods in order to better gauge the extent of exposure to various risk factors.

1.5. Risk Mitigation

Once we have identified and measured a risk, we must then proceed to mitigate it.

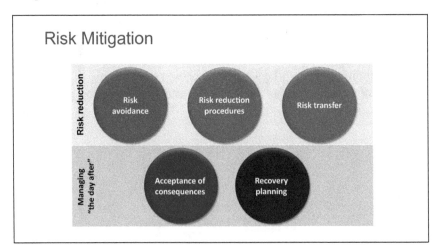

Risk management strategy consists of two parts: first, reducing vulnerability to a risk and second, managing the consequences of a failure, i.e., dealing with the consequences should the risk be realized.

1.5.1. *Risk reduction*

In general terms, there exist three main tools which may be employed to reduce risk:

- **Risk avoidance:** Let us suppose a company is examining the possibility of launching a product in another country. It turns out no one at the company is familiar with the trade regulations of that country; the company requires additional salespeople and is unfamiliar with the legislation in this country. Since marketing a product abroad requires a substantial financial commitment, one way of managing the expected loss from this investment would be to avoid it altogether.
- **Risk reduction procedures:** An example of risk reduction procedure might be fire detectors. Many factories install fire detectors in their facilities in order to ensure that the time elapsed from the moment a fire breaks out until it is discovered will be as short as possible. The sooner the fire is detected, the sooner the firefighters can arrive and minimize the damage it causes.
- **Risk transfer:** The most common way to transfer risk to other parties is by purchasing an insurance policy. In this way, even if parts of the factory are damaged in the fire, the insurance company will cover the costs.

1.5.2. *Managing the consequence*

The consequence of an event refers to the results of an incident in which damage was sustained. At this point, two management methods are available:

- **Accepting the consequences of the risk:** Let us suppose our investment portfolio consists of 98% bonds and 2% NASDAQ stocks. Should we purchase options to protect against the risk of an NASDAQ collapse? Very often the answer is no: even if NASDAQ were to fall by 50%, the entire portfolio would only lose 1% of its total value.

In such cases, we may simply choose to accept the consequences of the market risk, rather than hedging the portfolio against it.

- **Planning a recovery:** Many organizations have emergency protocols instructing their employees on the proper conduct in extreme circumstances. Nations mobilize firefighting services, rescue services, police and military forces in response to fires, traffic accidents, robberies or even attacks by foreign nations. This array of security forces will often dedicate much of its efforts to preventing situations in which it might be required, e.g., by instructing on proper use of electricity or safe driving. However, its primary purpose remains to assist in recovering from events that have already occurred.

In the financial realm, banks are required to establish a backup array of computers, which are capable of performing all the functions of the primary array in case of a system failure. If the main system fails, the backup will activate automatically, and the bank's clients will probably not even notice that a malfunction has occurred.

1.5.3. *Example: Risk mitigation in the event of a car accident*

Example

Risk mitigation in the case of a car accident

- Risk avoidance
  - Not buying a car

- Risk reduction procedures
  - Driving carefully, using seatbelts, verifying airbags

- Risk transfer
  - Renting a car, buying insurance

Let us use the example of a car accident to demonstrate how risk mitigation is applied:

The first method is **risk avoidance**. The practical way to apply this method is by not buying a car at all.

The second method is risk reduction procedures in the event of an accident. We should make sure to fasten our seatbelts, check that the airbags are working properly, fill up the tires with air and, of course, drive slowly and carefully. These methods will reduce both the probability of being involved in a car accident and the amount of damage if an accident does occur.

The third method is to **transfer the risk to another party**. In this example, the two most common ways to do this would be either to purchase car insurance, thus transferring the cost of any damages to the insurance company, or to rent a car, in which case the rental company will be responsible for the car in the event of an accident.

Example

Risk mitigation in the case of a car accident (continued)

- Acceptance of consequences
  - Tow truck, garage, insurance agent — loss of work days for no return

- Recovery planning
  - Substitute vehicle

The fourth method is to **accept the consequences of the risk**. In the case of an accident, there are several consequences which we simply accept, without attempting to reduce the risk of their occurrence. For instance, we waste time waiting for the tow truck, dealing with the garage and contacting the insurance agent. This wasted time has an opportunity cost measured in lost work days. In many cases, once the accident has occurred, we accept these consequences without any attempt to reduce the risk.

The fifth and final method is to **plan a recovery**. In our example, this means making sure in advance that a substitute vehicle is available, ensuring we can continue to drive about in another vehicle while ours is under repair at the garage.

1.6. Risk Management

Risk management is a continuous process which consists of the following elements: identification, assessment and measurement of exposure to risk, followed by reduction and reporting of risk.

Risk Management

- ▪ Risk management
  - Risk management is the process of identifying and assessing risks, measuring exposure to them, reducing those risks and reporting them.

  - Risk management in the banking system:
  International Convergence of Capital Measurement and Capital Standards, June 2006, http://www.bis.org/publ/bcbs128.pdf, p. 113.

  - Risk management according to ISO guidelines:
  ISO 31000 – Principles and guidelines, 2015, https://www.iso.org/iso-31000-risk-management.html.

In fact, many financial entities go much further than this basic definition: they monitor risk exposure through appropriate controls, set priorities for risk mitigation, they put metrics of risk reduction, allocate resources for their implementation, devise risk reduction plans, they conduct periodic risk assessments, they make decisions regarding the scope of risk taking and they deliver reports on risk exposure to senior management and to the board of directors as well as reports on risk-related developments to the various regulators.

This somewhat 'boring' definition has far-reaching business consequences:

First, someone must be charged with carrying out these processes.[11] The organization must allocate the necessary resources in manpower, time, budget, etc.

---

[11] The role of the risk management supervisor is described in the chapter on ERM.

Second, "identification, assessment, and measurement of exposure to risk" is a function which requires considerable skill and expertise. Some risk measures demand complex statistical analysis and a thorough understanding of the field of knowledge encompassed by risk management. For comparison, a medical checkup involves the taking of measures such as temperature, pulse and blood pressure. Each test measures different physiological symptoms, but only by combining them all is it possible to derive a professional opinion regarding the patient's illness. Similarly, many different measures are involved in the measurement and assessment of risk, each of which measures a different aspect. Only by combining all of these can we correctly qualify and quantify risks. From a business perspective, this highlights the importance of professional qualification, periodic training and constant study of new developments in the field of risk management.

Third, risk management has an impact on the work plan of an organization. For instance, an upswing in the number of cases of credit card fraud may compel an organization to adopt countermeasures in an attempt to minimize its financial losses. Such steps must be planned and executed, and their results monitored; this frequently means integrating new technological systems, updating protocols, creating new job positions for risk management professionals, training employees, etc.

Fourth, the very fact that risk management is being conducted, when combined with various changes in the business environment, is itself a factor which affects changes in the extent of exposure, which consequently results in changes to the work plan as well. This may be overcome by allocating a budget reserve to materialized risks whose adverse effects must be mitigated. The extent of this reserve is the result of calculations which much be learned.

Fifth, as with any type of report, the manner in which reports are given to management and to the board of directors has an impact on the entire risk management process. A report which is careless, overly detailed, lacking crucial information, confused, long-winded, etc. may itself pose a risk to the organization.

1.6.1. *The risk management process*

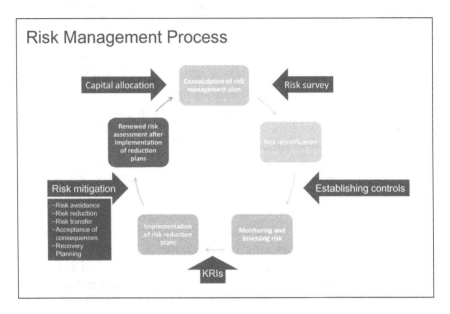

Risk management is a circular process. In fact, to adequately reflect the temporal dimension, it would be most aptly described as a spiral process over time.

The process begins with the **consolidation of a risk management plan**, which specifies who is responsible for conducting risk management, which resources are allocated to it, what the appropriate organizational structure is, to whom reports should be sent, etc.

In most organizations, the person or persons responsible for this process start out by conducting a **risk survey**, often with the assistance of outside consulting firms which specialize in this area. Most consulting firms maintain lists of hundreds or even thousands of different risks which they examine as part of the survey. These firms may also assist in **risk identification** and classification in order to allocate **controls** which allow us to regularly **monitor and assess risks** and gauge their magnitude. For example, the smoke detectors installed in many modern buildings serve as a *control* which alerts us to the risk of a fire outbreak.

Some, but not all, organizations also make use of Key Risk Indicators (KRIs), which are measures that allow us to identify potential risks. For instance, if by 7:30 AM only 70% of nurses have shown up at the emergency department of a hospital, hospital management receives an alert. While a shortage of nurses in and of itself is not a risk, it does increase the likelihood that other risks will materialize, e.g., wrongly diagnosed illnesses as a result of nurses not checking a patient's vital signs, medical complications and even death due to delays caused by understaffing.

An organization which has identified the risks, assessed their magnitude and monitored them using various controls will now wish to apply **risk reduction plans** using the risk mitigation methods outlined earlier. For example, in addition to smoke detectors, which provide warning of a fire, it is also possible to install sprinklers which activate automatically the moment a fire is detected. This way, even if a fire were to break out while the factory was closed, the sprinklers would help put it out before it spread to the rest of the factory. Now that the risk reduction plans are in place, we perform a renewed, **post-reduction plan risk assessment**. The remaining risk is hedged through **capital allocation** in the form of a budget reserve in case the risk materializes.

As soon as it ends, this process begins anew, resulting in the spiral model we used earlier to describe the risk management process.

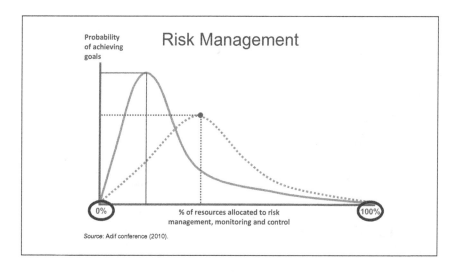

The above diagram demonstrates the connection between risk management and goal achievement. The x-axis reflects the resources allocated to risk management, monitoring and control by the organization. The y-axis reflects the likelihood that the organization will achieve its goals.

The origin of the graph represents organizations which irresponsibly choose to allocate no resources at all to risk management, monitoring and control (0% of resources). Such organizations will not be able to meet their goals at all. Their employees will soon realize no one is monitoring their hours at work or their output, not out of trust but simply because no one at the organization cares. The employees will eventually stop showing up for work but continue receiving their paychecks because no one bothered to check if they were even there.

At the extreme right end of the x-axis is the point representing an organization which allocates all of its resources (100%) to risk management, monitoring and control. Such organizations will also be unable to meet their goals — all their employees will be too busy monitoring other employees to actually do the jobs for which they were hired.

Using a few simplifying mathematical assumptions, we may draw the dotted line which connects the leftmost extreme (0%) and the rightmost extreme (100%). Although the precise course of the line is open to discussion, it can be stated that there is a point at which asset allocation to risk management, monitoring and control is optimal, ensuring the highest probability of achieving goals.

The purpose of risk management is to make the dotted line conform as closely as possible to the continuous line, to ensure the highest odds of success for the lowest possible allocation of assets.

1.6.2. *Concluding exercise*

Questions	Answers
What do we see in this image?	Two rock climbers.
What is their objective?	To get to the top, to climb higher.
What could this mean from an economic perspective?	Two insurance scenarios.
How do we manage the risks?	According to the risk management circle.
Which risks can we identify?	• Falling down from a high altitude • Rocks falling from above
What is the exposure the two climbers face?	• Falling from a high altitude: major damage • Rocks falling from above: comparatively minor damage
How do we assess risk? Which measures do we use?	• Probability of injury • Extent of financial damage
Which of the two climbers has put in place a better reduction plan? Why?	The climber on the right has a better risk-reduction system in place: • Better rope • Harness • Anchors • Helmet
After the risk has been reduced, which of the two climbers is exposed to greater risk?	The climber on the left is more exposed, as he uses a rope with no additional equipment.
Who needs to allocate more capital before climbing?	The climber on the left must allocate more capital before climbing as he is not managing his risk properly. The capital will be used to pay for the rescue team.
Who is a better risk manager?	The right-hand side climber.
Who has better odds of reaching his goal?	The right-hand side climber.
Who has better odds of reaching higher goals?	The right-hand side climber.

Chapter 2

Market Risk*

Part I

Accompanying presentation: 2. Risk Management — Market Risk (Part I)

2.1. Trading in Financial Markets

2.1.1. *Markets*

Before we can understand the meaning of "market risk", we must first define the term "market". A market is a medium which facilitates transactions between buyers and sellers. Markets differ from one another in various aspects, including but not limited to the following:

- **Location of trade:** This might be a physical location (e.g., Venice's fish market), where buyers meet vendors face to face, or it might be a virtual setting (e.g., the Tokyo Stock Exchange — TSE), where buyers and sellers may be physically situated in different countries, linked by computer programs which allow them to conduct trade without ever meeting in person.
- **Type of assets and/or services traded:** For example, flowers at the Amsterdam Flower Market or options at the Chicago Board Options Exchange.

---

*In this chapter, we will describe some of the advanced methods used to measure loss. Part I and Part II share the same numbering sequence.

- **Trading methods:** Ranging from barter (e.g., swapping tomatoes for eggs) to electronic currency trading.
- **Target population:** Working-class individuals, professional brokers, etc.
- **Extent of trade:** Measured in kilograms of apples per week, hundreds of millions of U.S. Dollars per day, etc.

Trade in Financial Markets

▪ Stock exchange trade
  - Computerized trade
  - Standardized contracts (derivatives)

▪ Over-the-counter (OTC) trade
  - Traders at financial firms, large companies, fund managers
  - Contracts may be non-standard

We shall here focus on financial markets, which may be further subdivided into two distinct categories:

- **Stock exchange**

The stock exchange[1] is a well-organized and highly regulated market, in which a particular type of asset is traded (stocks, bonds, currency, indices, futures, options, etc.). These assets are traded according to clearly defined standards which dictate the minimal amounts which may be traded and how precise the prices should be, fix the term to maturity, determine trading priorities, specify the rights and obligations of both buyers and sellers,

---

[1] Some interesting facts...

Another name for the stock market is "bourse". Although somewhat less commonly used in English, this word, or variants of it, is the most popular term for the stock exchange in many languages.

The term acquired the modern sense of "stock exchange" from the *Huis ter Beurze*, an inn established in the city of Bruges (in present-day Belgium) in the 13th century. The inn took its name from its owners, the van der Beurze family. Traders from across Europe would meet at the inn to conduct business and receive financial counsel from the owners. This system was formalized in the 15th century. The idea spread rapidly, and similar institutions were established across Europe, adopting not only the concept but also the name of the original inn.

provide collateral, etc. The trade conducted in modern stock exchanges is almost entirely computerized, allowing for countless transactions to be performed simultaneously.

Usually, traders who operate in the stock market enjoy greater liquidity. In order to purchase a futures contract on gold, for instance, the buyer need only launch the appropriate trading program, select the desired contract out of a list and complete the purchase. The deal is typically closed within a fraction of a second with the contract registered in the buyer's name. The process of selling the contract may be performed just as quickly.

On the other hand, the apparent advantage of standardized stock exchange trading can be a double-edged sword in some circumstances. Let us take as an example the case of a Jordanian exporter who wishes to hedge a deal with an Icelandic importer, which would require an immediate payment in the local currency (Jordanian dinars, JOD) and a future receipt in a foreign currency (Icelandic króna, ISK), over a period of 37 days. The exporter will find it difficult to find an appropriate contract at the stock exchange, where such an asset is not tradable. The disadvantage of the stock exchange lies in the type of assets traded and in the duration of contracts, which are predefined and cannot be modified to suit every possible demand. The solution to this issue may be found in over-the-counter trading.

- **Over-the-counter trading**

Over-the-counter (OTC) trading is conducted directly between the two parties, without the stock market as an intermediary. OTC trading has a number of advantages: it allows greater flexibility in the type of asset, duration, quantity, etc. Thus, using this method, the Jordanian exporter would be able to hedge the aforementioned deal by purchasing a JOD/ISK futures contract for a period of 37 days.

OTC trading, however, suffers from a **lack of liquidity** compared to stock market trading — should the deal be canceled, the Jordanian businessman would be unlikely to find buyers for his futures contract. Furthermore, OTC trade is only **partially regulated** — although various regulatory measures have been put in place and those who violate them face severe penalties, this system is not nearly as extensive as that which has been established in the stock market. OTC trading **is not always conducted at market prices** — rather, the price is agreed upon during the negotiations between the two parties. Further disadvantages exist, mostly due to the lack of transparency in OTC trading.

2.1.2. *Long and short*

Traders make use of two basic concepts, "long" and "short", which are essential to proper management of market risks:

Long

Examples of long trades:
- Purchase of 100 IBM shares at the stock exchange
- OTC exchange of 1M GBP for USD
- OTC purchase of 1,000 ounces of gold
- Sale of 1M General Motors bonds at the stock exchange

- Such deals are often referred to as spot trades as the asset is immediately transferred from one party to the other.

- **Long:** The classic type of deal, in which the trader *buys* the asset and intends to profit from an *increase* in the value of the asset. For example, a long purchase of Apple shares will return a profit if the share price rises, and a loss if the share price falls.
  - o In a long transaction, the buyer may make a very large profit (potentially infinite, at least in theory) if the price of the shares rises. However, the maximum loss cannot exceed the value of the shares, even if the share price drops all the way to zero.
  - o Having purchased the shares, the buyer now owns the asset.

Short

- In a short sale, the stocks are not owned by the trader.
- The financial intermediary borrows the stocks from another trader and proceeds to sell them on the market like any other stocks.
- Such deals require collateral.
- If the asset returns benefits and/or dividends, the trader must pay these to the shareholder.
- The cash flow may include a fee for lending the share.

- **Short:** A more complex form of transaction in which the trader *sells* the asset before buying it and intends to make a profit from a *decrease* in the price of an asset (e.g., if a company's share price drops to zero). For example, a short sale of Apple shares will return a profit if the share price falls and a loss if it rises.
  - o In a short transaction, the trader can make a profit equal to the value of the asset if the asset value drops to zero. However, the loss potential is infinite if the asset price continues to rise (theoretically, all the way to infinity).
  - o In a short sale, the stock being traded is not owned by the trader. It is equivalent to a loan whose value is linked to the share price. Therefore, in such a deal, the trader does not become the asset owner.
  - o A different trader lends the asset to a financial intermediary, who then proceeds to sell it in the free market.
  - o A short sale requires the employment of collateral by the trader to ensure that the loan will be repaid when it expires.
  - o If the asset returns benefits and/or dividends, the trader must pay these to the shareholder.
  - o The cost of a short deal is higher, as the trader must pay a fee to the intermediary from whom the asset was lent.

Despite the financial complexity of such transactions, performing a short transaction using a trading platform is quite a simple action. Having selected the type of asset we wish to sell and set the amount, method of execution and other parameters, the only thing which remains is to press the "sell short" button and wait for the system to carry out the transaction.

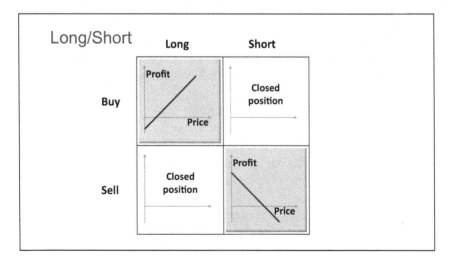

Once a long transaction has been performed, it is said that the trader has **"opened" a long position** or "extended" an existing long position, and from this point forth is taking a long position which exposes him or her to asset price depreciation (the top left in the diagram).

Meanwhile, the trader who has **"closed" a long position** or "reduced" an existing one and therefore is not exposed or at the very least less exposed to asset price depreciation. The chart in the presentation represents a trader who has closed a long position.

Once a short transaction has been performed, it is said that the trader has **"opened" a short position** or "extended" an existing short position, and from this point onwards is taking a short position which exposes him or her to asset price appreciation (the bottom right in the diagram).

The trader, by contrast, has **"closed" a short position** or "reduced" an existing one and therefore is not exposed or at the very least less exposed to asset price appreciation. The diagram represents a trader who has closed a short position.

Position is essential to risk management — whether the loss is expected to originate from a decrease or an increase in asset prices will, to a considerable extent, determine the risk reduction measures which should be adopted. This last sentence may seem obvious, but there have been many instances of companies committing basic errors with regard to the direction of trade: long and short. Instead of hedging the risk of an asset portfolio according to an open position, the company acquired the "wrong" form of protection. The supposed protection, in fact, covered the opposite direction, serving only to increase the exposure to market risks instead of reducing them.

2.1.3. *Financial derivatives*

Financial Derivatives

- Forwards
- Futures
- Swaps
- Options
- Exotic options

Financial derivatives are a type of security whose price is derived from, or depends on, the price of another asset. Derivatives are often used to manage market risk. Here, we shall list some of the most widespread types of financial derivatives:

- **Forwards**

Forward

- A contract between two parties which sets the amount and price for the future purchase of an asset, according to terms and conditions agreed upon in the present.
- Traded OTC.
- The contract is binding for both sides.
- However, there is always a certain risk that one of the sides will not honor its commitment.

A forward is a contract between two parties, which sets the amount and price for the future purchase or sale of an asset in accordance with the terms of the contract.

For example, an Italian energy company predicts a rise in the local demand for oil in the coming months and would like to guarantee the price of the oil it intends to import from Saudi Arabia in two, three and four months. Thus, the company signs a contract with the Saudi oil supplier, which fixes the price per barrel and the number of barrels for the relevant period. Forward contracts are traded over the counter. The contract is binding and compels both sides to fulfill its terms. However, there is always a certain risk that one of the parties will be unable or unwilling to comply with the terms of the agreement.

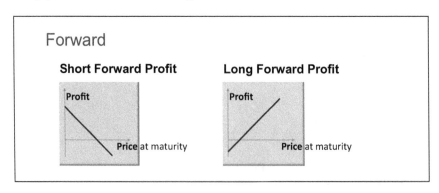

In a long forward contract, profits increase as the price rises. The Italian energy company, which has purchased a long forward, will make a profit if oil prices go up, since it is still able to purchase oil at the lower price which was set two months before.

By contrast, in a short forward deal, profits go down as the price goes up. Thus, for example, the Saudi supplier, who has sold a short forward contract, will lose money if oil prices go up, i.e., the oil could have been sold for a higher price than that agreed upon two months in advance.

In forward contracts, reckoning is performed at the end of the contractual period. At its conclusion, rather than paying the entire price, only the difference between the price named in the contract and the actual price is transferred from one party to the other.

- **Futures**

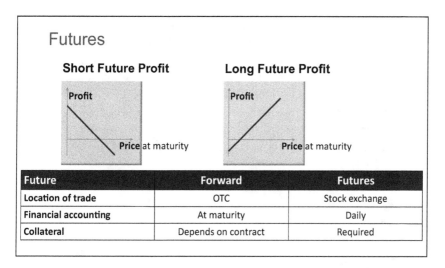

Future	Forward	Futures
Location of trade	OTC	Stock exchange
Financial accounting	At maturity	Daily
Collateral	Depends on contract	Required

A futures contract is a type of forward contract which is traded in the stock market. Futures have standardized features, e.g., asset type, duration and future value. For instance, a chocolate manufacturer, having signed a deal to provide fifty thousand chocolate bars every month for the next year, will have to purchase a precise amount of cocoa every quarter — not so little as to render the manufacturer incapable of meeting the terms of the deal but also not so much that part of the cocoa will be thrown away. To ensure that the deal remains profitable year-round, the chocolate manufacturer can purchase a futures contract today for each quarter of the year in order to guarantee the price of cocoa for the entire year.

Forward and futures contracts differ from each other in the following aspects:

o **Location of trade:** Forward contracts are traded over the counter, whereas futures contracts are traded in the stock market.

o **Financial accounting:** In forward contracts, financial accounting is only performed at the end of the specified period, whereas in futures contracts, financial accounting is conducted on a daily basis, i.e., at the end of each day, the difference between the stated price in the contract and the market price on that day is transferred from one party to the other, according to the position taken by each party.

o **Collateral:** Forward contracts lack a mechanism to guarantee that both sides will fulfill their obligations. It is possible to acquire such a mechanism, but it is not built into the contract by default. For futures contracts, however, the stock exchange guarantees that the contract will be honored by both sides. This is done by continuously tracking market prices as well as the liquid balance of each party. The stock exchange ensures that, at any given moment, the side which is in debt has a sufficient cash balance to honor the agreement (the process of assessing the financial situation of each party is termed "mark to market").

- **Swaps**

Swap

- A deal in which two sides swap financial assets
- Example:
  - The ICBC signs a three-year agreement, according to which it will receive a variable interest from JPMorgan Chase, set to match LIBOR* rates. In parallel, the ICBC pays JPMorgan Chase a fixed interest of 5% per year every six months. The extent of this deal is $1M U.S.

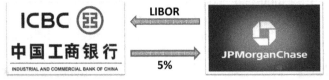

Note: *London Interbank Offered Rate.

A swap is a contract in which two parties swap financial assets. For example, the Industrial and Commercial Bank of China (ICBC) signs a three-year agreement with JPMorgan Chase, which stipulates that the latter will pay a variable interest rate to the former, with the interest rate determined according to LIBOR.[2] At the same time, ICBC will pay JPMorgan Chase every six months at a fixed annual interest rate of 5%. The scope of the deal is USD 100 million.

Swap

Potential cash flow according to fluctuations in LIBOR interest rates.		--------Millions of Dollars--------		
Date	LIBOR Rate	*FLOATING* Cash Flow	*FIXED* Cash Flow	Net Cash Flow
Mar. 5, 2016	4.2%			
Sept. 5, 2016	4.8%	+2.10	−2.50	−0.40
Mar. 5, 2017	5.3%	+2.40	−2.50	−0.10
Sept. 5, 2017	5.5%	+2.65	−2.50	+0.15
Mar. 5, 2018	5.6%	+2.75	−2.50	+0.25
Sept. 5, 2018	5.9%	+2.80	−2.50	+0.30
Mar. 5, 2019	6.4%	+2.95	−2.50	+0.45

Source: Hull (2014).

The fluctuations in LIBOR interest rates are largely responsible for determining the profitability of the swap contract from the perspective of ICBC. For instance, for the first six months, the LIBOR interest rate was 4.2% per year (2.1% for six months) while the fixed interest rate was 5% per year (2.5% for six months). The bank accordingly lost 0.4% during this six-month period. Subsequently, the LIBOR interest rate increased up to 6.4 during the second half of the year, resulting in a profit of 0.45% for ICBC during the whole period.

---

[2]The London Interbank Offered Rate (LIBOR) and London Interbank Bid Rate (LIBID) are used in interbank trading in London. Their use has expanded significantly, and they currently serve as a benchmark for the interest rates of several of the largest financial entities in the world.

A swap deal can make a lot of sense from a risk management perspective. An analysis of the example above from a business viewpoint uncovers that, before performing the swap deal, ICBC signed a second deal with one of its clients for a three-year period, during which the bank has promised to pay a variable interest rate according to LIBOR. Meanwhile, JPMorgan Chase has signed another deal in which it pledges to pay a real estate company a fixed annual interest rate of 5% for a period of three years. In signing these deals, each of the banks created exposure which was subsequently completely eliminated through the swap deal between the two banks, as described earlier.

- **Options**

Option

- A contract granting the buyer the right to **choose** to conduct a future transaction.

- The transaction is defined in advance according to various parameters, typically quantity, price and timing.

- By contrast, the seller **must** conduct the transaction according to the predetermined terms.

An option is a contract which grants the buyer the right to perform a transaction at some point in the future. The seller, on the other hand, is obligated to perform the trade according to the predetermined terms. When the transaction is defined in advance according to standard parameters — underlying, quantity, price and duration — the option is termed a vanilla option.

For example, an energy company would like to hedge its market risk and ensure that the price of an oil barrel does not exceed USD 50 for the next three months. For this purpose, the company seeks to purchase an option from the oil supplier, predefining the deal as a purchase of 1,000 barrels of oil at USD 50 per barrel for the next three months.

Exercising this option will be worthwhile if, during these three months, oil prices exceed USD 50 per barrel. The oil supplier will be obligated to perform the deal according to the terms defined in the contract. Conversely, if the price drops below USD 50, the company will choose not to exercise the option, as buying the oil at the market price would be a cheaper and more profitable alternative. Regardless of the circumstances, the company will not have to pay more than USD 50 per barrel.

Why would the oil supplier agree to such a deal at all? After all, the market risk is not eliminated but rather transferred in its entirety to the oil supplier. The motive for accepting the deal would be the risk premium charged by the seller. The oil supplier does not offer the option free of charge but demands a fee in return. This fee is called a risk premium (or just a premium for short).

The risk premium is intended to serve as recompense to the risk-bearing party (the oil supplier in the example above) for the risks involved in the deal. Such risks depend on market conditions and on various parameters defined in the contract. Thus, in the example above, the primary risk would be fluctuations in oil prices. The greater the fluctuations predicted for the next three months, the higher the risk premium.

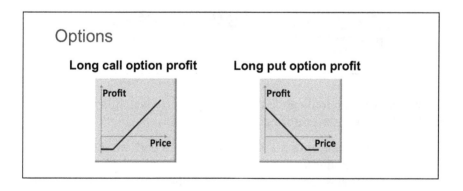

We distinguish two types of options — call options and put options:

o   A **Call option** allows the buyer to perform a *purchase* in the future.
o   A **Put option** allows the buyer to perform a *sale* in the future.

In the example earlier, the energy company has acquired a call option to purchase oil barrels, and the oil supplier has sold (or "written", to use the professional term) a call option.

A vine grower wishes to ensure that the price of grapes during the harvest, in four months' time, will remain at least GBP 6 per kilogram. The vine grower purchases a put option from the winemaker. If the market price falls below GBP 6, the vine grower will still be able to sell his grapes at GBP 6 per kilogram, and if the price exceeds GBP 6, he will be free to choose not to exercise the option and instead sell his grapes at the higher market price.

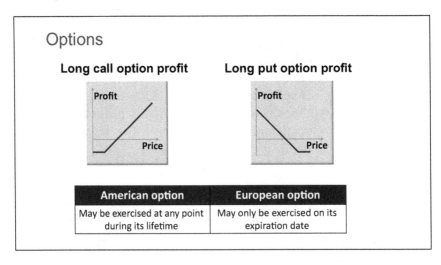

There are two commonly traded types of options, which differ in the manner in which they are exercised:

o   An **American option** allows the buyer to perform the transaction at any point during the option's lifetime.
o   A **European option** only allows the buyer to perform the transaction at the end of the option's lifetime.

Options on stocks are usually of the American type, whereas options on indices are usually European.

Options

122.02 +0.08 (+0.07%)
As of 12:01PM EST Market open.

Calls for January 27, 2017

▲ Strike	Contract Name	Last Price	Bid	Ask	Change	% Change	Volume	Open Interest	Implied Volatility
117.00	AAPL170203C00117000	5.55	5.50	5.60	-0.05	-0.89%	242	2,587	31.35%
118.00	AAPL170203C00118000	4.70	4.70	4.80	-0.20	-4.08%	74	3,593	31.10%
119.00	AAPL170203C00119000	3.98	3.95	4.05	-0.12	-2.93%	88	4,177	30.81%
120.00	AAPL170203C00120000	3.27	3.25	3.30	-0.08	-2.39%	1,933	19,786	29.61%
121.00	AAPL170203C00121000	2.63	2.62	2.64	-0.14	-5.05%	1,152	6,712	28.86%
122.00	AAPL170203C00122000	2.08	2.06	2.10	-0.10	-4.59%	2,631	12,033	28.76%
123.00	AAPL170203C00123000	1.58	1.58	1.61	-0.14	-8.14%	1,400	15,938	28.32%
124.00	AAPL170203C00124000	1.18	1.16	1.18	-0.10	-7.81%	902	4,116	27.59%
125.00	AAPL170203C00125000	0.84	0.83	0.85	-0.09	-9.68%	2,289	12,543	27.20%
126.00	AAPL170203C00126000	0.57	0.57	0.58	-0.09	-13.64%	941	3,570	26.61%
127.00	AAPL170203C00127000	0.38	0.37	0.38	-0.07	-15.56%	590	5,294	26.12%
128.00	AAPL170203C00128000	0.25	0.24	0.25	-0.06	-19.35%	253	3,143	25.98%

Source: Yahoo Finance.

In the above table, we can see the quoted price of tradable call options on Apple shares for January 27, 2017, to be exercised on February 3, 2017. The options differ only in the price at which they are exercised (or "strike price"), which is shown in the leftmost column. The options marked in first six rows are "in the money" (ITM) whereas the unmarked options are "out the money" (OTM).

The price of an Apple share, as can be seen in the table, is USD 122.02. Supposing we would like to purchase the share on 3 February, 2017, and wish to guarantee its purchase at a price no higher than USD 123, we may buy an option for USD 1.61 (see "ask" column).

On February 3, 2017, we would be faced with two possibilities. In the first, the price of an Apple share remains below USD 123, and in the second, the price of a share has exceeded USD 123. In the first scenario, we will purchase the share directly, losing the option premium (USD 1.61). The second scenario may be further split into two possibilities. If the price of the share is below USD 124.61 (123 + 1.61), we will minimize our loss by purchasing the share at USD 123 while losing the premium. However, if the price is above USD 124.61, we will gain the difference between the market price and the option.

It is evident, therefore, that in the case of a call option, the higher the strike price, the lower the price of the option (or "last price").

- **Exotic Options**

Exotic Options

- Asian options
- Barrier options
- Basket options
- Binary options
- Compound options
- Lookback options

An exotic option is a non-vanilla option. It may differ from a vanilla option in the type of underlying, exercise rules, how returns are calculated, etc. Here are a few examples of exotic options:

o **Asian options** yield profits according to the average price of the underlying for the entire lifetime of the option. Asian options were first issued in 1987 by Japanese banks, on futures contracts for crude oil. The main features of this type of option are as follows:

  – They are less sensitive to market fluctuations and their standard deviation is smaller. They therefore tend to be cheaper than equivalent vanilla options.

  – The standard deviation of an Asian option decreases over time, as part of the average is already known.

  – Asian options are less vulnerable to manipulations to the date of exercise (e.g., inside information), thus giving the option writer a significant advantage.

  – Asian options are well suited to the needs of businesses which trade continuously in a certain type of underlying and wish to hedge the risk involved in this type of trade (for instance, an airline which continuously purchases fuel over the course of a year may hedge itself from fluctuations in jet fuel prices by using an Asian option on fuel prices).

o **Barrier options** have barriers for entry or exit:
  – **Knock in:** An exotic option with a single barrier, which activates if the price of the underlying hits the barrier price during the option's lifetime.
  – **Knock out:** An exotic option with a single barrier, which becomes invalid if the price of the underlying reaches the barrier price during the option's lifetime.
  – **Double barrier:** An option with two barriers separated by an interval. These barriers may be either both knock ins or both knock outs, or there may be one of each (such an option is termed KIKO — Knock In/Knock Out).
o **Basket options** are options on an average of a basket of assets. This type of option is suitable for hedging the market risks associated with indices.
o **Binary options**[3] are True/False options. If a certain event occurs, the buyer of the option will receive a payment. If it does not, the buyer

---

[3] Some interesting facts…

• Binary options have ushered a golden age for online gambling companies, which offer their customers big, quick and, above all, legal profits.
• At the same time, illicit gambling, of the sort that tends to cause significant financial losses on most customers, has also seen significant growth. For instance, gambling companies may make it exceedingly difficult for customers to collect their earnings. Another example is the price quote of the underlying asset, the timing of which is often controlled by the gambling company in such a way that being off by just a few milliseconds could mean the difference between profit and loss for the client.
• As a result, over the years, binary options trading has largely become a synonym for gambling, fraud, deceit and deception — both regulators and the legal system have come to view binary options in a negative perception and consider them undesirable.
• Let us, therefore, take the opportunity to clarify a number of things regarding binary options, in an attempt to remedy their bad reputation:
  o Gambling is an act which combines luck with considerations of risk and return. "Luck" here refers to randomly occurring events, whose occurrence cannot be controlled and certainly not predicted. This fact is just as true of ordinary stock market trading as it is of filling out a lottery form, both of which are either difficult (stock market) or impossible (lottery) to predict, and yet perfectly legal in many countries.
  o It turns out that certain companies are indeed capable of predicting the direction in which stock and currency indices are headed, making use of physical and

must pay a certain amount. For example, if in three hours the USD/ EUR exchange rate increases above 1.1, the buyer will receive USD 70, and if it does not the buyer will have to pay USD 90.

– **Compound options** are options which activate other options. The first option may be a binary option, for instance, a type of option well suited for tenders. Let us suppose a company is participating in a tender for building infrastructure and must allocate extensive collateral which it needs to borrow from the bank. If the company wins, it will have no problem to repay the loan. If it does not win, however, it may have to pay back the loan with substantial interest. In order to hedge the risk, the company may choose to purchase a compound option for a cheap price. This compound option will, in turn, activate the option to take a loan only if the company makes the winning bid.

– **Lookback options** are options which are exercised on their expiration date, according to the best price recorded during the lifetime of the option (typically the maximum or minimum price during this period).

Despite their exotic name and their implied speculative connotations, exotic options are an effective tool for reducing many forms of market

---

mathematical algorithms (these methods are only partially effective, but they do result in predictions at an accuracy of greater than 50%). This means that it is in fact possible to make a profit from binary options trading, i.e., not all depends on luck.

o In between two investment extremes — an investment in AAA-rated bonds on the one hand, where the probability of receiving zero interest is extremely high, and an investment in the lottery on the other, where the probability of winning large sums of money is almost zero — binary options are situated somewhere in the middle, with a probability greater than 50% of making a profit. From a risk/return perspective, binary options are therefore just another legitimate form of investment.

o Furthermore, in 2016, the New York Stock Exchange (NYSE) launched a form of binary options called Binary Return Derivatives (ByRDs), in order to offer traders a wider variety of investments.

o Those many companies commit fraud, refusing to return interest payments on bonds or tampering with legitimate lottery gambling, which is an issue that the authorities must combat with resolve, regardless of the financial instrument these companies use to commit their crimes.

risk which are a part of everyday business activity and in fact anything but speculative (see the infrastructure tender and crude oil examples above).

2.2. Market Risk

2.2.1. *Definition*

> **Market risk**
>
> *"Market risk" is the possibility of incurring losses in profits or capital as a result of unforeseen changes in market prices.*

Before we explore deeper into the precise definition of "market risk", let us first explore the manner in which this risk is defined.

The first part of the definition refers to the "possibility of incurring losses" and appears in the definition of any type of risk. In the realm of financial risks, this loss materializes in the form of damage to future profits or present capital. However, the loss can certainly vary in nature. It can be a breakup with your great love, the loss of a dear friend, harm to one's physical well-being, etc.

This definition also applies to negative projected profits, i.e., losses. In such a case, the risk is of incurring even greater losses than the already projected loss. Similarly, the definition also applies to negative capital, i.e., an increase in current debt.

The second part of the definition, "due to…", refers to the causes for the potential loss. Such causes are not hard to find. A crisis of trust may lead to a breakup from a great love, moving to another town may result in the loss of a friend and carelessly crossing a road could quite possibly damage one's health.

In the world of financial risks, the cause is typically an unforeseen event which could have an adverse effect on profits or capital.

If the event is predictable, this is then an example of certainty. In this case, assuming proper risk management measures are in place, the risk has already been mitigated.

The third and final part of the definition, "in...", describes the risk factor. Some examples of risk factors are inflation, interest rates, exchange rates, earthquakes and fire.

2.2.2. Risk factors

The risk factor "market prices", which appears in the definition, is a general term for various prices. The following image gives some examples of such prices:

Market Risk Factors

- Price of goods
- Price of services
- Share prices
- Bond prices
- Option prices
- Exchange rates
- Stock indices

For instance, if we were to hold a long position on 100 Coca-Cola shares worth USD 150 each, or USD 15,000 overall, the most significant risk factor on our total Coca-Cola holdings would be the market price of the share. Should the market price per share drop by USD 1, we would lose USD 100 overall.

It is important to note that a decline in share prices does not necessarily correspond to a loss. Were we to hold a short position on Coca-Cola stock, a fall in share prices would, in fact, represent a profit. For both long and short holdings, the share price is a market risk factor. The two cases differ in the direction the price might go. For long holdings, a decrease in share prices would pose a risk to the value of this investment, whereas for short holdings, an increase in share prices would be a risk to that investment.

2.2.3. *Measurement*

Having identified the risk factor, we must now attempt to measure and quantify the scope of risk embodied in this factor. By doing this, it is possible to determine whether a share is a riskier asset than a bond and to what extent holding an option on the stock index of the Shanghai Stock Exchange is a riskier venture than investing in the EUR/GBP exchange rate.

However, measuring the scale of risk embodied in market prices is far from simple.

Unlike risk, measuring profit and return is relatively straightforward. When we measure profits, we compare the total value of financial assets at the end of a given period of time with their value at its beginning. The profit may then be divided by the value of financial assets at the beginning of the period to calculate the return on investment in percentage. The result of this calculation may be substituted with cash, concrete products, services or other assets. Measuring profit and return is so simple that almost no additional methods have been developed to compare the holdings at the end of a given period with the holdings at its start.

Measuring risk is a considerably more complex process, in part because what we attempt to measure is the "possibility" of losing profit or capital (see the definition of market risk mentioned earlier). Several methods exist for measuring risk:

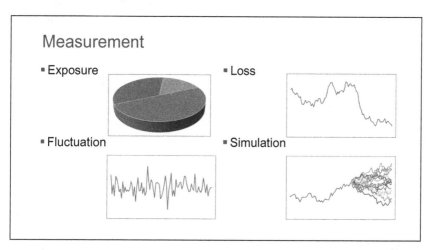

- **Exposure:** Measures the potential damage in case of a failure event, regardless of the probability of the damage materializing. For instance, if we hold a long position worth USD 15,000 on Coca-Cola shares and a USD 30,000 long position on General Electric (GE) bonds, our exposure to Coca-Cola is USD 15,000 and is therefore smaller than our USD 30,000 exposure to GE. This measure makes it very easy to estimate the potential of damage at any given point during a time period and at its end.

- **Fluctuation:** Over a period of time, the value of an asset may increase or decrease. For some assets, these fluctuations are greater and more frequent than those for others. Fluctuations may be calculated using statistical measures (see the following) such as standard deviation, implied volatility, variance, volatility index (VIX) and vega. For example, if the standard deviation of Coca-Cola share prices is greater than that of GE bonds, one may say that the risk embodied in a Coca-Cola share is greater than that of a GE bond.

- **Loss:** Unlike exposure, which only measures the potential damage, loss is a measure which incorporates probability as well. Measuring loss can be done using Value at Risk (VaR), maximum drawdown (MaxDD), etc. For example, at a probability of 99%, loss on Coca-Cola shares over the coming month will not exceed USD 1,300 as a way of loss quantification.

- **Simulation:** Risk assessment using various scenarios in which changes are applied to the risk factor. This may be a simulation of a worst-case scenario, a what-if or Monte Carlo simulation, etc. It is possible to simulate a worst-case scenario in which market prices fall drastically, e.g., by one-third over the next month, and then examine how such a scenario might affect the value of Coca-Cola and GE holdings. In this scenario, the total accumulated value of our holdings is USD 45,000 (USD 15,000 Coca-Cola + USD 30,000 GE), and it might drop to USD 30,000 in the worst-case scenario (a loss of USD 15,000).

The measurement and assessment of risk feature a wide variety of measures, each one examining a different aspect of the risk. Accurate classification and correct quantification of risk are only possible when all of these are utilized in combination.

We have already dedicated a section exposure in the first chapter. In the following sections, we shall continue discussing measurement of loss, as well as expand upon the topic of simulation.

2.2.3.1. *Preliminary calculations*

Preliminary Calculations

- Rather than performing calculations based on the portfolio value, *P*, we base our calculations on *Ln(P)* for the following reasons:

  - Simpler calculations (linear rather than exponential structure)
  - Uniform scale
  - Mathematically continuous interest rate

The various methods for quantifying risk require preliminary mathematical transformations of the portfolio value. Rather than performing calculations directly upon the portfolio value (which we shall refer to as *P*), they are performed upon *Ln(P)*. Why is this transform necessary?

- This method makes it much easier to perform calculations, as they are performed within a linear framework rather than an exponential one. Thus, for example, the formula for calculating compound interest is not a product, e.g., $(1 + r)(1 + r)-1$, but a sum such as $i + i$.
- This method ensures that a consistent scale is maintained, even in cases where the portfolio value varies significantly over time. A failure to perform these preliminary calculations may confuse our understanding of how the risk has evolved.

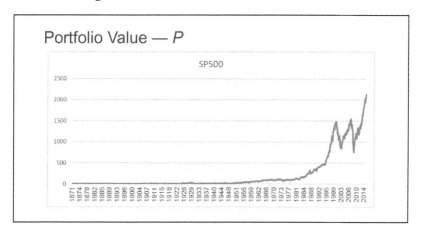

For example, a chart of the S&P 500 Index for the years 1871–2014, drawn without the preliminary calculations, would give the impression that the largest financial crisis of the last 150 years occurred in 2008, with the second-largest occurring in 2000. The various other crises which occurred between these years are simply not represented in the chart. From this chart, we might conclude, by mistake, there were no crises before 2000.

This happens because, when the index is worth USD 10, a 10% change will amount to USD 1, whereas if the index is worth USD 1,000, a 10% change will equal USD 100. Therefore, the same crisis event, in which the index lost 10% of its value, would register as a dramatic event for the high index value but would be almost indiscernible at the lower value.

If one first performs the preliminary calculation and only then draws the chart, this ensures that such an event is represented in a similar manner in both cases.

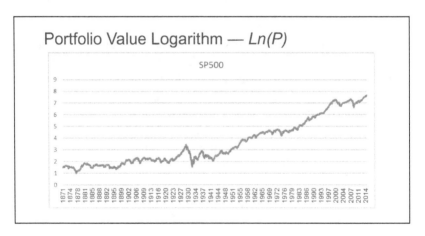

This image shows the development of the S&P 500 Index during almost 150 years. It also clearly shows that during the past 150 years, the index experienced its most severe crisis in the 1920s and 1930s.

- Mathematical continuity of interest rates ensures that it is possible to derive the portfolio value at any point and, for example, calculate the value of options which assist in determining risk pricing. The conversion from discrete to continuous yearly interest is done in the following manner:

Preliminary Calculations

Annual interest rate on investment, r:
$$P_2 = P_1(1+r)$$

It is also possible to receive $\frac{r}{2}$ after six months and then reinvest for six additional months:

$$P_2 \cong P_1\left(1+\frac{r}{2}\right)\left(1+\frac{r}{2}\right) = P_1\left(1+\frac{r}{2}\right)^2$$

$$\vdots$$

$$P_2 = P_1\left(1+\frac{r}{n}\right)^n$$

$$\lim_{n\to\infty}\left(1+\frac{r}{n}\right)^n = e^r$$

The value of the investment at the end of the period, P_2, equals its value at the beginning of the period, P_1, multiplied by 1, plus the interest, r.

Many banks allow for a semi-annual interest, which equals $\frac{r}{2}$ for half a year, and $\left(1+\frac{r}{2}\right)\left(1+\frac{r}{2}\right)$ all together for the entire year. The year may be further divided into smaller segments, e.g., a triannual interest of $\left(1+\frac{r}{3}\right)\left(1+\frac{r}{3}\right)\left(1+\frac{r}{3}\right)$, and so forth. More generally, the value of the investment at the end of the period may be written in the following way: $P_2 = P_1\left(1+\frac{r}{n}\right)^n$, with n standing for the number of times per year interest is received. n may, in theory, be increased all the way up to infinity, in which case the coefficient of $\left(1+\frac{r}{n}\right)^n$ is reduced to e^r.

Preliminary Calculations

$$\frac{P_2}{P_1} \cong e^r$$

$$Ln_{(P_2)} - Ln_{(P_1)} \cong r$$

The formula for calculating continuous interest is now very simple:

$$Ln(P_2) - Ln(P_1) \cong r$$

In much the same way, it is also possible to calculate the continuous yield of a portfolio:

$$Ln(V_2) - Ln(V_1) \cong y$$

where V is the portfolio value.

Excel
Some useful Excel functions for performing the calculations described above are as follows:

$(1 + r)^n$	$r = 0.02; n = 2$	$= (1+0.02)^{\wedge}2$
e^r	$r = 0.03$	$= \text{EXP}(0.03)$
$Ln(P)$	$P = 101$	$= \text{LN}(101)$

2.2.3.2. *Standard deviation*

As a general rule of thumb, due to statistical considerations, the various risk calculations are based on the yield rather than on the portfolio value. In the following example, we calculate the daily standard deviation of a portfolio value. In order to calculate the standard deviation, we must first calculate the average.

Standard Deviation

Portfolio average and standard deviation:
$$Ln(V_t) - Ln(V_{t-1}) = y_t$$
V_t = portfolio value on day t
y_t = difference in portfolio value between day t and day t-1

Average daily yield: $\bar{y} = \frac{1}{T}\sum_{t=2}^{T} y_t$

Daily standard deviation:
$$Std(y) = \sqrt{Var(y_t)} = \sqrt{\frac{1}{T-1}\sum_{t=2}^{T}(y_t - \bar{y})^2}$$

Let us use y_t to represent the change in portfolio value between day t and day $t-1$.

The average daily yield is

$$\bar{y} = \frac{1}{T}\sum_{t=2}^{T} y_t$$

And the standard deviation is

$$\text{Std}(y) = \sqrt{\frac{1}{T-1}\sum_{t=2}^{T}(y_t - \bar{y})^2}$$

In order to calculate the average yield and standard deviation for a period of 10 days, we multiply the daily result by the number of days and by the square root of the number of days, respectively:

Standard Deviation

Conversion to annual average and standard deviation:

Average:	$t\bar{y}$
Standard deviation:	$\sqrt{t}Std(y)$

The advantage of using standard deviation when measuring risk is that it is very simple to calculate. Almost any data analysis software contains built-in functions for the various calculations required.

For example, let us assume the yield on our portfolio is as described in the following image, with a probability of 25% for each possibility:

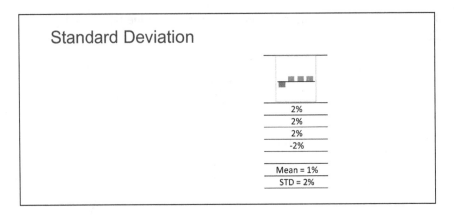

The average yield is 1% and the standard deviation is 2%.

Excel
Some useful Excel functions for performing the calculations described above are as follows:

$$\bar{y} \qquad 2; 2; 2; -2 \qquad = \text{AVERAGE}(2,2,2,-2)$$
$$\text{Std}(y) \qquad 2; 2; 2; -2 \qquad = \text{STDEV}(2,2,2,-2)$$

2.2.3.3. *Skewness*

Skewness, occasionally referred to as "inclination angle of the distribution", is a measure of the symmetry of a statistical distribution.

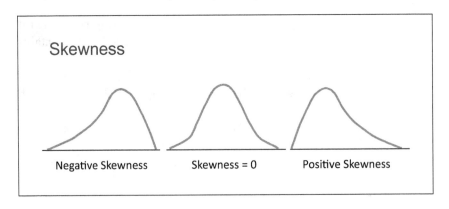

Skewness is calculated according to the following formula:

$$\text{Skewness}(y) = \frac{N}{(N-1)(N-2)} \sum_{n=1}^{N} \left(\frac{y_t - \bar{y}}{\text{Std}(y)} \right)^3$$

Skewness is often used alongside average and standard deviation, as the latter two are not always sufficient to reveal the complete understanding.

The following example shows two distributions whose average and standard deviation are identical but whose skewness levels are very different:

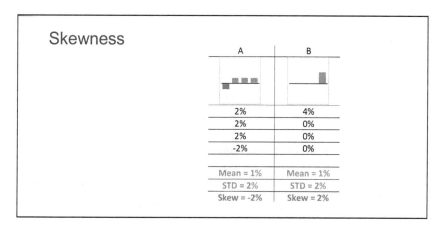

The average yield is 1% and the standard deviation is 2% in both examples. However, distribution A is left-skewed whereas distribution B is right-skewed.

Were we to compare only the average and the standard deviation of the two investments, we might conclude that both involve similar levels of risk. The difference in skewness, however, indicates that distribution B is less risky than distribution A, containing no possibility of loss at all.

Excel
This is the Excel function which may be used for performing the calculations above:

Skewness(y)   0; 0; 0; 4 = SKEW(0,0,0,4)

2.2.3.4. *Kurtosis*

Kurtosis is a statistical measure which allows us to determine whether a distribution is higher or flatter than a normal distribution. A positive measure reflects a leptokurtic distribution, i.e., a greater likelihood of outliers; whereas a negative measure represents a platykurtic distribution, meaning outliers are less likely to occur.

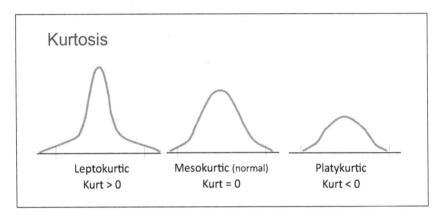

Kurtosis is calculated in the following way:

$$\text{Kurtosis}(y) = -\frac{3(N-1)^2}{(N-2)(N-3)} + \frac{N(N+1)}{(N-1)(N-2)(N-3)} \sum_{n=1}^{N} \left(\frac{y_t - \bar{y}}{\text{Std}(y)} \right)^4$$

A kurtosis ("Kurt") measure of zero represents a normal distribution.

If Kurt is greater than zero, the distribution has "thick tails", i.e., a greater probability of outliers than a normal distribution.

If Kurt is smaller than zero, most of the observations are concentrated around the center and the distribution therefore has fewer outliers than a normal distribution.

The following example shows two distributions with identical average, standard deviation and skewness measures but with different kurtosis measures:

	C	D
	3.45%	2.9%
	1%	2.55%
	1%	-0.55%
	-1.45%	-0.9%
	Mean = 1%	Mean = 1%
	STD = 2%	STD = 2%
	Skew = 0%	Skew = 0%
	Skew = 1.5%	Kurt = -5.7%

The average yield is 1%, the standard deviation is 2% and the skewness is 0% in both cases. However, distribution C has a higher kurtosis than distribution D.

Were we to compare average, standard deviation and skewness alone, it might appear as though both investments involve a similar level of risk. However, the positive skewness of distribution C reveals that this is the riskier option, as we should expect more outliers for distribution C than for distribution D.

Excel
This is the Excel function which may be used for performing the calculations above:

Kurtosis(y)   2.45; 0; 0; –2.45 = KURT(2.45,0,0,–2.45)

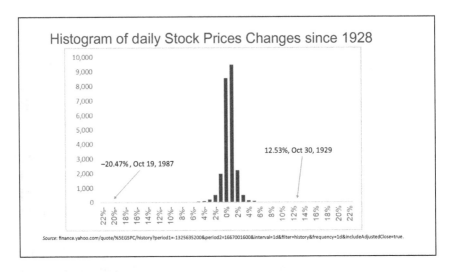

Source: finance.yahoo.com/quote/%5EGSPC/history?period1=-1325635200&period2=1667001600&interval=1d&filter=history&frequency=1d&includeAdjustedClose=true.

If one constructs a histogram of the daily changes to the U.S. stock index in the 20th century, several interesting phenomena become apparent:

First of all, most observations are concentrated within a margin of ±2%. This means that on most days we can expect returns or losses of up to 2%.

Second, the two columns at the center of the histogram and the additional two columns flanking them indicate a positive average return overall. Over time, the returns slightly outweigh the losses, and thus, in the long run, an investor can expect to make a profit by investing in the stock market.

Third, outliers are relatively uncommon but not small in number. The most extreme outliers are the worst day of 1987, on which the index fell by almost 20.5% in a single day(!), and the best day, which occurred in 1929 (to be precise, the day after Black Tuesday, during the Great Depression), when the index went up by over 12.5%.

When managing market risks, one would be wise to pay attention to the enormous difference between average daily losses and an extreme outlier, which has the potential to eliminate more than 20% of all capital in the market in a single day.

2.2.3.5. *Maximum drawdown*

Maximum drawdown (MaxDD) is a financial measure which represents the greatest difference measured between peak prices and low prices for an asset over a period of time.

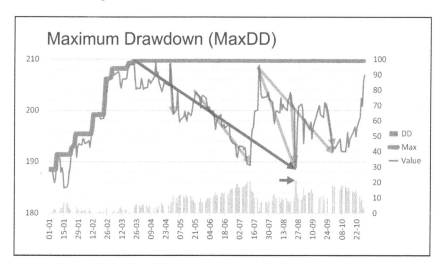

This is the formula for calculating maximum drawdown:

$$\text{MaxDD}(P) = \max_{\{T\}}\left[P_t, \text{Max}\left(P_{t-1}\right)\right]$$

In the example given in the image, the chart shows the value of an asset portfolio increasing from 198,000 Jordanian Dinars (JOD) to 207,000 JOD at the end of the period.

In the first quarter, the portfolio quickly soared to 210,000 JOD and subsequently began to descend. It then rose again dramatically at the middle of the period but immediately afterwards fell to the lowest point observed during the entire period.

During this time, various losses are shown (in gray arrows). These are called drawdowns (DD). Some of these, where the gray line is steepest, represent severe losses over a short period of time.

Out of these, the greatest accumulated loss, MaxDD, is the one marked by the thickest arrow.

Excel

Here is a fairly simple method for calculating MaxDD in Excel:

The **Value** column lists the values of the asset portfolio.

The **Max** column contains the formula = MAX($\bullet$,$\bullet$) as shown in the following:

	A	B	C	D
1	**DATE**	**Value**	**Max**	**DD**
2	01-01-15	188		
3	04-01-15	188	= MAX(C2,B3) Result: 188	0
4	05-01-15	187	= MAX(C3,B4) Result: 188	1
5	06-01-15	186	= MAX(C4,B5) Result: 188	2
6	07-01-15	187	= MAX(C5,B6) Result: 188	1
7	08-01-15	191	= MAX(C6,B7) Result: 191	0
8	11-01-15	191	= MAX(C7,B8) Result: 191	0
9	12-01-15	188	= MAX(C8,B9) Result: 191	3
10	13-01-15	189	= MAX(C9,B10) Result: 191	2
				= MAX(D2:D10) Result: 3

The column **DD** contains the difference between **Max** and **Value**.

Finally, we find the highest value in the **DD** column. This is the MaxDD value, which in this case equals 3, i.e., the greatest loss during this ten-day period is 3,000 JOD.

Market Risk

Part II

Accompanying presentation: 2. Risk Management — Market Risk (Part II)

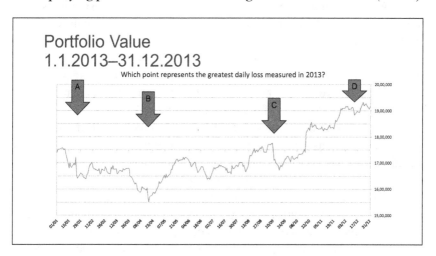

The chart in this image represents the daily value of an investment portfolio during the year 2013. From the chart, we can conclude that during the first few months of 2013, the portfolio value mostly went down. This trend reversed in late April, with the portfolio beginning to rise in value, marking a 10% increase by the end of the year.

The description above is short and dull while the real story is more dramatic. This is about an investment house managing a mutual fund for its clients. At the beginning of the year, neither the managers nor their clients knew that the year would end with profit, nor could they know what financial hurdles they would have to overcome. Let us outline the evolves in the order in which they occurred, without assuming prior knowledge of the evolution of the portfolio value during the year.

In late January, clients noticed that the fund was losing money and thought of selling their holdings. The fund managers claimed this was only a passing phase and managed to keep most of their clients from leaving. Indeed, in early February, the portfolio value started to go back up, although its value remained low compared to the beginning of the year. With clients now reassured that their investments were safe, the portfolio plodded along for two more months, until, for a short period of time beginning in late March, it began to experience sharp drops every day. Many upset clients sold their holdings at this point, incurring a loss of more than 10%. For the investment house, this represented both a loss of income from discontinued management fees and damage to their reputation.

In April, the portfolio began to recover. However, those clients who had left — the loss still fresh in their minds — were reluctant to return. Furthermore, new clients did not join up.

The fund continuously made a profit until mid-May but failed to recruit new clients. In June, the portfolio lost money once again, which served to further reinforce the conviction of potential clients that it would be unwise to invest in this "failed" mutual fund.

In August, the investment house managed to recoup all of its losses.

At this point, its clients were divided into two groups: those who had stayed true to the fund, who had recovered all the money they had lost, and those who had abandoned and lost money.

The fund experienced additional substantial losses in September but had recovered and even turned a profit by October. By December, those clients who had remained loyal had made a profit of almost 10%.

At this point, some of those clients who had left sought to reinvest in the portfolio and reap the rewards of the fund's upswing.

Let us here comment on the conduct of the clients and the investment house in the case study earlier:

(i) Inexperienced traders tend to act rashly, selling at cheap prices and buying at higher prices.

   At the core of this financial behavior often lie irrationality, fears and concerns rather than a genuine understanding of the financial risks involved and how to manage them. In our example, this caused clients to sell their holdings when the portfolio value was at its lowest and buy them only after the value had gone back up.

(ii) Loyalty to an investment house is no guarantee of return on an investment, however. In this example, we used the term "loyal clients" and showed how it was this group that had made a profit. This fact in and of itself does not mean that remaining loyal to a particular investment house will necessarily earn us money or, conversely, that not remaining loyal will cause us to lose money. Investment decisions are usually more complex than being loyal or not.

(iii) Many financial entities tend to mischaracterize their clients' risk profiles, and thus they might match a risky portfolio to a risk-averse client.

Although regulations stipulate that the risk profile of a client should be mapped in an accurate and reliable manner, many financial entities continue to ask the wrong questions despite the significant progress which has been made in this area. As a result, the investment brokers in this case had to deal with an outflow of clients whose risk profile did not match the largely foreseeable jolts experienced by the investment portfolio.

If we were asked to identify the worst day of the entire year, i.e., on which day during 2013 the portfolio suffered its greatest losses, we would concentrate on the four options marked by arrows in the below image.

Whenever this question is posed to students, along with the accompanying image, they tend to point to B and C as showing the greatest daily losses. Occasionally, option D is selected as well. Only once have we been told that A was the correct answer, and this was from a student who had arrived late to class and had not even heard the question.

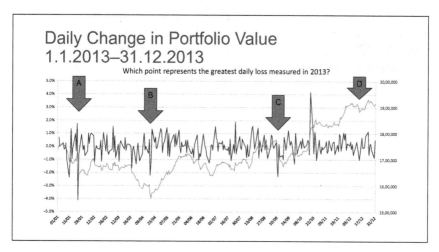

The presentation of data affects the way in which the brain interprets the facts and draws conclusions from them. In order to come up with a precise answer, we must use suitable measurement methods. In this case, all that means is calculating the daily changes in portfolio value and displaying them in a separate graph. In this way, it is evident that option A is the correct one, as on that day the greatest loss was *measured*.

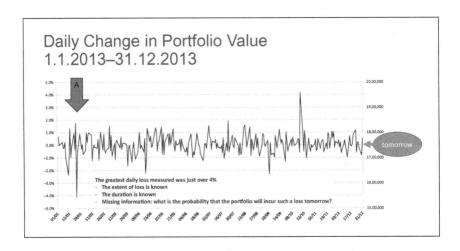

The greatest loss measured in a single day was 4%, making A the correct answer.

However, this is not sufficient for the purpose of risk management. There is a significant difference between a scenario where such a loss may be expected once a year and one where it is likely to occur on a weekly basis. We therefore wish to measure the probability that such a loss will be incurred tomorrow. In the example above, the calculation is simple. The probability is one out of 260 trading days (0.3846%).

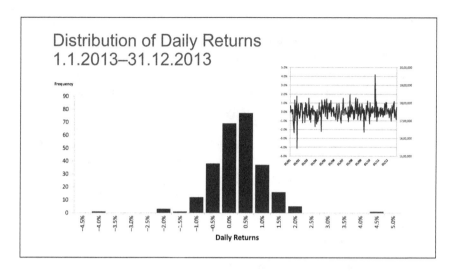

We have seen again that a different presentation of the data can improve our understanding of the risks of a portfolio.

Now that we have at our disposal all the daily value changes for 2013, we may proceed to arrange them in a different format. For instance, we may display the data as a histogram showing the number of days (*y*-axis) on which the change in portfolio value (*x*-axis) was within the bounds of 0.5% intervals.

For instance, the number of days on which the change was between 0% and 0.5% is 77. The number of days on which the change was between −0.5% and 0% is 69.

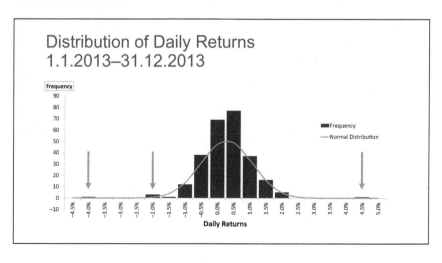

On top of our histogram, we may superimpose the normal distribution of value changes, based upon the average (0.037%) and the standard deviation (0.79%) of the portfolio's value changes.

This method of displaying the data reflects the distribution of daily changes for 2013 both as an empirical distribution and as a constrained normal distribution. This visual representation of the distribution reveals that it is more or less symmetrical, with most days seeing changes of ±1%, and that it has "thick tails", i.e., a higher probability of outliers than a normal distribution.

Now that we have examined the distribution of daily changes, we may proceed to discuss the concept of "Value at Risk".

2.2.3.6. *Value at risk*

Value at risk is a statistical method for assigning a monetary value to portfolio risk, reflecting the greatest potential loss which could, at a given probability, materialize during a given period. The Value at Risk is marked as VaR.[1] A higher value represents a higher risk level.

---

[1] Some interesting facts...

- In 1997, many financial institutions began to publish the results of their VaR calculations in order to more accurately disclose the levels of risk to which their portfolios were exposed.
- In 1999, banks worldwide began to employ VaR calculations in accordance with the recommendations put forward in Basel II.
- Many financial professionals erroneously use the initials VAR (with an uppercase A) in their reports on value at risk in investment portfolios. This three-letter combination can be rather confusing, as it represents three different concepts which differ only in letter case:

VaR	Value at Risk	
VAR	Vector Autoregression	An econometric model for capturing linear interdependencies in time series
Var	Variance	Statistical variance

VaR

- VaR is the greatest potential loss which could occur at a given probability over a given period of time.

Value at risk is a measure which answers the following question: "What is the potential loss of an investment portfolio, at its current composition, in the near future?"

Loss is typically measured in terms of money or percentage out of the total portfolio value.

Potential refers to the probability that the loss will materialize (typically 95% or 99%).

The **portfolio** includes all existing assets and liabilities, including derivatives such as forwards and options.

The **current composition** is a combination of the assets and liabilities which make up the portfolio at the moment of the value at risk calculation, in terms of the number of securities held in each asset (as opposed to a portfolio composition which also takes into account the price of the assets).

The **near future** is typically the next day, week, month, quarter or year.

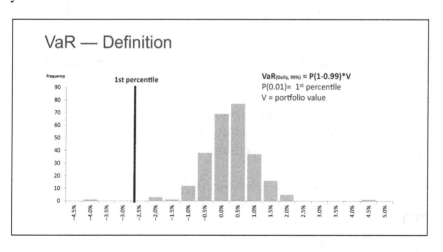

Value at risk is calculated using the following formula:

$$\text{VaR}_\alpha(y) = \text{Percentile}(y, 1 - \alpha) \times \text{Value}$$

where y represents all the changes in portfolio value at its current composition.

In the example earlier, over the entire period, the composition of the portfolio did not change in terms of the number of securities held. The value at risk for the portfolio at the end of 2013 was USD 42.7 thousand, or 2.23% of the portfolio value.

There are three widely used methods for calculating value at risk.

2.2.3.6.1. Historical method

Calculation Methods

- Historical method (based on past data)
  - Advantage: easy to implement
  - Disadvantage: sensitive to the length of the time windows selected

---

The historical method is based on past data. The advantage method is that it is fairly easy to implement. It is therefore frequently used in business risk management and integrated into many information systems.

The weakness of the method lies in the fact that specific time windows must be selected in order to perform the calculation. One window refers to the frequency of changes (daily, weekly, monthly, quarterly, yearly, etc.). The other refers to the historical time period we wish to examine for the sake of our calculation.

Having set the frequency and historical depth, the calculation according to the historical method is performed as follows:

(1) The composition of the portfolio is determined. For instance, 100 Apple shares and 150 Google shares.
(2) The units of time for which the calculation is performed are set (day, week, month, quarter, year, etc.).
(3) The reference period is set (last 360 days, last 206 weeks, last 60 months, etc.). In order to calculate the changes in the value, we need

to increase the number of observations by one (i.e., 361 days, 207 weeks and 61 months).

(4) The portfolio value is calculated at the end of each interval, according to the historical prices recorded for that point in time.

(5) The changes in price[2] between the end points of the intervals are measured (hence the additional interval added to the number).

(6) The 1st and 5th percentiles of all the changes are calculated.

(7) The result is multiplied by (−1) and by the portfolio value at the end of the period.

The following table gives an example of the data needed to calculate value at risk using the historical method:

Historical Method

#		#		#		#		#	
1	-0.475%	21	-0.237%	41	-0.025%	61	0.154%	81	0.310%
2	-0.470%	22	-0.227%	42	-0.020%	62	0.154%	82	0.356%
3	-0.465%	23	-0.219%	43	0.000%	63	0.162%	83	0.361%
4	-0.456%	24	-0.206%	44	0.015%	64	0.173%	84	0.364%
5	-0.415%	25	-0.206%	45	0.025%	65	0.173%	85	0.364%
6	-0.405%	26	-0.173%	46	0.025%	66	0.186%	86	0.366%
7	-0.387%	27	-0.144%	47	0.026%	67	0.187%	87	0.382%
8	-0.385%	28	-0.128%	48	0.035%	68	0.200%	88	0.406%
9	-0.371%	29	-0.122%	49	0.042%	69	0.210%	89	0.416%
10	-0.368%	30	-0.119%	50	0.050%	70	0.230%	90	0.421%
11	-0.340%	31	-0.118%	51	0.060%	71	0.258%	91	0.432%
12	-0.326%	32	-0.102%	52	0.105%	72	0.262%	92	0.433%
13	-0.321%	33	-0.095%	53	0.106%	73	0.267%	93	0.459%
14	-0.279%	34	-0.093%	54	0.112%	74	0.272%	94	0.461%
15	-0.271%	35	-0.089%	55	0.118%	75	0.277%	95	0.481%
16	-0.270%	36	-0.084%	56	0.131%	76	0.278%	96	0.491%
17	-0.265%	37	-0.057%	57	0.133%	77	0.293%	97	0.494%
18	-0.261%	38	-0.034%	58	0.146%	78	0.298%	98	0.495%
19	-0.256%	39	-0.034%	59	0.149%	79	0.308%	99	0.495%
20	-0.238%	40	-0.030%	60	0.152%	80	0.310%	100	0.497%

$P(0.01) = -0.470\%$

Value = 100,000$

VaR = 470$

---

[2] This refers to changes in market price which are not the result of technical reasons such as a stock split or devaluation resulting from a dividend payout. There are two possible courses of action in such a case:

The first is to remove the problem, i.e., omit the day on which it is known that the technical change will occur. The advantage of this is the ease with which this may be done. The disadvantage is that data are omitted.

The second method is to "string" the data to create a consistent asset price index over the entire period: For instance, if the share price was USD 250 on 2.3.2013 and at the end of the day a 1:2 stock split was performed, on the following day (3.3.2013), the share price would be USD 125 and the change would register as 50% due to a technicality. In such instances, all that needs to be done is to double the share price starting from 3.3.2013.

The advantage of the second method is that it preserves all the available data. The disadvantage is that operating errors may occur in its application.

The values table contains 100 observations of returns, sorted in ascending order according to size.

The first percentile equals –0.47%. If the total portfolio value is USD 100,000, the VaR will equal USD 470.

At the start of this chapter, we showed a chart representing the value of an investment portfolio over the course of 2013. According to the historical method, the value at risk at a 99% probability is USD 42,699, which means that in 99%, the maximum loss of this portfolio during the next day will not exceed USD 42,699.

Excel
This Excel function may be used for performing the calculations above:

$$P(y,\alpha) \quad y = 1,2,3,4,5; \; x = 0.05 \quad = \text{PERCENTILE}(\{1,2,3,4,5\},0.05)$$

2.2.3.6.2.   Analytical method

Calculation Methods

- Historical method (based on past data)
  - Advantage: easy to implement.
  - Disadvantage: sensitive to the length of the time windows selected.
- Analytical method (based parametric structure of distribution)
  - Advantage: maintains consistency with the selected time windows and with other risk measures (e.g. standard deviation).
  - Disadvantage: requires an *a priori* assumption regarding the form of distribution (difficult to apply to derivatives).

The analytical method for calculating value at risk requires an *a priori* assumption regarding the breakdown of the distribution of portfolio value changes. Generally, a normal distribution is assumed for the changes in value of the assets composing the portfolio. This approach aids greatly in maintaining consistency in VaR calculations. For instance, there is no need to set the time windows in advance, as the calculations already take them into account (naturally, when reporting VaR, it is necessary to mention the time horizon to which it pertains). Furthermore, it ensures consistency with other risk measures, such as standard deviation. Thus, if one measure indicates an increase in risk, the other will necessarily do so as well, and vice versa. The analytical method is widely used in academic research.

The disadvantage of this method is that it requires an *a priori* assumption regarding the distribution breakdown. In many cases, the theoretical distribution model does not match the empirical (historical) distribution and may even cause businesses to reach the wrong conclusions. For example, if there is a correlation between the prices of several assets in a portfolio, we must learn the nature of this correlation and incorporate it into our VaR calculations. In addition, if the portfolio contains non-standard assets, e.g., derivatives, it becomes apparent that they do not conform to an analytically structured distribution which is dependent on the distributions of the other assets contained in the portfolio.

The most common form of analytical distribution is normal distribution, which is defined only by average and standard deviation. Therefore, with this approach, the differences between various assets are simply the result of the differences in average and standard deviation between them.

The values of different assets may show a positive correlation, negative correlation or zero correlation. For the sake of simplicity, let us here assume zero correlation.

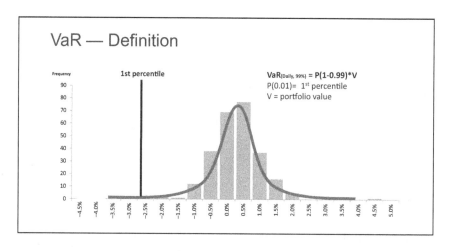

The calculation of value at risk according to the analytical method is done in the following manner:

(1) The composition of the portfolio is determined. For instance, 100 Apple shares and 150 Google shares.
(2) The units of time for which the calculation is performed are set (day, week, month, quarter, year, etc.).
(3) The reference period is set (last 360 days, last 206 weeks, last 60 months, etc.). In order to calculate the changes in the value, we need to increase the number of observations by one (i.e., 361 days, 207 weeks and 61 months).
(4) The portfolio value is calculated at the end of each interval, according to the historical prices recorded for that point in time.
(5) The changes in price[15] between the end points of the intervals are measured (hence the additional interval added to the number).

Analytical Method

▪ Assumption: Normal distribution

$$VaR_\alpha = -\mu + \sigma Z_\alpha$$

$$Z_{0.99} = 2.33$$
$$Z_{0.95} = 1.645$$

---

(6) The average (μ) and standard deviation (σ) of changes between the end points of the intervals are calculated.
(7) Value at risk is calculated according to the formula:

$$VaR_a = -\mu + \sigma Z_a$$

If $a = 0.99$ then $Z_{0.99} = 2.33$
If $a = 0.95$ then $Z_{0.95} = 1.645$

where Z is the normally distributed random variable and a is the level of confidence (equals 1-α when α is the significance level).

At the beginning of this chapter, we showed a chart representing the value of an investment portfolio over the course of 2013. Using the analytical method results in a value at risk of USD 34,504 at a 99% probability.

Why is there such a difference between the historical method and the analytical method? We will let our readers attempt to answer this question themselves (hint: refer to the image about the definition of VaR, showing both the historical distribution and the normal distribution in the same diagram).

Excel

This Excel function may be used for calculating Z_α:

$$Z_a \quad a = 0.99 \quad = \text{NORMSINV}(0.99)$$

It is then possible to create a user-defined VaR function in Visual Basic using the following code:

```
   Public Function myVaR (myMean, myStd As Variant, a As
Double)

       'Main equation
       If myStd > 0 And a > 0 And a < 1 Then
       myVaR=-myMean+myStd*Application.WorksheetFunction.
NormSInv(a)
       End If

       'Return error message if STD is not positive
       If myStd <= 0 Then
           myVaR = "ERROR: Standard deviation must be positive"
       End If

       'Return error message if confidence level is not between 0
       and 1
       If a <= 0 Or a >= 1 Then
           myVaR = "ERROR: Confidence level must be greater than 0
           and less than 1"

       End If

   End Function
```

where myMean is the average, myStd is the standard deviation (must be a positive value) and a is the level of confidence (between 0 and 1).

Now, we may run the function =myVaR(Mean, STD, a) from the datasheet itself, entering the different values in the appropriate places.

2.2.3.6.3.   Monte Carlo simulation method

Calculation Methods

- Historical method (based on past data)
  - Advantage: easy to implement.
  - Disadvantage: sensitive to the length of the time windows selected.
- Analytical method (based parametric structure of distribution)
  - Advantage: maintains consistency with the selected time windows and with other risk measures (e.g. standard deviation).
  - Disadvantage: requires an a priori assumption regarding the form of distribution (difficult to apply to derivatives).
- Simulation method (Monte Carlo)
  - Advantage: copes well with time windows, derivatives and complex forms of distribution.
  - Disadvantage: relatively complex to implement.

This method relies upon the ability to perform a computer simulation of various future scenarios. This approach overcomes the disadvantages of both the historical and the analytical approaches. The simulation may be performed for variable time windows, taking derivatives into account and implementing complex distribution breakdowns. The more future scenarios we test (iterations), the more precise the result of the simulation. This method is relatively less common due to its complexity, as it requires a deeper understanding of statistics, especially of time-series econometrics.

In this context, we will not detail the statistical proofs for this method, but we will outline the rationale for it. We shall start with a simple case study and subsequently proceed to make matters increasingly complicated.

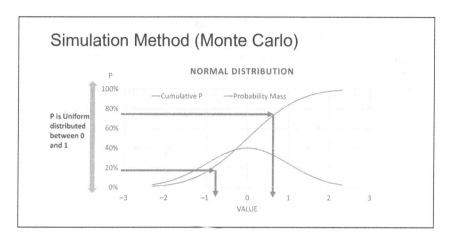

We might not know what the value of the portfolio will be exactly in one day, or even in one hour or one second, but we usually do possess sufficient information on the projected distribution of the portfolio's value. For instance, we know the average and the standard deviation of daily changes in value. Assuming a normal distribution, we may run a computer simulation of value changes based on said normal distribution.

In many programs, assuming normal distribution, it is possible to run a simulation with just a single command. All these programs rely on the same concept, which we will attempt to explain using an image which shows distribution (in this example, normal distribution) alongside cumulative distribution.

It is evident that for the cumulative distribution, every value on the *x*-axis has only a single P on the *y*-axis, and vice versa. In this example, for a probability of 20% on the *y*-axis, we would return a value of –0.842 on the *x*-axis.

A probability of 70% on the *y*-axis corresponds to a value of 0.524 on the *x*-axis.

All that remains is to let the computer randomly select a value between 0% and 100% and return a value from the normal distribution.

This process may be repeated as often as desired, each time returning a different value out of the normal distribution.

The appeal of this concept is that it may also be applied to cases where the distribution breakdown is significantly more complex.

How do we get our computer to randomly select a number?

Many programs contain a function which allows us to sample numbers between 0 and 1 at equal probabilities (this is called "0 to 1 Uniform distribution"). Some programs even allow us to calculate a value from the distribution based on the probability of its selection. Let us demonstrate how this works:

Excel

The Excel functions which may be used for sampling random numbers are as follows:

= RAND()	Random real number between 0 and 1
= RANDBETWEEN(Bottom, Top)	Random integer between Bottom and Top

Press F9 to recalculate manually.

To get a random number between −0.5 and 0.5, we may write the following:

= RAND()−0.5

To get a random number between 0.9 and 0.95, we may write the following:

= RANDBETWEEN(90,95)/100

To get a random number between 0.9000 and 0.9500 (more precise), we may write the following: = RANDBETWEEN(9000,9500)/10000

More generally, the formula is

= RANDBETWEEN(90*Scale,95*Scale)/Scale

where Scale determines the number of digits that will appear after the decimal point.

The function which converts probability into a normal distribution value is as follows:

$N(P, \text{Mean}, \text{STD})$ $P = 0.75; \text{Mean} = 0; \text{STD} = 1$ $= \text{NORMINV}(0.75, 0, 1)$

In order to get a random number out of a random distribution with an average of 0 and a standard deviation of 1, we may write the following:

= NORMINV(RAND(),0,1)

In order to get another number, we must press F9.

Should we wish to get two numbers simultaneously, we may copy the same formula to another cell in our Excel sheet.

The probability may also be modified to suit other types of distribution, such as a Chi-squared distribution of the standard deviation:

= CHIINV(RAND(),1)

Now that we understand how to return a randomly selected number, we may proceed to calculate the value at risk using a simulation. We run a simulation of the portfolio value for the following day according to the average change in portfolio value for the previous year. In addition, in order to verify the standard deviation which has been calculated for the entire year, we would like to randomly sample it out of a Chi-squared distribution. We would also like to restrict the range of random values the standard deviation will receive, and for this, we employ scale. The complete formula may be written thus as follows:

= NORMINV(RAND(),0.000367,CHIINV(RANDBETWEEN (0.904/0.025,0.954/0.025)*0.025,1))

Should we wish to repeat the process 30,000 times simultaneously, we must simply copy the formula to 30,000 rows in Excel.

Now that we have a column with all the results, we may calculate the VaR as in the historical method.

Every time the F9 key is pressed, 30,000 iterations are calculated again and a new VaR is given. We can see that these values are fairly close to each other. To further reduce the variation between the results each time the F9 key is pressed, all we need to do is increase the number of rows.

Some notes on VaR calculation in general:

(1) In all the calculations earlier, we must determine the composition of the portfolio for which the calculation is performed, e.g., 100 Apple

shares and 150 Google shares. There exist two approaches to performing this calculation:

- One approach is to calculate the portfolio value throughout the
  entire period according to a composition which has been determined in advance and only then calculate the VaR. The advantage
  of this approach is the relative simplicity of the calculation. The
  disadvantage is that it also inadvertently measures the correlation
  between stocks.
- The other method is to first calculate the VaR for Apple and
  Google stocks separately and only then combine them, taking into
  account the correlation between the two stocks. The advantage of
  this method is that there is no *a priori* assumption regarding the
  nature of the correlation between the stocks. This is important for
  measuring risk as empirical findings show that, in times of crisis,
  the correlation between assets increases, and the measured loss is
  accordingly greater as well. We will not expound on this method
  any further in this book.

(2) After the VaR has been measured, deviations from it must be
    recorded. Management must be informed whenever the VaR is
    exceeded. After approximately 100 days, five observations may be
    expected to exceed VaR(95) and only one is expected to exceed
    VaR(1).

(3) Every once in a while, backtesting may be performed on the VaR
    found at the beginning of the period. Having more exceptions than
    predicted will require a re-examination of the calculations.

(4) VaR must be matched to the time intervals we wish to examine. If we
    were to measure daily VaR but wished to calculate its value for ten
    days, we would have to use the following formula:

$$VaR * VaR(10\,days) = VaR(1\,day) \times \sqrt{10}$$

and more generally:

$$VaR * VaR(t\,days) = VaR(1\,day) \times \sqrt{t}$$

Many regulators use VaR as a basis for calculating capital adequacy
(see the following). The required capital is usually calculated according to
the following formula:

$$Required\,Capital = K \times VaR(99) \times \sqrt{10}$$

where $K = 3$.

2.2.3.6.4. Applications, advantages and disadvantages of
            value at risk

What are the Applications of VaR?

- Assessment of market risks
- Assessment of operational risks
- Calculations of capital

Value at risk is a measure used primarily for assessing market risk, but it has some wider applications. For instance, in the field of operational risks, which we will discuss in detail later on, the VaR approach allows us to assign a monetary value to risk more effectively than many other methods.

Furthermore, this method allows us to calculate the extent of loss at a given probability we seek to hedge. Banking supervisors in many countries use value at risk to determine the budget reserve each bank under their jurisdiction must hold. This is calculated separately for each bank.

Value at risk has considerable benefits compared to other measures:

- It is easy to understand and expresses the projected scope of damage in a single number.
- The value is given in both monetary value and percentage.
- It allows for a risk comparison between various assets as well as a comparison with overall market risk.
- It allows us to assess risk even for portfolios with an asset composition which includes derivatives.
- It takes the entire distribution of asset value changes into account (unlike standard deviation, for instance).
- It is very widely used.

However, the measure also has a number of weaknesses:

- It is not additive, i.e., the VaR for a portfolio containing two assets is not necessarily the sum of the separate VaRs of those assets.
- Its widespread use has led to its being regarded by traders and bankers as a form of "ultimate truth", lulling them into a false sense of security which may lead to excessive risk taking.
- All too often, the data upon which VaR is based are historical and bear no relevance for the future (there are those who equate risk management based exclusively on VaR to driving a car forward while relying only on the information one can see in the mirrors, which may reflect the straight road we have driven over but not the curve coming up ahead).
- Yet another disadvantage is that VaR only measures one side of the distribution — it measures loss without taking into account the potential gain from an investment.

2.2.3.7. *Measures of risk and return*

How can we compare two investments, one of which has an annual return rate of 6% with a 2% standard deviation and the other with a 12% annual return rate and 4% standard deviation?

Clearly, the return on the latter investment is twice as great as that of the former, but it is also twice as risky.

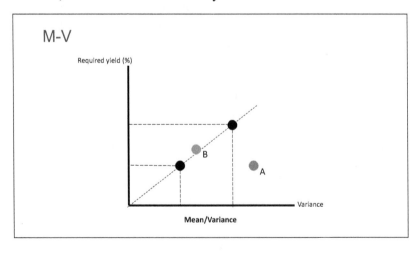

One way to choose between the investments is to look at the return-to-risk ratio, a method called **Mean-Variance (MV)**. In the example earlier, the ratio for the first investment is 3 (6/2%), as is that of the second investment (12/4%), giving no indication that either investment is preferable over the other.

The MV method is mainly used to rule out irrelevant investments with both lower return rates and higher standard deviation.

For instance, in the above image, we can rule out the investment marked (A), whereas one marked (B) may be worth examining further.

In addition, the annual return rate must be compared to the return of a risk-free asset. This method, which looks at the risk/return ratio and also takes into account the return on a risk-free asset, is called the **Sharpe ratio**:

$$Sharpe\,ratio = \frac{\bar{y} - r}{Std(y)}$$

where $\bar{y}$ is the average return and r is the risk-free interest rate.

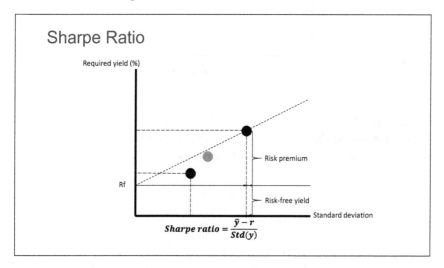

Let us suppose the risk-free interest rate is currently 2%. We will now attempt to calculate once more which investment is preferable.

In the first case, the investment will yield 6% less 2%, i.e., 4%, giving a Sharpe ratio of 2.

In the first case, the investment will yield 12% less 2%, i.e., 10%, resulting in a Sharpe ratio of 2.5.

2.5 is a better ratio than 2, and we should therefore select the latter option. This investment is also preferable to the one marked with (B) in the previous image.

2.2.3.8. *CAPM*

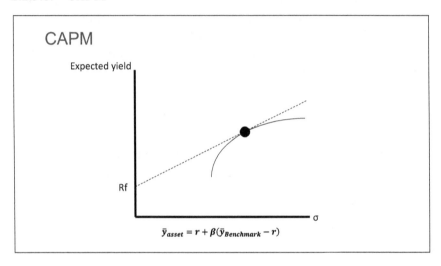

The Capital Asset Pricing Model (CAPM)[3] offers an approach to capital asset pricing which takes into account the risk and return inherent in these assets compared to those of a benchmark asset:

$$\bar{y}_{\text{asset}} = r + \beta\left(\bar{y}_{\text{Benchmark}} - r\right)$$

$$\beta = \rho_{\text{Asset, Benchmark}} \frac{\text{Std}\left(y_{\text{asset}}\right)}{\text{Std}\left(y_{\text{Benchmark}}\right)}$$

---

[3] CAPM is a very comprehensive model, but in this book, it is mentioned without further elaboration. The model features a vast array of useful concepts with which risk managers would be wise to acquaint themselves:

Capital allocation line, capital market line, *ex ante* return (expected return), *ex post* return (actual return), yield, market return, nominal risk-free rate, Sharpe ratio, security market line, correlation, weight of stock in portfolio, etc.

where $\bar{y}_{\text{asset}}$ is the average asset return, $\bar{y}_{\text{Benchmark}}$ is the average benchmark return, r is the risk-free asset return, β is the indicator comparing asset risk to benchmark risk, $\rho_{\text{Asset,Benchmark}}$ is the statistical correlation coefficient and $\frac{\text{Std}(y_{\text{asset}})}{\text{Std}(y_{\text{Benchmark}})}$ is the ratio of asset to benchmark standard deviation.

CAPM is one of the models most commonly employed to assist in portfolio selection. It may be used to measure to what extent an investment in a particular asset would be riskier than the pre-existing risk in the market (as reflected in the benchmark portfolio).

Unlike risk measures which try to estimate the extent of risk inherent in a portfolio, CAPM is used to select the optimal asset combination out of a multitude of options, based on both risk and return.

Excel

These are the Excel functions which may be used for performing the calculations above:

$\beta(x,y)$ $x = 1;2;3 \; y = 2.5,3,5$ $= \text{SLOPE}(\{1,2,3\},\{2.5,3,5\})$

$\rho_{x,y}$ $x = 1;2;3 \; y = 2.5,3,5$ $= \text{CORREL}(\{1,2,3\},\{2.5,3,5\})$

2.2.3.9. *Greeks*

The Greeks are a group of measures used to quantify financial derivative risk. These include Delta, Vega, Theta, Rho, Lambda, Gamma, Vanna, Vomma, Charm, Veta, Vera, Color, Speed, Ultima and Zomma.

Beyond mentioning their existence and the fact they are used to assess financial derivative risk, we will not discuss these measures any further in this book.

2.2.3.10. *Stress, scenario and sensitivity testing*

The various risk measures introduced thus far have largely been based on historical data. Even VaR, which answers the question "what the potential loss of an investment portfolio is, at its current composition, in the near future?", is typically calculated based on historical data. In other words, if fluctuation in market indices has been low recently, this will result in a low VaR. Conversely, if the indices have recently experienced very high fluctuation levels, the VaR will correspondingly be high as well.

Stress, Scenario and Sensitivity Testing

Tools for measuring risk in abnormal financial environments or situations:

- Stress tests
- Scenarios
- Sensitivity tests

Stress, scenario and sensitivity tests are measures which overcome the need for historical data, and we shall expound on them in this section. What these three measures have in common is their ability to quantify risk in abnormal financial environments and for varying time ranges. However, the greatest weakness of these three measures is their inability to measure the probability that these abnormal environmental conditions will indeed take place.

2.2.3.10.1.   Stress testing

A stress test measures the loss to the portfolio in a hypothetical scenario where one of the risk factors of the portfolio has experienced extreme changes.

Stress Tests

- Test the sensitivity of the portfolio to changes in one out of a variety of risk factors:
  - Prices
  - Exchange rates
  - Volatility
  - Change in ranking
  - etc.

An example of an abnormal occurrence in the stock market would be a 50% crash of stock indices. Using the stress test, we can estimate the scope of loss to the portfolio in such a scenario. A portfolio consisting exclusively of shares will lose 50% of its value, whereas the value of a portfolio with no shares will not be affected at all.

In order to obtain a complete understanding of the risks inherent in a portfolio, several extreme risk factor scenarios are examined, such as higher/lower exchange rates, higher/lower inflation, extreme interest rate changes and increased fluctuation.

Stress tests may be performed for a single change to one particular risk factor, or they may be performed for a scenario where multiple risk factors undergo simultaneous changes. For instance, the value of a stock portfolio traded overseas is subject to both share price risk and exchange rate risk. If the overseas share were to lose 10% of its value at the same time that the exchange rate appreciates by 10%, the overall loss in value to the portfolio would reach 19%.

2.2.3.10.2.   Scenario testing

A scenario test measures the loss to a portfolio resulting from an extreme hypothetical event where several risk factors are expected to change simultaneously (though the extent of the change to each individual factor need not be extreme itself).

Scenarios

- Test the portfolio within the framework of extreme real-life events:
  - Changes in interest rates, stock prices, exchange rates, etc. in the aftermath of the 9/11 crisis.
  - Changes in interest rates, stock prices, exchange rates, etc. during the subprime crisis.
  - Changes in interest rates, stock prices, exchange rates, etc. in the event of an earthquake.
  - etc.

When investment committees discuss stress scenarios, there are frequent disagreements over precisely what constitutes "stress". Is a 20% drop in share prices considered a stress scenario or should the threshold be 60%?

Risk managers frequently make use of real, historical scenarios which occurred during times of crisis, examining how the risk factors changed during the crisis. They examine, for instance, changes in interest rates, stock prices, exchange rates, etc., trying to estimate how such a scenario would have affected the portfolio in question.

The use of a uniform set of scenarios across all companies allows regulators to compare the severity of damage between vastly different companies and portfolios.

2.2.3.10.3. Sensitivity testing

A sensitivity test measures the *change* in the scope of loss to an investment portfolio dependent upon *changes* to risk factors.

Sensitivity Tests

- Test the change in the extent of loss to the portfolio dependent upon changes in risk factors:
  - How much to divert from one investment channel to another?

Let us suppose we wish to convert an investment in stocks to an investment in bonds. We would like to answer the following question: "By how much will the interest rate risk to the bond element increase, and, at the same time, by how much will the price risk to the stock element be reduced?" The answer will help us determine how much money to divert from one element to the other.

Stress tests, scenarios and sensitivity tests are used to assess various risks.

What are They Used for?

- Assessment of market risks
- Assessment of operational risks, credit risks, liquidity risks, etc.
- Policy decisions

We may also use these tests to determine policy. For instance, we may assume different portfolio compositions and measure the risks and rewards of these portfolios in various scenarios.

2.2.4. *Market Risk Management*

We have so far discussed the various methods used to measure market risk (exposure, fluctuation, loss and simulation). Once we perform the calculations and make sure the values are correct, what do we do next?

Do a daily VaR of USD 42,699 and a daily standard deviation of 0.79% indicate a risky portfolio?

We are now at the stage of "monitoring and assessing risk" in the risk management process (see introduction). How do we proceed from here?

Managing Market Risks

- To what should we compare the values of the various risk measures?
- How do we reach a decision?
- How can we minimize the risk?

Generally speaking, we must now answer the following questions:

- **To what should we compare the results?**

  Having measured and quantified the risk, we now wish to compare it to other values in order to tell, for instance, whether it is substantial or not. The values to which our portfolio's risk measures are compared are as follows:

  o **Historical values:** The various risk measures may be traced over the course of time, telling us whether the risk has increased, decreased or remained at similar levels compared to previous points in time.

  o **Risk values of other assets:** The risk measures of multiple assets may be compared to each other; that is, the risk embodied in one asset may be compared to that of another asset.

- o **Return:** The greater the risk, the higher the projected return. We may use measures which combine risk and return and compare them between various assets.
- o **Alternative portfolios:**
  - **Benchmark:** When examining the risk levels of a portfolio, it is common to compare it to a benchmark portfolio which represents a predetermined investment policy. In this way, it is possible to tell if a portfolio has strayed too far from the policy which was originally set.
  - **Market portfolio:** This represents the risk measures of an average market portfolio. Examples of these are the general stock index, bond index, etc.
  - **Competing portfolio:** What were the risk measures of competing portfolios in our category? We may compare our portfolio to a single competing portfolio, to an average of the measures of several competing portfolios, etc. Typically, the comparison is made with competitors in the same category, e.g., investment firms specializing in government bonds.

Now that we have performed these comparisons, we know whether our portfolio has a higher or lower level of risk compared to the alternatives, and we can even attach a numerical value to this difference.

- • **What is our decision?**

Even with precisely quantified answers regarding the risk in our portfolio compared to other investment options, human judgment is still required in order to decide whether to continue to invest in a portfolio in its current form, modify it or find an alternative investment.

For example, just because one portfolio is riskier than another does not necessarily mean that we will choose the one with lower risk. The choice ultimately depends to a large extent on the **risk perception** and **personal preference** of decision makers. Risk-averse investors may prefer the lower-risk investment, whereas more daring investors will choose the riskier investment. Furthermore, not every decision is necessarily dichotomous. It may be possible to select a mix of higher-risk and lower-risk portfolios.

- **How do we reduce the risk?**

  The risk may be reduced through risk management, according to the methods described in the introductory chapter of this book:

  o **Risk avoidance:** Avoiding investment in a risky asset altogether is often a reasonable option for managers. For example, many investment funds make an *a priori* decision not to invest in derivatives and to invest only in assets traded at the stock exchange.

  o **Risk reduction procedures:** Using suitable hedging tools such as options or forwards, it may be possible to reduce the loss of a portfolio in various scenarios. Risk reduction usually comes at a certain cost and must therefore be subjected to the appropriate cost-benefit calculations. For instance, it is possible to decide to invest in promising stocks overseas while at the same time purchasing an option to hedge against an increase in the exchange rate. Furthermore, many investment committees set minimum and maximum thresholds for the levels of risk they would consider acceptable for a portfolio, e.g., investing up to 30% of a portfolio in stocks, up to 50% in corporate bonds, up to 30% in government bonds and at least 10% in cash (the numbers do not necessarily add up to 100%).

  Many entities manage market risk by setting a portfolio structure (stocks, bonds, cash, etc.) and then requesting a report whenever the portfolio crosses certain minimum and maximum thresholds[4] (e.g., exceeds the VaR or certain values set by company policy).

  o **Risk transfer:** Some financial entities transfer their risk to other parties. To give an example, mortgage banks require their customers to have a life insurance policy. This way, should the customer pass away, the bank ensures that the insurance company will continue to pay the mortgage owed to the bank.

  o **Acceptance of consequences:** This is one of the most popular risk management methods in the world of investment. Most investments in stocks, bonds, real estate, public companies, private

---

[4]The composition of an investment portfolio varies over time. Sometimes this change is made actively by the portfolio managers, wishing to increase the weight of a particular asset (e.g., bonds) at the expense of another asset (e.g., stocks). However, most often, this change is passive and is merely the result of changing asset prices.

companies, etc. are made after an analysis of the potential risks and rewards involved. Though they might not readily admit it, investors accept a potential loss to their stock portfolio. For instance, were we to invest USD 10,000 in the stock of Chinese internet company Baidu because of its profit potential, we would have to acknowledge that we risk losing part of the money we invested.

o **Recovery plan:** Naturally, if our portfolio goes up by 10% and then down again by 10%, we have not returned to the original value but in fact dropped down to a value lower than that of the original investment. Therefore, to recover from a loss, we will generally require more capital for a renewed investment, in order to earn back what we have lost. In such a case, we must ensure in advance that we have a budget which will allow us to return to at least the original portfolio value. Putting together such a recovery plan is not a simple affair, and the relevance of our sources of funding for the aftermath of such a loss event must be taken into careful consideration. For instance, some of these sources may no longer wish to fund our investment once we have lost money, and others may have lost money themselves, rendering them incapable of assisting us.

Many financial institutions are required by regulation to allocate a certain minimum capital reserve which will allow them to recover even from an extreme outlier.

2.2.5. *Capital Allocation*

In order to counter the effects of market risk, financial entities are required to allocate a certain minimum capital reserve for times of crisis. This is alternately known as capital adequacy, regulatory capital or capital requirement.

Capital Allocation

- Capital reserve for times of crisis.
- The capital requirement is calculated as the ratio of risky asset exposure to the total extent of the portfolio in question.

This capital requirement is calculated as the percentage of risky assets out of the total asset array of the portfolio in question. Banking supervisors, for instance, demand that banks maintain a ratio of at least 8%. Sometimes, the requirement rises to 9%, and on occasion, the local regulator will modify the requirement according to developments in the economy and the state of the market. Banks which fail to meet these demands may have to pay substantial fines or even risk having their permits revoked. For this reason, many banks in fact allocate slightly more capital than the minimum requirement, thus hedging themselves from the risk of non-compliance with the law.

The exact manner in which each financial institution must allocate its capital reserve depends on the particulars of local regulations, which will not be explored here. Every country has its own rules regarding various forms of financial activity. Thus, for instance, even in the same country, different rules may apply for banks, insurance companies and other institutions.

Chapter 3

Credit Risk

Accompanying presentations: 3. Risk Management - Credit Risk (Part I)

3.1. Credit

Introduction

- Credit
The trust granted to a buyer or borrower for a certain sum of money.

- Loan
The credit granted to a borrower from the lender upon the condition that it will be returned at a certain point or points in time, as specified in the loan agreement. The borrower typically also commits to paying interest and sometimes linkage differentials as well.

Credit is the trust that a buyer or borrower will pay a certain sum of money in the future. Without trust, it is hard to imagine anyone giving money to someone else with any expectation of ever getting it back. The impact of trust on economic systems is dramatic, as it forms the foundation of business transactions between many financial entities. Based on the sheer number of businesses and consumers seeking to purchase goods around the world, it is evident that the financial systems we know incorporate rather more trust than mistrust, in part out of an understanding that, in the long term, we as a society would pay a heavy price if people refused to place trust in others.

Credit is given through a loan with clearly defined terms of repayment. These terms usually determine repayment dates, interest rates and occasionally also linkage differentials due to changes in inflation.

Introduction

<u>Examples</u>
Private individual
- I have paid for a product which I will not receive for two weeks (given credit).
- I have received a product for which I will only pay in two weeks (received credit).
- I have worked today but will only receive my wages at the beginning of next month (given credit).

<u>Business owner</u>
- I have provided goods and will receive payment up to 60 days later (given credit).
- I have issued a bond and received an advance payment (received credit).
- I have employed a subcontractor whom I will pay back to back (given credit to the customer and received credit from the subcontractor).

People give and receive credit every day. When a private individual purchases some shirt, the shirt is immediately transferred into the possession of that individual as soon as the payment is cleared. However, when buying a refrigerator, washing machine, car, etc., very often there is a delay between payment and the moment the buyer receives the product. If we have paid today but will only receive the product in two weeks, we have effectively given credit to the business owner.

Conversely, returning to the example of buying a shirt, if we have paid using a credit card, we have received credit from the credit card company.

On occasion, we give credit without referring to it as such. For instance, if I have worked throughout the month but will only receive my salary at the beginning of the following month, I have effectively given my employer credit.

Business owners provide goods but may receive payment up to 60 days later, granting their customers credit.

Bonds and advance payments are examples of credit being given to a business.

A repair contractor employs a subcontractor to complete the electricity works, and they have agreed that the electrician will only be repaid once payment has been received from the customer. In such a case, which is sometimes referred to as "back to back", the contractor gives credit to the customer (until the completion of the repair works) and, at the same time, receives credit from the electrician (until payment has been transferred).

Introduction

Why take credit?
- Maintaining continuous business activity (based on future inflows).

Why give credit?
- The creditor earns a profit (through interest).

How is this beneficial to the economy?
- Efficient allocation of resources.

What motivation do we have to grant or accept credit?

For the debtor, credit makes it possible to maintain continuous economic activity.

For example, in exchange for the customer's payment, which is due in two months, the business owner must today purchase raw materials, pay employees, etc. In order to maintain business activity, the owner may use credit to bridge the two months between the time the job is carried out and the moment the payment is received.

For the creditor, credit is a legitimate source of income by means of fees and interest. The banking system is founded on the ability to receive interest on the loans it grants to its clients.

Why is credit good for the economy?

Credit benefits the economy as it enables accelerated growth. Let us look at the following example.

There exists a farmstead with two corn farmers, each of whom owns two sacks of corn seeds.

Case I — no credit
The first farmer sows the seeds from two bags, and by the end of the growing season, he has managed to double the amount of corn in his possession to 4 bags.

The second farmer is more skilled and knowledgeable than the first, and his land is more fertile. By the end of the season, he has managed to quadruple his corn to 8 bags.

The total amount of corn on this farm at the end of the season will be 12 bags (4+8).

Case II — with credit
The first farmer lends his two bags to the second farmer, who, thanks to his superior skills and better land, manages to increase the number of bags to 16 by the end of the season (2 bags belonging to the first farmer plus 2 bags belonging to the second farmer times 4).

The first farmer may request interest in addition to the loan principal, ending the season with 5 bags rather than 4.

This leaves the second farmer with 11 bags (16 bags minus the 5 returned to the first farmer), making the total number of corn bags on the farm 16.

The farm where credit was used experienced more rapid growth than the one where no credit was given. From a more general perspective, it is evident that credit allows for a better allocation of resources — rather than 2 bags per farmer, the second farmer will have 4 bags and the first farmer none. This is a better allocation of resources as it leads to increased growth — 16 bags of corn rather than 12 at the end of the period.

In practice, however, borrowers do not always repay their debt. A certain percentage of borrowers are unable to fulfill their obligation to repay the loan they have taken. This is the element of credit risk we will discuss in the following section.

3.2. Credit Risk

> ## Credit Risk
> The possibility of a loss in profits or capital resulting from default on a loan.

Credit risk is the possibility of incurring a loss in profits or capital due to a default on a loan. The default may be due to either the loan principal or the interest — or both — not being repaid at maturity.

Financial institutions which grant their clients credit, such as banks, credit card companies, and bond purchasers, are all exposed to credit risk.

The subprime crisis in the United States was the result of materialized credit risk. The processes leading up to the crisis, the dramatic events of the crisis itself, the recovery period and the financial reality in its wake are all fascinating topics in their own right, but this book is too short to explore them all in detail. We will nevertheless state that the crisis was triggered when, at one point, it was discovered that borrowers who had taken credit from the banks as mortgage were unable to repay it according to the agreed terms. This phenomenon was so widespread that the banks themselves incurred severe losses, with some even driven to bankruptcy. The crisis then spread to other sectors of the American economy as well as to other parts of the globe.

In order to mitigate credit risk, we must first properly define it. It turns out that between full repayment of the loan according to its terms and complete non-repayment, there is a wide range of definitions for bad debt.

Credit Risk

- The money will not be repaid (bad debt).
- The money is unlikely to be repaid (doubtful debt).
- The money will be repaid but more than 90 days late (debt in arrears).
- The money will definitely be repaid, experiencing trouble right now (debt in temporary arrears).
- The principal will be repaid but not the interest (non-performing debt).

Borrowers who fail to meet the terms of a loan are called "bad borrowers" and the debt they owe may be divided into the following categories:

- The debt will definitely not be repaid (bad debt).
- There is a slight chance that the debt will be repaid (doubtful debt).

- The debt will probably be repaid, but there will be a delay of at least 90 days (non-performing debt).
- The debt will be repaid but there are issues at the moment, such as liquidity problems (debt in temporary arrears).
- The principal will be repaid but not the interest (non-profit debt).

Different states and regulators classify borrowers using different systems, and any further exploration of the topic therefore requires that the regulations of each individual country be discussed separately.

It is important to classify bad borrowers, as each type requires different mitigation. For instance, bad debt is registered as a loss on the income statement, whereas a debt in temporary arrears will affect a bank's cash flow but has almost no effect on its income statement.

3.3. Main Credit Risk Parameters

The field of credit risk management features many important concepts. Among these are credit exposure, counterparty credit risk, credit valuation adjustment, etc. In this section, we shall focus on the most important of these.[1]

3.3.1. *Probability of Default (PD)*

Components of Credit Risk

PD
Probability of Default

PD is the probability that a default (i.e., a failure to return credit) will occur. This event of default is defined in a binary manner — either a default occurred or it did not. For this reason, the precise definition of "default" is of critical importance. At one end of the scale, default may be defined as the conclusion of a legal process and a declaration of

---

[1]As mentioned by the Basel II Accord.

bankruptcy by the borrower, who is consequently unable to return the credit; at the other extreme, default may be defined as a delay in delivering just a single partial payment out of several.

For instance, if a company whose bonds are traded at the bond market is late in paying its coupons, even by one day, the company is considered to have defaulted. On the other hand, many banks allow their clients up to 90 days of arrears before determining that the client has defaulted.

Maximum Profit for Creditor

$$Max(Profit) =$$

$$(1 - PD)R_L L - \text{Expenses}$$

$PD \in [0\text{-}100\%]$

PD is measured in percent. For instance, if PD = 0.5%, this means the borrower has a 0.5% probability of defaulting in the coming year. The value 1-PD is the rate at which loans will be returned (sometimes referred to as the "survival rate" of the borrower). In this example, there is a probability of 99.5% that the borrower will repay the loan in accordance with the terms agreed upon when the loan was granted.

The PD value affects the income of the creditor.[2] If PD is zero (a hypothetical situation where failure is impossible), the rate of returned loans (or borrower's "survival rate") will be 100%, and the credit giver will enjoy a profit of $R_L L$, where R_L is the interest on the credit and L is the amount of money given as credit. A positive PD means a lower repayment rate and consequently reduced income and profits.

---

[2]Mugerman, Y., Tzur, J., & Jacobi, A. (2018). Mortgage loans and bank risk taking: Finding the risk "Sweet Spot". *The Quarterly Journal of Finance*, 8(4), 1840008.

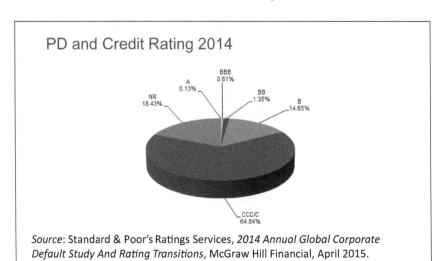

PD and Credit Rating 2014

Source: Standard & Poor's Ratings Services, *2014 Annual Global Corporate Default Study And Rating Transitions*, McGraw Hill Financial, April 2015.

PD values may be divided into categories such as those of Standard & Poor's Rating Services for business firms.[3] Each rating group is assigned upper and lower default rates on an annual basis. For instance, in 2014, firms with a PD of up to 0.14% were rated A. Firms with a PD between 1.35% and 14.65% were rated B.

Due to the nature of business cycles, high years see a thriving economy with generally low rates of failure, whereas low years will see higher rates of failure overall. As a result, while PD for the same company may change over time, its rating may remain stable, as the PD values for each rating group (AAA, AA, BBB, etc.) also change according to the state of the economy.

---

[3] Some interesting facts…

Different agents use different systems to mark their ratings. Following is a table comparing the various rating agents:

S&P	AAA	AA+	AA	AA−	A+	A−	BBB+	BBB	BBB−	BB+	BB−	B+	B−	CCC+	CCC−	CC	C	D
Moody's	Aaa	Aa1	Aa2	Aa3	A1	A3	Baa1	Baa2	Baa3	Ba1	Ba3	B1	B3	Caa1	Caa3	Ca	C	
Fitch	AAA	AA+	AA	AA−	A+	A−	BBB+	BBB	BBB−	BB+	BB−	B+	B−	CCC+	CCC−	CC	C	D

Source of Calibrations: Bank for international Settlements (2011).

PD and Credit Rating 2009

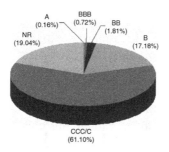

Source: Standard & Poor's Ratings Services, *2009 Annual Global Corporate Default Study And Rating Transitions*, McGraw Hill Financial, March 2010.

In 2009, a year after the subprime crisis, even a company with a PD value of 0.16% would have received a rating of A (as opposed to 2014, when a similar value would have seen that company receive a rating of BBB), and companies with a probability of up to 17.18% were rated B.

A risk manager, upon being informed that a company has been rated A, must at the very least check who has given it this rating, when it was rated and what its PD value is in order to properly assess its credit risk.

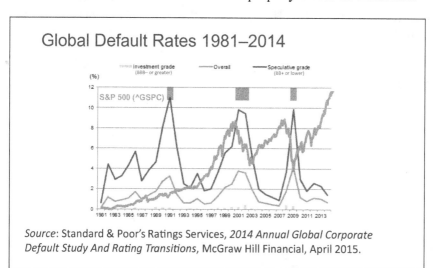

Global Default Rates 1981–2014

Source: Standard & Poor's Ratings Services, *2014 Annual Global Corporate Default Study And Rating Transitions*, McGraw Hill Financial, April 2015.

The chart in this slide shows the PD values for the rating categories BBB– and BB+ as well as a general average, for the years 1981–2014. Three peaks may be observed, in 1991, 2001 and 2009, indicating that in these years, companies with a BB+ rating maintained their rating, despite the fact that their probability of default had more than doubled compared to other years during this time frame.

These changes are connected to other financial developments:

- The Gulf War broke out in 1990, and the price of an oil barrel doubled, from USD 30 to USD 60. Although this change had little effect on the S&P500 index, it did significantly increase the probability of default for many companies.
- The year 2000 saw a stock crisis in the wake of the dot-com crash. Many companies went bankrupt the following year, affecting the rating system.
- The subprime crisis of 2007–2008 led to a readjustment of ratings the following year, to correspond with the increased probability of default at the time.

While adjusting the rating system to different PD rates may be seen as an expression of flexibility and understanding with regard to the effects of business cycles, it has also been the source of some criticism, as it is difficult to measure the risk of a company if the scale changes with such frequency.

Nevertheless, this system is very widespread, and it is a convenient method which allows us to distinguish between companies with high and low credit risk.

Probability of Default over Time (%)

	Time (years)						
	1	2	3	4	5	7	10
Aaa	0.000	0.013	0.013	0.037	0.104	0.244	0.494
Aa	0.021	0.059	0.103	0.184	0.273	0.443	0.619
A	0.055	0.177	0.362	0.549	0.756	1.239	2.136
Baa	0.181	0.510	0.933	1.427	1.953	3.031	4.904
Ba	1.157	3.191	5.596	8.146	10.453	14.440	20.101
B	4.465	10.432	16.344	21.510	26.173	34.721	44.573
Caa	18.163	30.204	39.709	47.317	53.768	61.181	72.384

Source: Moody's.

The probability of default is usually measured on a yearly basis. According to the table in this slide, the probability that a company rated Baa will declare bankruptcy within a year is 0.181%. The probability that the same company will file for bankruptcy within ten years is 4.904%.

Independent Probability

Probability of default in year *X* at time 0

	Time (years)						
	1	2	3	4	5	7	10
Aaa	0.000	0.013	0.013	0.037	0.104	0.244	0.494
Aa	0.021	0.059	0.103	0.184	0.273	0.443	0.619
A	0.055	0.177	0.362	0.549	0.756	1.239	2.136
Baa	0.181	0.510	0.933	1.427	1.953	3.031	4.904
Ba	1.157	3.191	5.596	8.146	10.453	14.440	20.101
B	4.465	10.432	16.344	21.510	26.173	34.721	44.573
Caa	18.163	30.204	39.709	47.317	53.768	61.181	72.384

What is the probability of default during the third year for a company ranked B?

$$16.344 - 10.432\% = 5.912\%$$

The table also allows us to calculate the probability that a company rated B will declare bankruptcy during year 3: 16.344–10.432% = 5.912%.

Independent Probability

	Time (years)						
	1	2	3	4	5	7	10
Aaa	0.000	0.013	0.013	0.037	0.104	0.244	0.494
Aa	0.021	0.059	0.103	0.184	0.273	0.443	0.619
A	0.055	0.177	0.362	0.549	0.756	1.239	2.136
Baa	0.181	0.510	0.933	1.427	1.953	3.031	4.904
Ba	1.157	3.191	5.596	8.146	10.453	14.440	20.101
B	4.465	10.432	16.344	21.510	26.173	34.721	44.573
Caa	18.163	30.204	39.709	47.317	53.768	61.181	72.384

What is the survival rate for a bond rated B until the end of the third year?

100-16.344% = 83.656%

Using the same table, we may also calculate the survival rate of various companies. For instance, the three-year survival rate of a company rated B is 83.656% (100−16.344%).

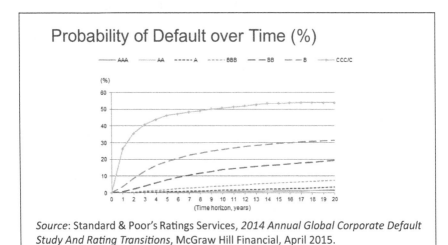

Probability of Default over Time (%)

Source: Standard & Poor's Ratings Services, *2014 Annual Global Corporate Default Study And Rating Transitions*, McGraw Hill Financial, April 2015.

This diagram shows the evolution of the PD values for different rating categories over the course of time. It is interesting to note that the probability of default for a company rated CCC quickly rises to 40% by the third year and then continues to rise at a more gradual rate, to 55% by year 20.

By contrast, companies rated AAA maintain consistently low rates of failure throughout the entire period.

One-Year Corporate Transition Rates (2014)

From/to	AAA	AA	A	BBB	BB	B	CCC/C	D	NR
Global									
AAA	100.00	0.00	0.00	0.00	0.00	0.00	0.00	0.00	0.00
AA	0.29	93.26	4.40	0.00	0.00	0.00	0.00	0.00	2.05
A	0.00	1.43	89.87	5.48	0.00	0.00	0.00	0.00	3.23
BBB	0.00	0.06	3.12	85.52	4.90	0.00	0.00	0.00	6.40
BB	0.00	0.00	0.00	3.63	79.97	6.87	0.24	0.16	9.13
B	0.00	0.00	0.00	0.15	3.58	76.04	4.57	2.39	13.27
CCC/C	0.00	0.00	0.00	0.00	0.00	5.85	49.71	25.73	18.71

Another table used for measuring credit risk is the transition matrix, which shows the probability that, for instance, a company with a rating of A will maintain its rating the following year (89.87%), be promoted to AA (1.43%) or pushed down to BBB (5.48%). The percentages must add up to 100%, and the rightmost column of the table contains the percentage of companies which were not rated the previous year. It is evident from the table that the probability of a company's rating falling is greater than of it rising.

Why do companies dedicate so much effort to preserving their rating? The answer is that this guarantees better credit terms. The greater the stability of a company, the lower its PD rate, the lower the interest it will receive on the credit it wishes to obtain and the greater the amount of credit it will be able to request compared to a similar company with a lower rating.

3.3.2. *Exposure at Default (EAD)*

Components of Credit Risk

EAD
Exposure At Default

EAD is the credit exposure in the event of default, measured in monetary terms. For example, a borrower owes ISK 100,000 to the Icelandic bank Íslandsbanki. It turns out, however, that this borrower is broke and will not be able to repay the bank. The bank's credit exposure toward this borrower is ISK 100,000.

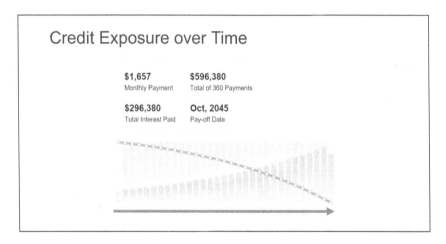

Credit Exposure over Time

$1,657 — Monthly Payment
$596,380 — Total of 360 Payments
$296,380 — Total Interest Paid
Oct, 2045 — Pay-off Date

The size of a loan with monthly repayments decreases over time. At first, the money being repaid mostly covers the interest rather than the principal. Over time, however, the portion covering the principal gradually increases and the portion assigned to the interest decreases until the loan is eliminated altogether. For such a loan, EAD goes down every month as a function of time.

EAD generally depends not only on time but also on the type of loan, its accounting value and any mitigating factor which might affect credit risk (e.g., execution of surety bonds).

The precise manner in which EAD is calculated varies by regulator, and in some cases even by individual banks, which may fall under the jurisdiction of the same regulator but use different methods for managing credit risk. For instance, banks subordinate to a regulator which has adopted the recommendations of Basel II, and which have adopted a Foundation Internal Rating-Based (F-IRB) approach, will use a different approach than banks which are subordinate to the same regulator but have been granted permission to employ an Advanced Internal Rating-Based approach (A-IRB). Banks using the F-IRB approach receive detailed instructions on how EAD should be calculated, whereas banks using the A-IRB approach enjoy greater flexibility with regard to the calculation of EAD.

Risk managers who specialize in managing credit risk must be familiar with the various types of calculations in general and in particular, the specific instructions required by the regulations under which they operate.

3.3.3. *Loss Given Default (LGD)*

Components of Credit Risk

LGD
Loss Given Default

LGD is the monetary loss in the event of default, measured as percentage out of the total credit exposure in case of failure. Suppose a borrower owes Íslandsbanki ISK 100,000 but is bankrupt and therefore unable to repay the debt. However, the bank can realize the borrower's collateral and recover ISK 60,000, reducing the bank's loss to just ISK 40,000, i.e., LGD in this case would be 40%.

Recovery Rate

The portion of a debt which may be recovered after the borrower has defaulted.

Examples of factors which may affect the recovery rate:
- Place on the list of creditors (higher place — higher recovery rate).
- Liquidation costs (greater liquidation capacity — higher recovery rate).
- Geographical spread (narrower spread — higher recovery rate).
- Length of recovery period (shorter length — higher recovery rate).

The recoverable part of the loan in the example earlier is 60%. This is often referred to as the recovery rate and equals 1-LGD.

The ability of the lender to recover at least a part of the loan is affected by various factors, including but not limited to the following:

- **Position on the creditor list:** Generally speaking, the higher a creditor's place on the list, the higher their recovery rate, i.e., they will recover a greater portion of the loan and will enjoy a lower LGD compared to other creditors.
- **Liquidation costs:** A factory which has declared bankruptcy will often own equipment worth hundreds of thousands of U.S. Dollars and, on occasion, will also hold bank deposits, tradable stocks and other forms of property which may be liquidated in order to eliminate a portion of the debt.

    Deposits and stocks are relatively easy to liquidate, and the money received from their sale may be used to cover the debt. The liquidation of types of property, however, is often a more complicated process, and the search for a buyer often entails additional costs. Furthermore, liquidation in the wake of bankruptcy often results in a forced sale, leaving the creditors with little bargaining room and compelling them to sell at lower prices than they would have succeeded in obtaining under different circumstances. As a rule, the easier it is to liquidate a company's property, the higher the recovery rate and the lower the LGD.
- **Geographical spread:** When the property is scattered across distant areas or even countries, it is often more difficult to sell. Sometimes, the same type of property (e.g., real estate) may be sold with greater ease in one country than in another, due to differences in national legislation, etc. As a rule, the smaller the geographical spread, the higher the recovery rate and the lower the LGD.
- **Length of recovery period:** Stocks may be sold fairly quickly, whereas selling factory buildings might require some time. During this time, the debt continues to accumulate and the interest continues to accrue. A shorter recovery period signifies a higher recovery rate and a lower LGD.

3.3.4. *Collateral*

One way to ensure a low LGD and a high recovery rate is by pledging assets as collateral.

Collateral

The borrower's pledge of an asset or group of assets to guarantee the repayment of a debt.

<u>Examples</u>
- Equity (vs. liabilities)
- Deposits, savings plans and tradable securities
- Future commitments (post-dated checks and contracts)
- Real estate
- Supplies and equipment
- Personal assets of owners

Collateral is the borrower's pledge of a particular asset or group of assets to guarantee the repayment of a loan. For example, borrowers who take out a mortgage pledge their house or apartment as collateral to the bank. Should the mortgage not be repaid, the bank may repossess the apartment and attempt to sell it in order to recover the unpaid debt.

Many forms of collateral exist as follows:

- equity (weighed against liabilities);
- deposits, savings plans and tradable securities;
- future obligations (postdated checks and contracts);
- real estate;
- supplies and equipment;
- personal assets of the owners.

It is important to continuously re-evaluate the collateral throughout the loan's lifetime. For example, the value of tradable securities may change on a daily basis. It is certainly conceivable that the value of such securities may drop below the value of the loan itself. For this reason, changes in the value of the assets used as collateral must be constantly monitored.

Collateral has a substantial impact on LGD. Collateral which covers the full extent of a loan can greatly reduce LGD and ensure a recovery rate of almost 100%.

Collateral which is not sufficient to cover the full extent of the loan will not reduce LGD. Such a situation may occur for various reasons, most often in cases where the collateral was not properly evaluated to begin with or its value has dropped since the loan was taken out.

Financial institutions which grant their clients credit must dedicate resources to the re-evaluation and management of collateral in order to maintain high recovery rates for all the lines of credit they offer. While collateral is a tool for managing credit risk, financial institutions must also manage the risk embodied in the collateral itself.

3.3.5. *Term to Maturity, M*

Components of Credit Risk

PD	Probability of default	The probability that a borrower will not meet its obligations towards the bank (default) during a given time period (in percent)
LGD	Loss given default (1-Recovery Rate)	The share of monetary loss out of the total exposure in case of borrower default (1 minus recovery rate) (in percent)
EAD	Exposure at default	Exposure in the event of default: book value of assets minus any mitigating factor (e.g., execution of surety bonds) (in monetary terms)
M	Maturity	Time left until the maturity of the exposure (in years)

The term to maturity, M, is the time left until the loan must be repaid, measured in years. To give an example, let us return to the example of the Icelandic bank and suppose there is a borrower whose credit matures in six months. In this case, M would be 0.5.

Time is a vital factor in all the parameters we have reviewed so far: PD, LGD and EAD. For instance, a company's PD at the start of a year is not the same as its PD at the end of that year. For this reason, estimates of credit risk which factor in PD, LGD and EAD must relate to a specific value of M.

For one year, M equals 1. For half a year, M = 0.5. How is M calculated for a period of 45 days?

It turns out that the calculation of M for non-whole terms is not as simple as it might first seem. One may calculate the ratio of 45 days from 365, 0.123288. However, what happens during a leap year? In such a case, the year will be 366 days long, and the ratio will change to 45 from 366, i.e., 0.122951. To a reader unaware of the enormous sums of money concerned, a difference of 0.000337 might seem negligible. However, even for a bank with a loan balance of USD 1 billion (a modest balance in banking terms), this difference represents USD 336,000 per year. For the Industrial and Commercial Bank of China Limited (ICBC), whose credit balance is USD 1.8 trillion, this seemingly negligible difference will amount to USD 337 million every year.

The effect of time on financial calculations is substantial. The International Swaps and Derivatives Association (ISDA), which assists in the international regulation of financial derivatives trading, has issued guidelines regarding the manner in which the time element is to be calculated.[4]

The same time calculations must be employed when assessing credit risk and when referring to the loan for which the risk assessment is being conducted. In fact, it is necessary to examine each loan on an individual basis and calculate its credit risk separately. This typically involves large volumes of information and requires extensive computing capabilities (in both software and hardware).

---

[4]An example of day count convention may be found at https://www.isda.org/a/pIJEE/The-Actual-Actual-Day-Count-Fraction-1999.pdf.

3.3.6. *Expected Loss (EL)*

> ## Components of Credit Risk
>
> **EL**
> Expected Loss

EL is an estimate of the loss which could result from a failure to repay credit, and it is measured in terms of monetary value. Assuming information regarding the main components of credit risk is available, it is possible to calculate EL as soon as a loan is issued. Let us explain:

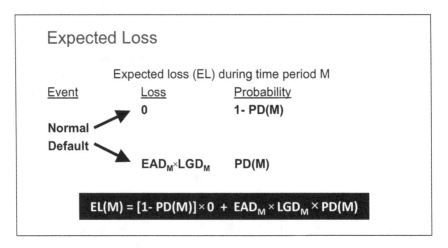

Where credit is concerned, there are two possible outcomes at maturity:

The **normal outcome**, where the borrower has repaid both the loan and the interest in full. In this case, the loss will be 0. The probability of a normal outcome is 1-PD.

A case of **default**, where the borrower does not repay the loan according to the agreed-upon terms. In this case, the loss will be EAD × LGD. The probability of such a failure event occurring is PD.

The time-adjusted (M) expected loss is calculated using the following formula:

$$EL(M) = [1 - PD(M)] \times 0 + EAD(M) \times LGD(M) \times PD(M)$$

As the first part of the formula equals zero, the formula may effectively be written thus as follows:

$$EL(M) = EAD(M) \times LGD(M) \times PD(M)$$

Components of Credit Risk

Credit risk during the time period M
Expected Loss (EL)

$$EL_M = EAD_M \times LGD_M \times PD(M)$$

To give an example, let us calculate EL for a borrower with the following data for the coming year:

Mortgage: EUR 100,000
Repaid thus far: EUR 20,000
Current house value (as collateral): EUR 70,000
Cost of house sale: EUR 10,000
Failure rate for mortgages: 40%

Calculating EAD: The exposure is EUR 80,000 (EUR 100,000 mortgage minus EUR 20,000 already repaid).

Calculating LGD: LGD is 25% (house value of EUR 70,000 less the EUR 10,000 cost of selling the house equals EUR 60,000 in total. The recovery rate is therefore 1-LGD, i.e., 75%, or EUR 60,000 out of EUR 80,000).

PD is a given, in this case, 40%.

EL may now be calculated as follows: EUR 80,000 $\times$ 25% $\times$ 40% = EUR 8,000.

3.4. Measurement

> # Main Components of Credit Risk – Measurement
>
> - EAD
> - LGD
> - EL
> - M
> - PD

In order to measure credit risk, we must first calculate each of the main risk components separately.

There may be some complications involved in calculating EAD, LGD, EL and M, but it is a relatively straightforward process of addition, multiplication and division. These calculations are determined by local regulations dictating which lines in the balance sheet must be included and in what capacity. These regulations vary from country to country.

> # Measuring PD
>
> - Scoring (score card and Altman's Z-score)
> - Profiling methods
> - Value at risk (VaR)
> - Merton's options pricing model
> - Binary regression (logit)

Calculating PD is a different matter altogether. In the previous sections, we were shown tables containing probabilities of failure with no explanation of how these values were obtained.

In this section, we will discuss the following main PD estimates in existence:

- scoring (score card and Altman's Z-score);
- profiling methods;

- Value at Risk (VaR);
- Merton's option pricing model;
- binary regression (logit).

3.4.1. *Scoring*

3.4.1.1. *Score card*

Scoring
Example Scorecard

Characteristic	Attribute	Scorecard Points
AGE	<22	100
AGE	22<=AGE<26	120
AGE	26<=AGE<29	185
AGE	29<=AGE<32	200
AGE	32<=AGE<37	210
AGE	37<=AGE<42	225
AGE	>=42	250
HOME	OWN	225
HOME	RENT	110
INCOME	<10000	120
INCOME	10000<=INCOME<17000	140
INCOME	17000<=INCOME<28000	180
INCOME	28000<=INCOME<35000	200
INCOME	35000<=INCOME<42000	225
INCOME	42000<=INCOME<58000	230
INCOME	>=58000	260

Let cutoff=600

So, a new customer applies for credit.....

AGE	35	210 points
INCOME	$38K	225 points
HOME	OWN	225 points
Total		660 points
Decision:		GRANT CREDIT

The scoring method for calculating the probability of default makes use of a questionnaire where each answer is assigned a different score. For instance, a borrower younger than 22 years old will be awarded 100 points, between 22 and 26 years of age 120 points and so on. A borrower older than 42 will be awarded the greatest number of points possible, 250.

A borrower who owns an apartment will get 225 points, but one who rents an apartment will only get 110 points.

A borrower with an income of less than USD 1,000 will only receive 120 points, but an income of over USD 58,000 will earn the borrower 260 points.

The questionnaire is completed in this manner, and at the end, all the points are summed up. If the total sum is higher than a set minimum value, e.g., 600, the applicant will be granted a loan. Otherwise, the loan will not be approved.

For example, a borrower has requested a loan for a sum of USD 100,000. She is 35 years old, her income is USD 38,000 and she owns a house. Should the bank approve her request?

In this case, the answer is yes, as according to the table her score is 660, above the minimum required score of 600.

The scoring method's primary strength is its simplicity. However, it can only return a binary yes/no answer. For instance, it is quite possible that we would agree to give credit to a potential borrower with a score of 580, but for a smaller sum of money and with a higher interest rate to make up for the greater risk. To make this possible, the questionnaire must contain a large number of scoring categories, negating the initial simplicity of the method.

This method is widely employed by financial institutions which provide large numbers of relatively small loans (typically to individual borrowers).

3.4.1.2. *Altman's Z-score*

Scoring

Altman's Z-score for predicting default

- X_1=working capital/total assets
- X_2=retained earnings/total assets
- X_3=EBIT/total assets
- X_4=market value of equity/book value of liabilities
- X_5=sales/total assets

$$Z = 1.2X_1+1.4X_2+3.3X_3+0.6X_4+0.99X_5$$

Score greater than 2.99 — low risk of default.

Score between 1.82 and 2.99 — some risk of default.

Score below 1.82 — high risk of default.

Source: Hull (2014).

Altman's scoring method is primarily used to classify firms into three categories: low risk, medium risk and high risk of bankruptcy.

Using this simple model, a number of financial ratios are multiplied, each by a different coefficient, and then summed up to give a final score.

The financial ratios are as follows:

- X_1 = working capital/total assets
- X_2 = retained earnings/total assets
- X_3 = earnings before interest and taxes (EBIT)/total assets
- X_4 = market value of equity/book value of liabilities
- X_5 = sales/total assets

The results of these ratios are then assigned to the following formula:

$$Z = 1.2X_1 + 1.4X_2 + 3.3X_3 + 0.6X_4 + 0.99X_5$$

Z is greater than 2.99 — low risk of bankruptcy ("safe zone").
Z is between 1.81 and 2.99 — medium risk of bankruptcy ("gray zone").
Z is lower than 1.81 — high risk of bankruptcy ("distress zone").

Scoring

Altman's Z-score for predicting default

Is a company with the following data at risk of default?
- Working capital 170,000
- Total assets 670,000
- EBIT 60,000
- Sales 2,200,000
- Market value of equity 380,000
- Book value of liabilities 240,000
- Retained earnings 300,000

Source: Hull (2014).

Example:
Is a company with the following data at risk of bankruptcy?

Working capital	170,000
Total assets	670,000
EBIT	60,000
Sales	2,200,000

Market value of equity	380,000
Book value of liabilities	240,000
Retained earnings	300,000

Let us now calculate the financial ratios:
- $X_1 = 0.2537$
- $X_2 = 0.4478$
- $X_3 = 0.0896$
- $X_4 = 1.5833$
- $X_5 = 3.2836$

This will result in the following formula:

$$1.2 \times 0.2537 + 1.4 \times 0.4478 + 3.3 \times 0.0896 + 0.6 \times 1.5833$$
$$+ 0.99 \times 3.2836 = 5.43$$

5.43 is greater than 2.99, i.e., the company is in the safe zone.

The Z-score's strength lies in its simplicity as well as its ability to divide companies into intermediate classes in addition to the main three. However, this method is mostly used for businesses and is not suited to rating individual borrowers.

3.4.2. *Profiling methods*

Profiling

- Calculating the probability of default according to categories:
  - Market sectors
  - Products
  - Geographical location
  - Entity type (individual, corporation, etc.)

Profiling is the calculation of bankruptcy rates for groups of borrowers. For instance, we may identify a group of borrowers who match certain criteria, e.g., real estate borrowers (industry sector) selling real estate for construction (product) in France (geographical area) who are private contractors (type of entity). We then proceed to check how many cases of default occurred for all the borrowers in this group, giving us its PD value.

Profiling allows for greater precision than the two methods previously discussed. Furthermore, it may be applied to both corporate borrowers and individual borrowers, and even to borrowers in the public sector, etc. However, the precision of this method drops sharply when smaller groups are examined. For instance, if a category contains only 10 borrowers, none of whom have ever defaulted, this will give us a PD of 0%. This is indeed the nominal value, but its statistical significance is somewhat questionable.

Profiling is an accepted method for banking systems where millions of borrowers take out hundreds of millions of loans, and the values provided by this method are statistically valid.

3.4.3. Credit VaR[5]

> ## Value at Risk
>
> | PD grade | 1 year | 2 years | Maturity 3 years | 4 years | 5 years |
> |---|---|---|---|---|---|
> | 1 | VaR(1,1) | VaR(1,2) | VaR(1,3) | VaR(1,4) | VaR(1,5) |
> | 2 | VaR(2,1) | VaR(2,2) | VaR(2,3) | VaR(2,4) | VaR(2,5) |
> | 3 | VaR(3,1) | VaR(3,2) | VaR(3,3) | VaR(3,4) | VaR(3,5) |
> | .... | VaR(...,1) | VaR(..,2) | VaR(...,3) | VaR(...,4) | VaR(...,5) |
>
> *Source*: Basel Committee on Banking Supervision, *An Explanatory Note on the Basel II IRB Risk Weight Functions*, July 2005.

---

[5]Some interesting facts…

One often encounters the abbreviation CVaR in reference to credit value at risk. This abbreviation confusingly refers two entirely different concepts:

- Credit VaR, as explained in this section.
- Conditional VaR — a numerical estimate of the expected loss given a certain VaR. This estimate takes on the following form:

10% of the time — USD 100 million loss;
20% of the time — USD 15 million loss;
35% of the time — 0 loss;

The VaR method allows us to estimate the expected loss for a given period of time at a given level of statistical significance. For instance, credit VaR of JPY 30 million, for a period of 100 days, at a probability of 99%, means that we may expect to see a credit failure in excess of JPY 30 million on one day out of the coming 100 days.

Credit VaR may be calculated either for the total credit portfolio or separately for specific rating categories for a particular time horizon.

This method offers considerable advantages in measuring credit risk and breaking down the structure of credit risk over time (credit risk term structure).

The main strength of this method is its great flexibility in calculating credit risk for varying time ranges and rates of risk. Its weakness is its technical complexity.

3.4.4. *Merton's option pricing model*

Options

Merton model (1974)
- The market value of a company, S:

$$\max(V_T - D, 0)$$

V_T = value of company assets during period T
D = value of company debt

According to Merton's option pricing model, the probability of default depends on the market price at which a share is traded.

The premise at the core of this model is that the value of a company is the difference between its assets and its liabilities. If this value is negative, the company's value is assumed to be zero.

20% of the time — 70M profit;
10% of the time — 90M profit;
This information facilitates more accurate and precise investment decisions.

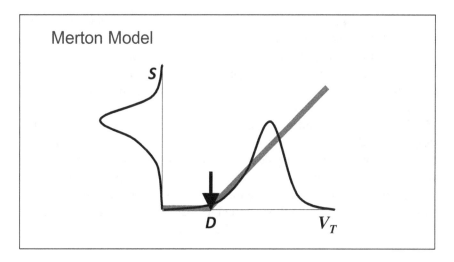

In this model, the x-axis represents the company's value and the y-axis represents its share price. The thick line on the graph marks the correlation between these two values. Up to the debt level marked D, the company's value is zero. From this point onwards, company value and share price are directly correlated.

Merton Model

$$S = VN(d_1) - De^{-rT}N(d_2)$$

$$d_1 = \frac{\ln(V/D) + (r + \frac{1}{2}\sigma_V^2)T}{\sigma_V \sqrt{T}}$$

$$d_2 = d_1 - \sigma_V \sqrt{T}$$

The formal framing of Merton's model resembles the pricing of an option on a base asset, V, where the exercise price of the option is D. As the option value approaches 0, the company draws ever nearer to failure. If the value of the option is close to V, the company is solvent.

Merton's model is relatively easy to apply to companies whose shares are traded in the stock market.

Another options pricing model worth mentioning is the KMV model, which is a development of Merton's model with a number of added parameters and simplifying assumptions, permitting more accurate prediction of a company's credit risk.

The strength of both the Merton model and the KMV model is the simplicity and ease with which they allow us to measure risk (despite their apparent mathematical complexity). Some would argue, however, that these models are flawed as they rely on historical market prices, which may be affected by unrelated economic factors. Their greatest weakness, however, is that they cannot be applied to individual borrowers or to companies which do not issue shares to the public.

3.4.5. *Binary regression*

Binary Regression

- A statistical model which allows us to estimate the probability that one out of the two outcomes will occur.
- In the context of credit risk, these two outcomes are as follows:
  - An event of default occurred
  - An event of default did not occur
- Calculation methods are as follows:
  - Logistic regression
  - Probit regression

Binary regression is a statistical model which allows us to measure the probability that one out of two outcomes will occur, given one or more explanatory variables. With regard to credit risk, the possible outcomes are as follows:

1 — a credit failure event occurred.

0 — a credit failure event did not occur.

For instance, using binary regression, it is possible to measure with great precision the probability of a failure event if the borrower is 40 years old, holds a senior position at a medium-sized real estate company, is married with two children and has no prior liabilities.

The two most widely used approaches use the models logit and probit, which differ in the form of statistical distribution each model assumes.

Binary regression is capable of grouping together all borrowers (reliable and risky alike) using a single model and measuring the probability of default for each one. This means a more precise measurement of credit risk may be assigned to each borrower. However, this approach requires extensive historical data, including on historical default events, and this is not always available.

3.4.6. *Stress testing, scenarios and sensitivity testing*

Stress, Scenario and Sensitivity Testing

Measuring tools which allow us to quantify the credit risk in an abnormal financial environment:
- Stress testing
- Scenarios
- Sensitivity testing

Stress, scenario and sensitivity tests may also be applied to credit risk. The purpose of these tests is to estimate the credit risk under exceptional circumstances, e.g., what would be the expected loss if the credit ratings of all current loans were to drop by one level all of a sudden, e.g., how would EL be affected if every single-firm-rated AA were demoted to a rating of A?

3.4.7. *Credit risk management*

Now that we understand what the components of credit risk are and how they are measured, how do we actually manage credit risk?

Credit Risk Management

- Risk identification (complete)
- Risk assessment (complete)
- Reduction and treatment of risk (not yet complete)

Suppose we are an institution which gives out loans, and we have been approached by the owner of a hypsometrical company named Grass Fragrance LTD., which produces and markets garden furniture. The owner wishes to obtain a loan of CAD 150,000 for a period of ten years. Let us also assume that we have measured a PD of 2.5% for the company. What should we do next?

In the risk management process, we are now at the stage of "monitoring and assessing risk" (see introduction). However, measuring PD alone is not sufficient for this purpose. We must also measure the expected loss (EL).

As the loan has not yet been granted, EAD is CAD 150,000. Assuming no collateral has been pledged, EL for one year will be CAD 3,750 (150,000 × 100% × 100% × 2.5%).

Money-lending and credit-providing institutions are typically risk averse and reluctant to support adventurous enterprises. They will therefore only approve the loan if its EL is lower than the greatest loss they are prepared to incur. For instance, if the annual interest rate on this loan is 7% (giving an expected profit of CAD 10,500 for the first year), and it covers operational costs and other risks as well, such an institution will be willing to approve the loan to Grass Fragrance LTD.

However, an interest rate below 2.5% would imply a risk greater than the expected loss, and the loan would be denied.

How can we reduce the risk?

The risk may be reduced through the process of risk management, following the methods described in the introduction of this book:

- **Risk avoidance:** The option of denying the loan altogether is perfectly reasonable from the standpoint of management. We may choose to deny Grass Fragrance the loan, thus avoiding the potential loss. This method reduces credit risk by reducing the exposure to the risk factor.

- **Risk reduction procedures:** The financial institution may demand that Grass Fragrance pledge collateral as a guarantee in case of failure.

  It is also possible to approve the loan but only grant a more limited sum of money (e.g., CAD 50,000).

- **Risk transfer:** For certain types of loans, such as mortgages, banks require that the borrower possess a life insurance policy. Thus, if the borrower were to pass away unexpectedly, the insurance company would still have to repay the bank.

  The most frequently employed method for managing credit risk is by charging higher interest rates to riskier borrowers. This means that those risky borrowers who do fulfill their obligations effectively subsidize those who fail to do so. Thus, the creditor creates a mechanism where the credit risk is transferred collectively to all the borrowers belonging to a particular risk group.

- **Acceptance of consequences:** This is one of the commonest methods in bond investment. A bond is a financial tool which allows investors to grant a loan to a business. Occasionally, the business defaults on its obligations to the bond owners. An investment in bonds is conducted according to the bond's risk rating and requires an analysis of the potential risks and rewards. Although they may not readily admit this, investors accept a potential loss in the event of credit failure. For example, when we invest USD 10,000 in the Italian government, we accept the fact that we may end up losing a part of our investment.

- **Recovery plan:** Collection of an unpaid debt constitutes the recovery process for a credit failure. Various aspects of the debt collection process must be planned in advance in order for it to succeed. For instance, any legal issues which may arise when we attempt to collect the debt (due to changes in the ownership of the collateral or an inability to realize the collateral as a result of laws which prevent us from doing so) must be resolved. It is also essential to allocate the manpower required for executing the debt collection. Occasionally, a financial investment is required in order to obtain the necessary documents or legal counsel in order to recover the debt, and so on. In addition, many financial institutions are required to allocate a certain minimum capital reserve which will allow them to recover even from rare instances when materialized credit risk results in exceptionally severe losses.

Another method for reducing credit risk combines the possibility of reducing damage with the option of transferring it to another party, using a financial tool called Credit Default Swaps (CDS).

Credit Default Swaps (CDS)

Tool used to hedge credit risk:

- Provides protection against failure to repay a debt.
- In an event of default, the CDS buyer maintains the right to sell bonds at a stated value.

CDS is a tool for hedging credit risk, which provides protection against failure to repay a debt. In such an event, CDS buyers reserve the right to sell their bonds at a stated value.

The annual sum paid in exchange for this protection is called the CDS spread, and it also serves as a measure of the perceived credit risk in the market. A higher spread implies greater risk perception. This measure makes it possible to track developments in the market over time (wider spread and narrower spread correspond to higher and lower risk perceptions, respectively), as well as compare the credit risk of various financial institutions.

3.4.7.1. *Capital adequacy*

Capital Allocation for Credit Risk

- Capital reserve for times of crisis.
- The capital requirement is measured as the rate of exposure to risky assets out of the total extent of the portfolio in question.

To protect against credit risk, financial institutions are required to allocate a certain minimum budget reserve for times of crisis. The Basel Committee on Banking Supervision has issued a number of documents on the subject of the minimum requirements for capital allocation as well as the regulation of capital adequacy, dealing in depth with the measurement of credit risk. In this section, we will outline some of the highlights of these various documents.

At the heart of the Basel recommendations stand two basic principles:

The first principle is the definition of the capital base which banks may hold to cushion against losses from the range of credit risks to which they are exposed.

In this context, Basel distinguishes between paid-up capital and undistributed profits, which are the stable part of the capital, referred to as Tier 1, and capital founded mainly upon subordinated debt, which represents the more volatile part, or Tier 2.

The second principle is that capital must be held in proportion to the bank's risk assets, where different risk assets are assigned a different weight: greater weight is assigned to credit given to the public (no distinction is made between businesses and households) and lower weight is assigned to less risky assets such as cash, deposits in commercial banks or at the central bank, and credit to the government.

Banks add up their risk assets in order to calculate the ratio of capital to risk assets (minimum capital requirement) in the following manner:

$$\text{Minimum Capital Requirement} = \frac{K}{\sum_{i=1}^{n} w_i A_i}$$

where K is the bank's capital requirement, w_i is a weight coefficient of asset i in percent, A_i is the book value of asset i and n is the number of assets listed on the bank's balance sheet.

A very similar formula, multiplied by conversion factors to adjust for the equivalent of credit value can also be applied to off-balance sheet activity which involves credit risk due to the bank's guarantees and commitments towards its clients. Examples of this are credit cards, sales guarantees, financial instruments, derivatives, etc.

Regulators in different countries set this ratio (typically, rates of 8% or more) and add conditions specifying the nature of this ratio, e.g., what is the ratio of relatively stable assets out of the total of all risk assets? The capital adequacy required by the regulator is frequently referred to as **regulatory capital**.

Independently of regulatory capital, many firms must also calculate **economic capital**, a realistic estimate of financial risk with the goal of maintaining the institution's financial stability.

In order to meet both regulatory demands and their own *de facto* risk assessment, banks must allocate the higher of these two values as a reserve.

Why are both values needed? On the one hand, the state wishes to preserve the stability of the individual bank, for which economic capital is preferred. On the other hand, the state also wishes to ensure the stability of the financial system as a whole by allocating capital to the entire banking system (which itself comprises hundreds of individual banks), for which regulatory capital is the preferred choice. The way to protect both the individual bank and the financial system as a whole is by requesting an estimate of both values from each bank and demanding that the bank allocate the higher of the two values.

With regard to credit risk, the Basel Committee recommends one of the two capital allocation methods:

- **The standard approach**, which features precise definitions of the weighting coefficients applied to credit risk. These coefficients may vary from 0% to as high as 150% depending on the asset's risk. Thus, for instance, the Committee allows banks to rely on the credit rating of business firms conducted by independent companies not related to the banks. These companies must be approved by the banking supervisor in each country according to several criteria, of which the main ones are objectivity, independence, transparency and reliability. The Committee allows institutions to conduct credit risk mitigation using collateral, guarantees and off-balance sheet financial instruments (including those traded in secondary markets such as mortgage-backed securities).
- **The Internal Ratings-Based (IRB) approach**, according to which banks may use their own internal systems to measure credit risk,

employing internal credit rating methods and advanced models. The Committee distinguishes between two IRB models:
- o **The Foundation Internal Ratings-Based (F-IRB) approach**, where banks calculate the probability of default (PD) of every borrower and group of borrowers, but the banking supervisor determines the manner in which the additional variables (M, LGD and EAD) required to determine the capital requirement are measured.
- o **The Advanced Internal Ratings-Based (A-IRB) approach**, which allows banks to determine independently all the necessary variables for calculating capital requirement: PD, M, LGD and EAD.

The Basel Committee stipulates that only banks which meet certain conditions (typically multi-national banks) may be granted permission to use internal models.

The Basel Committee recommended the following formula for calculating the capital ratio required to shield against credit exposure according to the Basel Committee:

$$k = \left[LGD \times N \left(\frac{N^{-1}(PD) + \rho^{\frac{1}{2}} N^{-1}(0.999)}{\sqrt{1-\rho}} \right) - (PD - LGD) \right] \times A^*$$

and the formula for calculating the capital requirement is

$$K^* = k \times EAD$$

where *LGD, PD* and *EAD* are as defined earlier in the chapter, namely monetary loss given default, probability of non-repayment of credit and extent of exposure to credit in case of default, respectively; *k* is the capital ratio required to protect against credit exposure; K^* is the capital required to protect against exposure; $N(x)$ is the function of the standard cumulative normal distribution of a random variable (i.e., the probability that a normal random variable with average 0 and variance 1 will be smaller or equal to *x*); $N^{-1}(x)$ is the inverse of the cumulative standard distribution of a normal random variable with average 0 and variance 1; $N^{-1}(0.999)$ is the value of the 99.9% confidence threshold, $N^{-1}(0.999) \approx 3.09$; ρ is a weighted correlation coefficient of the various exposures dependent on PD. Its formula is as follows:

$$\rho(PD) = 0.12 \times \left(\frac{1 - e^{(-50 \times PD)}}{1 - e^{(-50)}} \right) + 0.24 \times \left[1 - \left(\frac{1 - e^{(-50 \times PD)}}{1 - e^{(-50)}} \right) \right]$$

and A^* is a component which matches the required capital to the effective due date,[6] M, and to the insolvency rate. This component is defined in the following way:

$$A^*(M, PD) = \left[1 - 1.5b(PD) \right]^{-1} \times \left[1 + (M - 2.5) \times b(PD) \right]$$

where

$$b(PD) = \left[0.011852 - 0.05478 \times \mathrm{Ln}(PD) \right]^2$$

A rise in PD, LGD or EAD may result in an increased capital requirement. An increase in ρ, the correlation coefficient for the different exposures, will cause an increase in the required capital. An explanation for the positive correlation between ρ and K comes from portfolio management models which have proven that as the correlation between the components of a portfolio (borrowers or sectors) is smaller, the credit portfolio is more diverse and therefore less risky, i.e., requires less capital to cover unexpected losses.

---

[6]The formula for calculating the effective due date (duration) is

$$M = \frac{\Sigma t \times CF_t}{\Sigma CF_t}$$

where CF_t is the commodities' finance, predicted discounted cash flow from credit and t is the due date of above cash flow.

It is evident from the formula for A^* that adjustments are only required for effective due dates other than 1.

The Committee stipulated that ("economic") the capital reserve should cover unpredictable loss component of a credit portfolio, reflecting the bank's response to the potential materialization of risks in the future. By contrast, for the predictable loss component, the bank must set aside funds separately to cover doubtful debts.

The credit risk management methods proposed by the Basel Committee do not negate the need for careful and intelligent management of credit risks based on the correct pricing of credit (including pledging adequate collateral), proper filtering of clients, the option of credit rationing to troublesome clients, etc.

Criticism

Some would argue that the implementation of the Basel recommendations is likely to have a procyclical effect on the economy, i.e., it will result in greater fluctuations in the macroeconomic business cycle. We shall explain.

During a low period in the business cycle, credit risks increase, requiring greater allowances for doubtful debts. Because more money has been set aside, this in turn decreases the bank's capital. In such a scenario, assuming all other variables remain constant, the excess capital adequacy (above the minimum requirement) will decrease and the growth potential of credit given to the public will also decrease.

In professional literature, it is frequently stated that reducing credit may ultimately serve to deepen a recession and exacerbate the decline in the business cycle.

The reversed process will occur during the growth phase of the business cycle. During times of growth, credit risks go down, a smaller portion of the bank's capital will be tied down and as a result, the growth potential for banking credit will grow, accelerating market growth.

This causes business cycles to undergo greater fluctuation than would occur naturally, without the above credit risk management system in place.[7]

---

[7]Some interesting facts...

Two interesting points with respect to business cycles and credit are as follows:

- Generally speaking, the performance of the financial system is procyclical, i.e., during times of financial growth, the performance of financial institutions improves, and during a recession, their performance declines. Measurements of the cyclical nature of financial activity using the extent of loans and newly issued bonds would seem to point towards increased growth during times of financial growth than during times of financial recession. This procyclicality may be largely explained using the acceleration model, according to which high growth rates lead to increased potential returns and consequently to a relaxation of limits on credit and increasing financial debt.
- Opinion regarding the correlation between credit rating and procyclicality is divided into two schools of thought:
  - The first states that, unlike credit risk, credit rating should not change due changes in business cycles, as, at its core, it distinguishes safer companies, which are more resilient to financial shocks, from companies which are riskier and tend to file for bankruptcy every time a recession occurs.
  - The second believes there is plenty of empirical evidence which demonstrates that the opposite is true, namely that a procyclical connection between credit rating and business cycles does exist.

Chapter 4

Liquidity Risk

Accompanying presentation: 4. Risk Management - Liquidity Risk

4.1. Liquidity

```
Liquidity

▪ The ability of an economic agent to exchange his or her existing
  wealth for goods and services or for other assets.
                                            —Williamson (2008)


▪ The ability to finance an increase in assets and meet obligations
  as they come due, without incurring unacceptable losses.
                                            —Israel Supervisor of Banks
```

Liquidity is the ability of an economic agent to trade his or her existing wealth for goods and services or for other assets. For example, our ability to pay in cash for groceries at the supermarket is an indicator of financial liquidity.

Wealth is an important factor in determining liquidity; a penniless individual possesses nothing that may be traded for services, goods or other assets and therefore has no liquidity.

However, great wealth is not a guarantee of liquidity; a billionaire who owns three large buildings in Manhattan, New York, has decided to go backpacking around Machu Picchu, Peru. He then wishes to return to Cusco by train but discovers his pockets are empty — he does not have even a single Peruvian sol left. Although this man is a billionaire of indisputable wealth, he was unable to exchange even a small fraction of his fortune for basic transportation services. At this point, the billionaire would be said to lack liquidity.

For banks, liquidity is the ability to finance an increase in assets and meet obligations as they come due, without incurring unacceptable losses. For example, when clients wish to withdraw a large deposit, they expect the bank to transfer the money into their account. Banks typically hold a certain amount of "liquid" money which allows them to provide their clients with cash immediately upon demand.

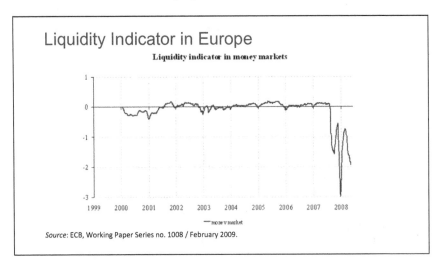

The subprime crisis affected many markets worldwide and caused a widespread liquidity crisis. Although we have not yet discussed the ways in which liquidity is measured, it is nevertheless clear that the liquidity index of Europe, which had previously enjoyed long years of stability, plummeted abruptly during the crisis.

Throughout the crisis, Europe's wealth did not change substantially. During this short time, the territorial extent of the continent remained the same, its population changed very little, structures both new and old remained standing and the natural resources of the continent were almost constant as well. However, Europe's substantial wealth was of little help to the financial system, which could not fulfill its obligations, drawing the continent into a severe liquidity crisis.

4.2. Liquidity Risk

Liquidity risk may be defined in various ways, according to the type of liquidity in question.

4.2.1. *Central bank liquidity risk*

Central Bank Liquidity Risk

- The inability of the central bank to cope with excess supply or demand for the local currency.
- The inability of the central bank to cope with excess supply or demand for foreign currency.

- Indicators of a potential central bank liquidity crisis
  - Inflationary pressures
  - Currency devaluation
  - Credit crunch

For states, liquidity risk is defined as either of the following two (related) situations:

- The inability of the central bank to cope with excess supply or demand for **local currency**.
- The inability of the central bank to cope with excess supply or demand for **foreign currency**.

Both of these situations are interconnected, as the tools employed by central banks to manage supply and demand for local currency simultaneously affect supply and demand for foreign currency. When the local currency is more attractive than other currencies (due to higher interest, lower inflation, an economic environment supportive of international investment, etc.), demand for the local currency grows. The local currency is bought by exchanging foreign currency. Therefore, if the exchange rate between local and foreign currencies remains constant, the supply of foreign currency must naturally grow in accordance with the growing demand for the local currency.

The problem with this model is that exchange rates rarely stay constant in practice. Many states have tried in the past to set a fixed exchange rate, with little success. As mentioned in the introduction chapter, many countries, in a futile attempt to protect their currency, ultimately found themselves in the midst of a financial crisis as soon as they could no longer provide the necessary liquidity to guarantee their financial stability.

Nevertheless, various countries around the world still attempt to keep their exchange rate within reasonable (though not always officially declared) limits, and central banks attempt to influence exchange rates by buying and selling foreign currency in exchange for the local currency. The ability of a central bank to do this depends in large part on its foreign exchange reserves. By contrast, the less foreign currency the central bank possesses, the smaller its ability to meet excess demand for foreign currency and the greater its liquidity risk.

A recent example of a central bank unable to cope with excess demand for local currency was the 2013 financial crisis in Cyprus. Following the crisis, the Cypriot government agreed with the European Union on a rescue plan worth approximately EUR 16 billion. According to this plan, the E.U. would lend Cyprus EUR 10 billion, and the government of Cyprus would raise the remaining EUR 6 billion through taxes on bank deposits. Deposit owners understood what this meant, i.e., that a significant portion of their money would be taken by the state in taxes and sought to withdraw their deposits. At this point, the government realized that the excess demand for the local currency would render the country incapable of raising the sum to which it had committed. The government ordered a bank shutdown, in the process creating a liquidity crisis for the local currency.

Indicators of a liquidity crisis in the economy
It is easy to identify an economy undergoing a liquidity crisis. It tends to experience inflationary pressures, such as frequent price rises and a devaluation of the local currency.

This is sometimes accompanied by a credit crunch, which is reflected in the inability of financial entities to borrow money from local banks in order to guarantee the necessary liquidity for their business operations.

4.2.1.1. *Measurement*

Central Bank Liquidity Risk

■ Measurement
- Foreign currency reserves
- Financial ratios
- Inflation/amount of money

The liquidity risk of a state or central bank is measured using macro-economic data:

- **Foreign currency reserves** reflect the ability of the central bank to prevent a significant drop in the exchange rate by selling foreign currency. The greater the reserves, the lower the liquidity risk.
  - **Financial ratios** such as the extent of accumulated short-term debt as a percentage of GDP, obligations to the local market as percentage of GDP, etc. can reflect financial pressures faced by market. Lower ratios indicate a lower liquidity risk. During the 1990s in Israel, the Ministry of Finance actively conducted a process of debt rescheduling, extending the repayment period of the national debt by many years. In this way, rather than searching for a new source of funding every three months to cover its short-term debt, Israel increased its liquidity by reducing the extent of its debt repayments, even if this meant drawing them over a longer period of time.
- **Inflation and money supply** are an expression of excess supply and demand for the local currency. The closer the inflation rate is to 2–3%, and the smaller the rate of change in money supply, the lower the liquidity risk.

4.2.2.   *Funding liquidity risk*

Funding Liquidity Risk

■ Inability to repay obligations as they come due

Liquidity	≠	Repayment capacity

The ability to make payments on time   More assets than liabilities (positive equity)

■ Indicators of a potential funding liquidity crisis
  • High costs required to raise capital
  • Bankruptcy

For businesses, liquidity risk is defined as the inability to repay obligations as they come due.

Liquidity allows us to make payments on time (e.g., when boarding a train), whereas repayment capacity signifies positive equity (more assets than liabilities).

While a lack of repayment capacity indicates a lack of liquidity by definition, the reverse is not necessarily true. Lack of liquidity does not always signify a lack of repayment capacity. The story of the billionaire stuck in Peru with no money to pay for a train ticket, used above as an example of a liquidity crisis, also serves to demonstrate the asymmetrical relationship between liquidity and repayment capacity. Although the billionaire had no liquidity, his repayment capacity was excellent.

Manifestations of a liquidity crisis in business firms
A company experiencing a liquidity crisis will have difficulty borrowing money or raising capital in other ways. Eventually, the company will no longer be able to raise money at all, at which point, in addition to lacking liquidity, it will lack repayment capacity and go bankrupt.

Northern Rock

- British bank, traded at the London Stock Exchange.
- Dealt in bonds and mortgages.
- In August 2007, due to the financial crisis, concern spread that the bank would not be able to meet its obligations.
- At the same time, the value of the bank's total assets was greater than that of its liabilities.
- This lack of trust resulted in a panic, leading to a bank run.

For many years, the British-based Northern Rock bank, whose stock was traded at the London stock exchange, dealt in bonds and mortgages. In August 2007, the bank earned the dubious distinction of being the first British bank to suffer a bank run[1] in 150 years. During the subprime crisis, concern began to grow that the bank would be unable to repay its obligations. However, from an accounting perspective, the bank had more assets

---

[1] Some interesting facts…

A bank run occurs when a large number of customers arrive at a bank simultaneously, seeking to withdraw their money.

- Banks typically receive deposits from different customers and then lend the money to other customers. A delicate situation is created as a result, where most of the time the bank does not possess sufficient cash reserves to return the deposits of all its customers at once.
- As it is quite likely that some customers will ask to withdraw their deposits, banks maintain a cash reserve to allow them to return money to depositors. As long as not all the bank's customers ask for their money at the same time, the bank may continue to operate properly.
- Although the bank may not at any given moment have the capacity to repay all of its customers, at the individual level, all the bank's customers are confident that they will receive their money back, and all they have to do is ask the bank to hand it over. In the event of a bank run, many depositors lose their confidence that the bank will be able to repay them and rush all at once to withdraw their deposits. When such a situation escalates and becomes a panic, this may even lead to a lack of confidence in banks in general, and other banks may experience a bank run as well.
- Although bank runs seldom occur, they do take place occasionally, even in the 21st century.

than liabilities, and it had a reasonable repayment capacity. Following the financial crisis, the bank's customers became increasingly concerned that they would be unable to recover their deposits. Customers lined up at the bank's offices in order to withdraw their money. These were joined by still more customers, which only served to increase the panic and make the lines at the bank's offices even longer. Although the bank possessed reasonable repayment capacity, it lacked the necessary liquidity to keep up with the enormous demand for cash.

In 2008, the bank was nationalized.

4.2.2.1. *Measurement*

> ## Funding Liquidity Risk
>
> ▪ Measurement
> - Liquid assets — compared to liabilities
>   - Cash and securities
>   - Short-term bonds
>   - Credit channels

The liquidity risk of business firms is measured by business indicators which compare the extent of the company's liquid assets with its liabilities:

- **Liquid assets** include cash, exchange-traded securities with high liquidity, short-term bonds and credit channels which may be activated in case additional liquidity is required.

   The liquid assets of a company are **compared to its liabilities** at any given moment.
- **Liquidity coverage ratio (LCR)** is a measure of the high-quality sources of liquidity which will be available for a period of one month if a stress scenario materializes.

Funding Liquidity Risk

▪ Liquidity Coverage Ratio (LCR)
  - Measures the ratio of high-quality liquid assets available for a period of one month, given a stress scenario.
  - The ability of a corporation to survive thirty days of liquidity disturbances.

$$LCR = \frac{High\ quality\ liquid\ assets}{Net\ cash\ outflows\ in\ a\ 30\ days\ period} \geq 100\%$$

	1 January 2015	1 January 2016	1 January 2017	1 January 2018	1 January 2019
Minimum LCR	60%	70%	80%	90%	100%

Basel III: The Liquidity Coverage Ratio and liquidity risk monitoring tools, January 2013.

This measure rates the ability of a corporation to survive thirty days of liquidity disturbances. It is calculated according to the following formula and must be greater than 100%:

$$LCR = \frac{High\ quality\ liquid\ assets}{Net\ cash\ outflows\ in\ a\ 30\ days\ period} \geq 100\%$$

In recognition of the fact that banks will require some time to rearrange their asset structure to conform to these recommendations, Basel III stipulates a gradual adoption of the new standards, with the threshold rising gradually from 60% in January 2015 to 100% in January 2019.

- **Net stable funding ratio (NSFR)** is a measure of longer-term stability, i.e., whether the corporation can survive a year of liquidity disruptions.

Funding Liquidity Risk

- **Net Stable Funding Ratio (NFSR)**
  - Measures longer-term stability
  - The ability of a corporation to survive a year of liquidity disturbances

$$NSFR = \frac{Available\ amount\ of\ stable\ funding}{Required\ amount\ of\ stable\ funding} \geq 100\%$$

Basel III: The net stable funding ratio, October 2014.

It is calculated according to the following formula and must be greater than 100%:

$$NSFR = \frac{Available\ amount\ of\ stable\ funding}{Required\ amount\ of\ stable\ funding} \geq 100\%$$

- **The liquidity ratios must be measured on a daily basis** in order to guarantee that the financial entity is prepared for a liquidity crisis at any given moment.

Funding Liquidity Risk

- Measurement of liquidity ratios on a daily basis.
- Preparation for a liquidity crisis.
- Pressure scenarios (systemic pressure, corporation-specific pressure or both).
- Liquidity gaps by payback period (up to a day, week, month, etc.).
- Based on contractual payback times and behavioral assumptions in various scenarios.

- **Preparation for a liquidity crisis** is an integral part of the management of liquidity risk in the aftermath of a liquidity crisis. In order to prepare for such a crisis, it is necessary to obtain sources which will provide cash in times of need. Particular care must be taken in the selection of financial entities (or even the central bank) upon which one chooses to rely for credit lines. Sometimes, during times of crisis, the financier we have chosen to rely on may be facing difficulties as well and therefore in no position to grant credit.
- **Pressure scenarios** include *systemic pressure*, which represents a widespread financial crisis affecting multiple financial entities simultaneously; *corporation-specific pressure* due to a crisis within the corporation itself, which might be the result of overdependence on a particular industry sector, specific liabilities, etc.; and even *a combination of the two types of pressures*, which may serve to further exacerbate the pressure scenario.
- **Measuring liquidity gaps by payback period** is another method for measuring liquidity risk. Using this method, the sum of liquid assets is compared to the total liabilities every day for a week, a month and so forth, in order to identify lapses where the total liabilities exceeded the total liquid assets.
- **Contractual payback times and behavioral assumptions** are the most complex aspect of liquidity risk measurement. Some regulators state that the financial behavior of clients during a crisis must also be taken into account as a factor in the pressure scenarios examined. It is not sufficient to determine the outlying values for a crisis — one must also guarantee that even under exceptional circumstances, the financial entity will be able to meet its obligations, for example, if its customers show signs of panic.

4.2.3.   *Market liquidity risk*

Market Liquidity Risk

- The inability to close a position before a change in the price of the asset or liability results in an unmanaged loss.

Source: TradeStation.

In financial markets, liquidity risk is defined as the inability to close a position before the change in asset/liability price results in an unmanaged loss.

Forex Capital Markets (FXCM) offered a platform for foreign exchange (forex) trading, making it possible to leverage and conduct deals as part of a contract for difference (CFD). The company had a questionable record with regard to compliance with regulations, and its conduct has tarnished the reputation of the entire forex sector since then until our time.

FXCM speculated on the Swiss franc, turning a sizable profit. This profit spurred the company to increase its exposure to the currency even further, to increase its earnings even more.

On January 15, 2015, the Swiss National Bank, having protected the Franc from revaluation for several years, decided to remove the value cap it had set on the currency, following which the value of the Swiss franc rose by 30% in just a few minutes. Although the exchange rate would drop back down later on, it had already caused a deep financial trauma for FXCM. The following day, January 16, FXCM announced that it had been forced to borrow USD 300 million to comply with the regulatory capital requirements. The company's value plummeted from USD 160 per share to just USD 6.58 per share in a few short minutes.

What does this story have to do with market liquidity risk? Traders who had held FXCM stock at USD 160 a share wanted to get rid of it as quickly as possible in order to minimize their losses. Attempting to sell their shares, these traders quickly discovered that the share price had already dropped to USD 120 per share. Those few who had managed to sell first had indeed cut their losses, but those who had failed to do so soon found that they could not get rid of their stock until the price had dropped all the way to USD 6.58.

During these few minutes, FXCM stock was illiquid, with many sellers but no buyers. No trader was willing to purchase the stock at any price higher than USD 6.58 per share. Traders who wished to sell their shares and close a position were unable to do so, and their losses spiraled out of control.

The earlier image shows a screenshot taken from the trading system Trade Station, which shows the evolution of the share price of FXCM during its several minutes of illiquidity. It clearly shows that during this time, there was no continuity in prices, and it was therefore impossible to close a position before the price had gone down substantially, causing an unmanaged loss.

Experienced traders, familiar with the intricacies of daily trading, will attest to the overwhelming sense of helplessness which accompanies such situations. Limit orders (LMT) are not carried out and market orders (MKT) give buyers the initiative, allowing them to take advantage of the circumstances and buy shares at outrageously low prices. A lack of liquidity in the market is a risk which traders must take into account when managing their portfolios.

Indicators of a liquidity crisis in financial trading:

Market Liquidity Risk

- Indicators of a potential market liquidity crisis
  - Slow market cycles
  - Bid/ask spreads
  - High slippage
  - Extended period of time required to close a position
  - Length of time from the moment the price changes due to a large transaction until it returns to its original, pre-transaction level

Stocks suffering from a liquidity crisis are traded at very slow cycles or not traded at all for extended periods of time. Sometimes, the stock is only traded once or twice over the course of an entire day or even not traded at all for hours or days at a time. Whereas the difference between the bid price and the ask price of a liquid share would be unlikely to exceed a single cent, for illiquid shares, this difference may amount to dozens of cents.

When a buy or sell order is issued for a given price, the transaction may in fact be executed at a different price from that stated: this phenomenon is called "slippage". For highly liquid stocks, slippage ranges from small to non-existent, whereas for illiquid stocks, it may reach dozens of cents per share.

One manager at an investment house was managing a large portfolio and attempted to sell corporate bonds in order to purchase another asset. During this time, the corporate bond was illiquid, and the manager had to wait two whole days until the sell order was executed. In these two days, the manager missed a more profitable alternative investment opportunity. Managing a portfolio with illiquid assets is a challenging prospect, and for this reason, investment managers typically prefer portfolios made up of liquid assets. In certain trading techniques, traders using computerized systems (algo-trading) make sure to select liquid shares, where sell orders issued automatically by the computer will indeed be carried out at the appropriate time.

Another way in which a liquidity crisis may be seen is in the length of time until the share price returns to its original value after a large transaction. Penny stocks, which are traded at very low prices, illustrate this very well. On occasion, after a transaction is performed, the share price may double from one cent to two. After that, many hours may pass until the next transaction lowers (or raises) the price by yet another cent. This rarely occurs with liquid stock, as, in almost all cases, for every order issued by one trader, another trader will issue an opposite order at a similar price.

4.2.3.1. *Measurement*

Various measures are used to assess liquidity risk in financial markets. Here, we shall present three of them.

4.2.3.1.1.   Bid–ask spread

The costs of a deal may contain several elements whose cost is known, such as operational costs and taxes, as well as other elements whose cost is not known, such as information asymmetry and bargaining skills. These costs are reflected in both the bid price and the ask price. The difference between these prices largely makes up for the costs, leaving a spread which reflects the liquidity of the asset.

Market Liquidity Risk

▪ Spread Bid/Ask

$$\frac{Ask \; - \; Bid}{\frac{1}{2}(Ask + Bid)}$$

The bid–ask spread, measured as a percentage of the average price, may be used as an indicator of liquidity risk. The greater the measure, the greater the liquidity risk, and vice versa. It is calculated in the following manner:

$$\frac{Ask - Bid}{\frac{1}{2}(Ask + Bid)}$$

Let us explain. When comparing stocks of a roughly similar price, it is possible to use the bid–ask spread directly. However, when we compare shares of substantially different prices (e.g., a cheaper share of around USD 10 compared to one of USD 100), we encounter a problem. An identical movement of 1% in both shares would mean a difference of 10 cents for the former share and 100 cents for the latter. In order to obtain a common base for the two spreads, we divide the bid–ask spread by the average price of the shares, resulting in a bid–ask spread as a percentage, which allows us to compare stocks of vastly differing prices.

In order to perform the calculation, we select the highest bid price and the lowest ask price recorded during the time period in question (minute, hour, day, etc.).

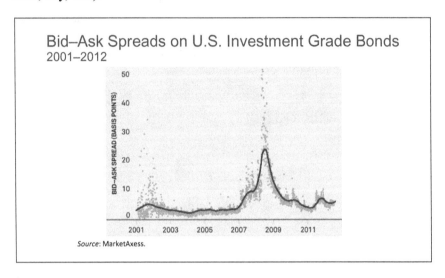

Bid–Ask Spreads on U.S. Investment Grade Bonds
2001–2012

Source: MarketAxess.

During the two most recent financial crises experienced by the American market — the dot-com crash of 2000 and the subprime crisis of 2008 — the market reacted with significantly reduced liquidity. Although it is important to proceed with caution when drawing a comparison between these two crises, as the liquidity risk shown in the above image is measured in bid–ask spreads only and not in percentage, a number of interesting findings stand out nonetheless:

- Although a loss of liquidity did occur during the 2000 crisis, this had little effect on the average measurement for the period.
  On the other hand, in 2008, the entire market responded with a lack of liquidity and the average value went up significantly.
- 2000 did not see any single dramatic event which affected liquidity risk. Rather, the risk rose intermittently on various days throughout the period.

For the later crisis, by contrast, a rise may already be noted in 2007, with steadily increasing variance compared to the average, culminating in a peak. In the days following this peak, the measure went back down but the spread around the average was narrower.

- The final point leads us to the most interesting aspect of this diagram, which may be seen more clearly in the following image:

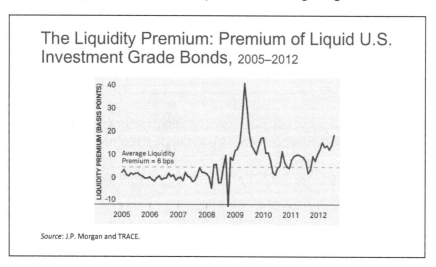

The Liquidity Premium: Premium of Liquid U.S. Investment Grade Bonds, 2005–2012

Source: J.P. Morgan and TRACE.

The liquidity risk measured immediately after the 2000 crisis was at a similar level to that measured shortly before the crisis.

However, after the 2008 crisis, the liquidity risk did not return to its original level. The market had learned the lessons of the liquidity crisis, and this would continue to affect the pricing of liquidity risk for years to come.

4.2.3.1.2. Turnover rate

The volume of trade reflects both the number of shares traded during a given period of time and their price at the time. The greater the volume of trade, the greater the chances of finding traders interested in buying and selling shares at any given moment. This ensures greater liquidity in the market.

Market Liquidity Risk

- Turnover Rate

$$Tn = \frac{V}{S \times P}$$

where

$V = \sum P_i \times Q_i$ (price and quantity of trade i)

S = outstanding of stock of asset
P = average price of the i trade

The turnover rate (Tn) examines liquidity risk from a different perspective, namely looking at the volume of trade out of the total outstanding stock of an asset. The greater the ratio measured, the lower the liquidity risk, and vice versa. It is calculated according to the following formula:

$$Tn = \frac{V}{S \times P}$$

where $V = \sum P_i \times Q_i$ (*Price and Quantity of trade i*), S = *Outstanding of stock of asset* and P = *Average price of the i trade*.

Let us explain. Suppose the stock of one company, *BIG*, and the stock of a second company, *small*, are traded at the same volume (V). Taken at face value, the liquidity risk of both would appear to be similar. However, let us now suppose that the total number of outstanding shares of *BIG* is ten times that of *small*. This means that, compared to their trade potential, *BIG* shares are traded ten times less than *small* shares.

In practical terms, the calculation is carried out by selecting a certain time period (minute, hour, day, etc.) and substituting the trading data of the stock during this period for the variables in the formula. S, which represents the number of outstanding shares available during this time, should remain constant. P represents the average of all the prices quoted during this period. P_i and Q_i are all the orders actually carried out during trade.

4.2.3.1.3. Market efficiency coefficient

In 1988, Hasbrouck and Schwartz published an article[2] in which they proposed a distinction between short-term price changes and long-term price changes to the share.

Market Liquidity Risk

▪ Market Efficiency Coefficient (MEC)

$$MEC = \frac{Var(R)}{T \times Var(r)}$$

where
$Var(R)$ = variance of long period return (in logarithm)
$Var(r)$ = variance of short period return (in logarithm)
T = number of short periods in each longer period

This new measure, which they termed the market efficiency coefficient (MEC), expresses the ratio between long-term variance and short-term variance during the same time period. For liquid shares, this ratio may be expected to be equal or almost equal to 1, whereas for illiquid shares, it will differ significantly from 1. It is calculated as follows:

$$MEC = \frac{Var(R)}{T \times Var(r)}$$

where $Var(R)$ = Variance of long period return (in logarithm), $Var(r)$ = Variance of short period return (in logarithm) and T = Number of short periods in each longer period

Let us explain. Some shares experience greater fluctuations in price than others. Within this framework, the fluctuation is measured using variance. For instance, it is possible to measure the evolution of the weekly

---

[2] Hasbrouck J. and Robert A. Shcwartz (1998), Liquidity and execution costs in equity market, *Journal of Portfolio Management*, Vol. 14, No. 3, pp. 10–16.

variance of the price of a certain share during the last two years. In the same way, it is possible to measure the evolution of its daily variance during this time. We would expect the ratio between the weekly variance and the daily variance to be similar throughout the measurement period.

However, if a certain week saw radical price changes, this might not be reflected in the weekly measure but only in the daily measure. In such a case, we might expect to see the ratio of variance rates change. MEC measures the changes in variance rates over time.

T remains constant throughout the measurement process and serves to standardize the time units.

From a practical standpoint, the measurement is carried out by calculating the moving variance of the share price, both for the longer periods and for the shorter periods.

4.2.3.1.4. Excel

In order to calculate the moving variance of a series of numbers, the familiar functions = Average( ) and = Var( ) may be employed in the following manner:

	A	B	C	D
1	**DATE**	**Value**	**Changes**	**Var(10)**
2	01-01-13	$ 1,740,877.64		
3	02-01-13	$ 1,752,480.39	0.66%	
4	03-01-13	$ 1,751,958.43	–0.03%	
5	04-01-13	$ 1,753,078.05	0.06%	
6	07-01-13	$ 1,757,491.25	0.25%	
7	08-01-13	$ 1,753,374.14	–0.23%	
8	09-01-13	$ 1,749,876.20	–0.20%	
9	10-01-13	$ 1,753,758.40	0.22%	
10	11-01-13	$ 1,737,076.30	–0.96%	
11	14-01-13	$ 1,696,372.56	–2.37%	
12	15-01-13	$ 1,679,924.42	–0.97%	0.00763% **= VAR(C3:C12)**

(*Continued*)

	A	B	C	D	
13	16-01-13	$ 1,702,333.23	1.33%	0.00957%	= VAR(C4:C13)
14	17-01-13	$ 1,686,160.32	−0.95%	0.00989%	= VAR(C5:C14)
15	18-01-13	$ 1,682,502.69	−0.22%	0.00969%	= VAR(C6:C15)
16	21-01-13	$ 1,698,231.51	0.93%	0.01115%	= VAR(C7:C16)
17	22-01-13	$ 1,691,873.90	−0.38%	0.01113%	= VAR(C8:C17)
18	23-01-13	$ 1,721,440.14	1.73%	0.01554%	= VAR(C9:C18)

In order to calculate moving variance for a period of ten days, the variance is calculated for the first ten days, and then the function is "stretched" downwards. We must then verify that the cells have been filled so that the function only calculates the variance for the previous ten cells.

4.2.3.1.5. Conclusion

The various methods outlined above measure different aspects of liquidity risk. Additional methods exist which require more extensive application of statistics and econometrics, and which have not been discussed in this chapter. The above methods, however, give a good overview of market liquidity, especially when employed in combination.

4.3. Capital Allocation

In practice, capital allocation for liquidity risk is today mandated by regulations for banks, insurance companies and other financial institutions. These regulations were set in accordance with the recommendations of Basel III for the banking sector and the Solvency II recommendations for the insurance sector. As a rule, financial institutions are required to maintain a minimal level of liquidity which should serve as their capital backbone for coping with unexpected obligations. For instance, even if a bank has studied the deposits of its customers in depth and is capable of predicting with great precision how much money its customers will withdraw from their deposits and when, it must nevertheless be prepared for an unexpected eventuality which could trigger a greater demand for cash than the bank has anticipated.

Capital Allocation

✓ Funding liquidity risk
× Central bank liquidity risk
× Market liquidity risk

With regard to central bank liquidity risk, in most cases, no capital requirement is specified by states or governments. However, extensive discussions have been conducted regarding the extent of foreign currency reserves a state must possess in order to ensure its ability to respond effectively to changes in market liquidity.

Finally, there is generally no regulatory requirement for maintaining market liquidity, mostly because other risk management mechanisms, such as mark to market, already ensure that any financial entity which has taken a short position will possess sufficient funds to be able to meet its obligations. However, various supervisory authorities do use liquidity measures in order to identify in real time any abnormal market events which might demand immediate intervention. For example, radical changes to the price of a stock may cause trade in this stock to be suspended temporarily.

Chapter 5

Interest Rate Risk

Accompanying presentation: 5. Risk Management — Interest Rate Risk

5.1. Interest

Interest

- Interest is a sum of money which is added to the sum of a loan or deposit (the "principal") at the end of a given period. It serves as a payment to the lender or a receipt for the borrower.

- The price of transferring money from the future into the present.

Interest is an essential concept in finance. We shall begin by attempting to explain what interest is, in the simplest terms possible.

Interest is the sum of money which is added to a loan or deposit (the "principal") at the end of a given period. It serves as a payment to the lender or a receipt for the borrower. Interest rates are typically measured as a percentage[1] out of the principal, for a period of one year. For instance, for a bank loan of USD 100,000 (principal) for a period of one year, the borrower will have to pay the bank an interest of USD 4,000 (4%).

Interest may also be thought of as the "price of money"; in other words, the price of transferring money from the future into the present. In the example above, as part of the loan agreement, in order to "buy" USD 100,000 today, one must "pay" USD 104,000 in one year's time (USD 100,000 plus the annual price of USD 4,000).

Interest rates have an impact on most market prices. For this reason, the nominal interest rate[2] is frequently employed as a key tool for managing monetary policy, in virtually every country in the world. The central bank of the country is charged with managing national monetary policy, and it does this by periodically setting the nominal annual interest rate for the country (typically on a monthly basis).

---

[1] Some interesting facts...
Professionals often measure interest rates in "basis points" (BPS). Each point is equivalent to 0.01%. Following is an example of a conversion table between percentage and basis points:

BPS	%
1	0.01
10	0.1
50	0.5
100	1
1,000	10
10,000	100

[2] The nominal interest rate does not take into account changes in the prices of products and services. Therefore, if we have deposited USD 100,000 in our savings account at the bank, the annual interest rate is 3% and prices have not changed during this year, we will have earned USD 3,000 in both nominal and "real" terms. "Real" in this context means we can purchase more goods with the money we have earned.

If, however, prices have also gone up by 3% during this year, we have not gained any money in "real" terms, as our purchasing power has not increased. The relation between the nominal interest rate and the real interest rate may be expressed in the following way: **Nominal interest rate = Real interest rate + Inflation rate.**

Interest Rates in Selected Economies (May 2017)

Name of interest rate	Country	Interest rate
Australian interest rate (RBA)	Australia	1.500 %
Brazilian interest rate (BACEN)	Brazil	10.250 %
Canadian interest rate (BOC)	Canada	0.500 %
Chilean interest rate (Banco Central)	Chile	2.500 %
Chinese interest rate (PBC)	China	4.350 %
Korean interest rate (Bank of Korea)	South Korea	1.250 %
Swedish interest rate (Riksbank)	Sweden	−0.500 %
Swiss interest rate (SNB)	Switzerland	−0.750 %
U.K. interest rate (BoE)	Great Britain	0.250 %
U.S. interest rate (FED)	United States	1.000 %
European interest rate (ECB)	Europe	0.000 %

Source: World Bank. https://data.worldbank.org/.

As interest rates are used as a tool in the management of monetary policy, the nominal annual interest rate has become the most extensively managed price in the financial world. While some central banks may attempt to manipulate currency exchange rates, and some states set fixed prices for basic goods, etc., no price is managed as consistently, intensively or for longer periods of time than the market interest rate.

Central bank interest rates of selected countries May 2017

Name	Economy	Interest rate (%)
Australian interest rate (RBA)	Australia	1.50
Brazilian interest rate (BACEN)	Brazil	10.25
Canadian interest rate (BOC)	Canada	0.50
Chilean interest rate (Banco Central)	Chile	2.50
Chinese interest rate (PBC)	China	4.35
Czech interest rate (CNB)	Czech Republic	0.05
Danish interest rate (Nationalbank)	Denmark	0.05
European interest rate (ECB)	Europe	0.00
Hungarian interest rate (MNB)	Hungary	0.90

(*Continued*)

(*Continued*)

Name	Economy	Interest rate (%)
Indian interest rate (RBI)	India	6.25
Indonesian interest rate (BI)	Indonesia	6.50
Israeli interest rate (BOI)	Israel	0.10
Japanese interest rate (BoJ)	Japan	0.00
Korean interest rate (Bank of Korea)	South Korea	1.25
Mexican interest rate (Banxico)	Mexico	6.75
New Zealand interest rate (RBNZ)	New Zealand	1.75
Norwegian interest rate (Norges Bank)	Norway	0.50
Polish interest rate (NBP)	Poland	1.50
Russian interest rate (CBR)	Russia	9.25
Saudi Arabian interest rate (SAMA)	Saudi Arabia	2.00
South African interest rate (SARB)	South Africa	7.00
Swedish interest rate (Riksbank)	Sweden	−0.50
Swiss interest rate (SNB)	Switzerland	−0.75
Turkish interest rate (CBRT)	Turkey	8.00
U.K. interest rate (BoE)	Great Britain	0.25
U.S. interest rate (FED)	United States	1.00

The earlier table shows the interest rates set by the central banks of various countries, as of May 2017.

The table above reveals that in May 2017, the nominal annual interest rate on the U.S. Dollar was 1.00%, on the Brazilian real 10.25% and on the Euro 0%. Meanwhile, the central bank interest rates of Sweden and Switzerland were in fact negative! In these countries, the nominal value of money is gradually decreasing. The practical significance of this is that if prices in Sweden remain constant, people will start to show an increased preference for spending their money on products and services right now rather than depositing it in their savings accounts.

The nominal interest rate, set by the central bank of each country, affects almost all prices in the market. These include interest rates on loans and deposits, mortgages and savings plans, bonds, stocks, exchange rates, insurance premiums and market value of corporations.

Interest — Examples

- **Credit interest** — the interest depositors receive on their savings
- **Debit interest** — the interest borrowers pay for the credit they receive

- **Fixed interest** — the interest rate is fixed in advance for the entire lifetime of the deposit or loan
- **Floating interest** — the interest rate varies over the lifetime of the deposit or loan, according to changes in market interest rates

- **Indexed interest** — a fixed interest which is added on top of changes in another value, e.g., changes in the consumer price index; in such cases, the interest rate is pegged to the inflation rate

- **Foreign interest** — the interest rate on foreign currency

- **Short-term interest** — the interest rate is set for a short period of time (typically up to three months)

- **Long-term interest** — the interest rate is set for longer periods of time (typically longer than a year)

- **Capitalization** — used to measure the present value of assets or liabilities of varying time ranges

---

The prices most strongly affected by the central bank interest rate are the many other forms of interest that exist in the market. Let us present a number of these:

- **Credit interest** — the interest depositors receive on their savings.
- **Debit interest** — the interest which debtors pay for the credit they receive.
- **Fixed interest rate** — the interest rate is fixed in advance for the entire lifetime of the deposit or loan.
- **Floating interest rate** — the interest rate varies over the lifetime of the deposit or loan, according to changes in market interest rates.
- **Indexed interest rate** — a fixed interest rate which is paid in addition to changes in another value, e.g., changes in the consumer price index. In such a case, the interest rate is pegged to the inflation rate.
- **Foreign interest** — the interest rate on foreign currency.
- **Short-term interest** — the interest rate is set for a short period of time (typically up to three months).
- **Long-term interest** — the interest rate is set for longer periods of time (typically longer than a year).
- **Capitalization** — used to measure the present value of assets or liabilities of varying time ranges.

As this short list demonstrates, many types of interest exist in the market. While all of these are greatly affected by the local central bank interest rate (with the possible exception of foreign interest, which is affected by the interest rate of the relevant foreign central bank), each type is also subject to the effects of a variety of other factors. For instance, although credit risk is essentially determined according to the central bank's interest rate, it is also affected by the size of the savings account. If a bank wishes to encourage its customers to deposit more money, it will offer them higher interest rates for larger savings accounts in an attempt to persuade them to choose this particular bank over its competitors. A customer who pledges not to withdraw any money from a savings account for at least five years will enjoy a higher interest rate than a customer who wishes to retain the right to withdraw his or her money at any point during these five years.

Similarly, debit risk is affected by the amount of credit concerned, borrower risk, supply and demand of loans, etc.

Credit interest rates tend to be lower than the central bank interest rate. In contrast, debit interest rates are most often higher than the interest rate set by the central bank.

Commercial banks exploit this difference between credit and debit interest rates, turning it into a source of income — they purchase money at a cheap price from depositors (credit interest) and sell it as credit at a higher price (debit interest).

As the difference between credit and debit interest rates grows, banks will enjoy greater profits. Conversely, if the gap between the two types of interest shrinks, banks risk incurring severe losses, particularly if this change occurs abruptly.

A sudden shift in interest rates may put banks at risk, but banks are not the only ones who stand to suffer such an event. For example, a married couple, having taken out a mortgage with a variable interest rate, may discover several years later that the interest rate has risen and that they can no longer keep up with the monthly payments.

Let us give yet another example: a man who has deposited his money in a savings account with a fixed interest rate may discover some years down the road that the interest rate on his savings is lower than the rate at which prices have risen during the same period, and he has effectively lost money. These examples demonstrate the interest rate risk involved in many financial activities. We shall describe this risk in greater detail in the following sections.

5.2. Interest Rate Risk

Interest rate risk is the possibility of losing profits or capital due to changes in interest rates.

Interest Rate Risk

▪ Interest rate risk is the possibility of losing profits or capital due to changes in interest rates.

- Repricing risk
  - The result of differences in payback periods (for fixed interest) or in the repricing schedule (for variable interest) of assets, liabilities or off-balance-sheet positions.
- Yield curve risk
  - Occurs due to unforeseen movements in the yield curve which have a negative impact on profits or capital.
- Basis risk
  - Occurs when the shifts in interest rates very between different financial markets or instruments with similar repricing characteristics.
- Options risk
  - Occurs when shifts in market interest rates result in a change in the timing or value of a cash flow from a financial instrument.

The main forms of credit risk are as follows:

- **Repricing risk:** Repricing risk is the result of differences in payback periods (for fixed interest) or in the repricing schedule (for variable interest) of assets, liabilities or off-balance-sheet positions.
- **Yield curve risk:** Yield curve risk occurs due to unforeseen movements in the yield curve which have a negative impact on profits or capital.
- **Spread risk:** Spread risk occurs when the shifts in interest rates vary between different financial markets or instruments with similar repricing characteristics.

- **Derivatives risk:** Derivatives risk occurs when shifts in market interest rates result in a change in the timing or value of a cash flow from a financial instrument.

We shall now describe each type of credit risk in detail.

5.2.1. *Repricing risk*

Repricing Risk

Year	Assets with fixed interest	Assets with variable interest	Profit
1	6%	4%	2%
2	6%	6%	0%
3	6%	7%	−1%

Repricing risk is the most frequently encountered form of interest rate risk. This type of risk is the result of differences in payback periods (for fixed interest) or in the repricing schedule (for variable interest) of assets, liabilities or off-balance-sheet positions. Such differences in scheduling may expose the profits and the capital to losses.

To give an example of a loss in profits, let us suppose we possess assets worth one million Mexican pesos (MXN), on which we receive a fixed interest rate of 6%. During the next three years, we may expect to receive MXN 60,000 per year. At the same time, we also have liabilities worth one million MXN, with a variable interest rate on these liabilities. In the first year, the variable interest rate was 4%, i.e., we paid MXN 40,000. Overall, we made a profit of MXN 20,000 during the first year.

In the second year, the variable interest rate increased to 6%. In that year, we received MXN 60,000 but also had to pay MXN 60,000 and therefore neither earned nor lost money during this year.

In the third year, the variable interest rate rose to 7%. In this year, we received MXN 60,000 but were also forced to pay MXN 70,000.

Therefore, during the third year, we lost MXN 10,000 overall. In this example, the repricing risk of the interest materialized during the third year.

Another example of materialized repricing risk causing a loss in profits may be found in the realm of mortgages. When interest rates are low, many investors augment their credit component and invest in higher-yield assets. In particular, private individuals will take out a mortgage in order to purchase an apartment and rent it out. The income from the rent is intended to cover the monthly mortgage payments, and once the mortgage has been repaid, the investor will be able to sell the apartment at a profit.

Such an investment contains an element of interest rate risk, as, even if the rent payments remain stable over time, the mortgage payments may vary due to the variable interest rate. Over the years, the interest rate on the mortgage may grow, and with it the monthly mortgage payments. Once these payments exceed the income from the rent, the investor will begin to lose money.

A loss in capital due to materialized interest rate risk may occur when we measure the value of assets. An investor holding a ten-year bond, for which he will begin to receive a coupon worth CNY 10 million starting from the end of the fifth year, wishes to sell the bond. The net present value of the bond depends on the interest rate and is calculated according to the following formula:

$$NPV = \sum_{i=1}^{N} \frac{C_i}{\left(1+r\right)^i}$$

where NPV is the Net Present Value, the current value of the bond, C_i is the sum of the coupon at time i (in the example above, 0 until the end of year four and CNY 10 million from year five), r is the interest rate, i is the time unit (in our example, each unit is one year) and N is the number of time units (ten years in the example above).

If the interest rate is 1%, the bond's NPV will be CNY 55.7 million. If the interest rate rises to 2%, the bond's value will drop to CNY 51.7 million. In this example, an increase in the interest rate from 1% to 2% will result in a loss of just under CNY 4 million. Were the interest rate to reach 3%, the loss would amount to approximately CNY 7.5 million.

Excel

In order to calculate NPV using Excel, we may employ the function = *NPV()* in the following manner:

	A	B	C	D	
1	r	1%	2%	3%	
2	C1	0	0	0	
3	C2	0	0	0	
4	C3	0	0	0	
5	C4	0	0	0	
6	C5	10,000,000	10,000,000	10,000,000	
7	C6	10,000,000	10,000,000	10,000,000	
8	C7	10,000,000	10,000,000	10,000,000	
9	C8	10,000,000	10,000,000	10,000,000	
10	C9	10,000,000	10,000,000	10,000,000	
11	C10	10,000,000	10,000,000	10,000,000	
12					
13	NPV	55,693,390	51,748,563	48,131,044	= NPV(D1,D2:D11)
14			–3,944,827	–7,562,345	

5.2.2. *Yield curve risk*

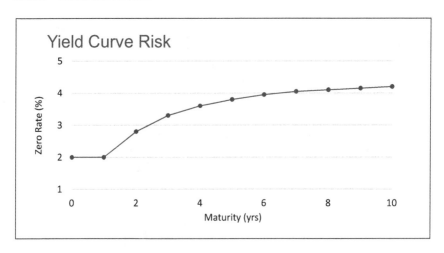

Yield curve risk occurs due to unforeseen movements in the yield curve which have a negative impact on the profits or capital of the entity exposed to the risk.

Let us first explain the meaning of the term "yield curve".

There exists a correlation between the payback period and the interest rate. This correlation may be displayed as a graph, called a yield curve. Normally, the longer the payback period, the higher the interest rate (positive/normal yield curve). During times when interest rates are expected to go down, the opposite correlation may be observed, i.e., the interest rate goes down as the payback period grows longer (negative/inverted yield curve). An intermediate state exists, where the interest rate is constant regardless of the payback period (flat yield curve).

Let us use a positive yield curve to demonstrate the main forms of yield curve shifts.

5.2.2.1. *Parallel shift in yield curve*

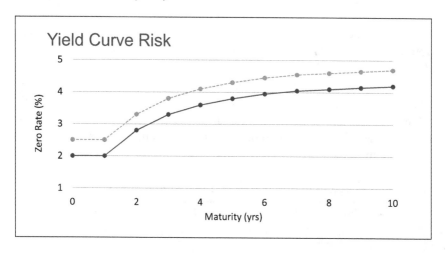

A parallel shift in the yield curve occurs when the growth in interest rates is constant over time. The example in the above image shows a consistent growth of 0.5% in the interest rate throughout the payback period.

It is important to note that a parallel shift in the yield curve does not necessarily correlate to a parallel shift in the associated interest rate risk!

To clarify this assertion, let us straighten the yield curve into a flat yield curve and assume that the interest rate remained constant at 2% every year, and the parallel shift was an increase of 0.5% in all periods.

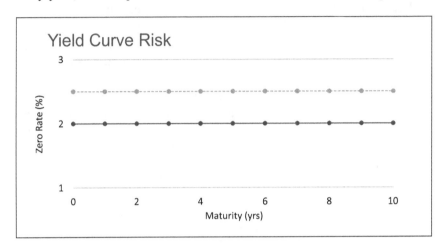

Let us suppose we have two ten-year bonds worth USD 100,000 each. Both pay USD 20,000 for one of those years and zero for the remainder of the time.

The only difference between these two bonds is that one of them pays USD 20,000 at the end of the first year, whereas the other pays an identical sum at the end of the last year. In every other year, the bonds pay nothing. The following table represents the payments received for each of the bonds over the course of ten years:

Year	1	2	3	4	5	6	7	8	9	10
Bond A	0	0	0	0	0	0	0	0	0	120,000
Bond B	20,000	0	0	0	0	0	0	0	0	100,000

The net present value of these two bonds, at a 2% interest, would be as follows:

Year	NPV(2%)
Bond A	98,442
Bond B	101,643

The difference in value between these two bonds is not due to the amount of money they pay (which is identical) or their interest rates (which are identical as well). It is also not the result of differing lifetimes (ten years for both) or a different currency (both bonds are in USD). The only difference between the two bonds is in their payment dates (year one for bond B and year ten for bond A).

Let us now suppose that a parallel shift has occurred, and the interest rate each year is higher by 0.5%. Although the shift in interest rates is identical throughout the period, the NPV of the two bonds will differ:

Year	NPV(2%)	NPV(2.5%)	NPV(2%) — NPV(2.5%)
Bond A	98,442	93,744	−4,698
Bond B	101,643	97,632	−4,011
			−687

A parallel shift in the yield curve does not necessarily correlate to a parallel shift in the NPV of the bonds.

In the example above, a parallel shift of 0.5% affects the NPV of bond A, where the payment is received at the end of the ten-year period, to a greater extent than it affects bond B, where the payment is already made at the end of the first year. Bond A is exposed to greater interest rate risk as a result of the parallel shift than bond B. We may measure just how much more vulnerable it is and see that the difference is USD 687. This difference is exclusively due to the differing payment dates. There is no other factor at play.

One might consider a loss of USD 687 to be fairly minor. However, for large financial institutions, whose holding in such bonds may amount to billions of U.S. Dollars, the amount of money they stand to lose in such a scenario would have been sufficient to fund the operations of the risk management department for an entire year and still allow the institution to keep a handsome profit.

This example demonstrates that a parallel shift in the yield curve does not necessarily correspond to a parallel shift in the interest rate risk.

5.2.2.2. *Change in yield curve slope*

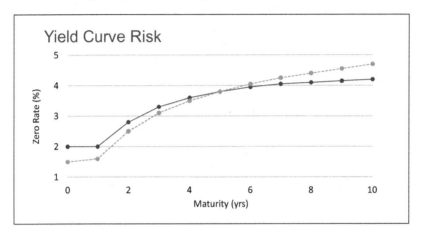

A change in the slope of the yield curve occurs when the interest rate grows at different rates for different payback periods. In the example in this image, the short-term interest rate has fallen by 0.5%, whereas the long-term interest rate has risen by 0.5%. The five-year interest rate remains unchanged.

Such changes are more difficult to measure, as the interest rate must be measured separately for each year. Further on in this chapter, we shall discuss the various measurement methods which may be employed in such circumstances and learn how this obstacle may be overcome.

5.2.2.3. *Isolated movement in the yield curve*

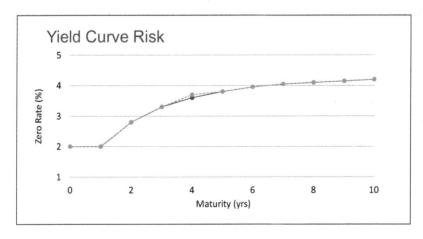

An isolated movement occurs when the interest rate for a certain period goes up or down, whereas the interest rate for the remainder of the time remains constant. In the example in the image earlier, it can be seen that the four-year interest rate went up by approximately 0.25%, whereas the other rates remained constant.

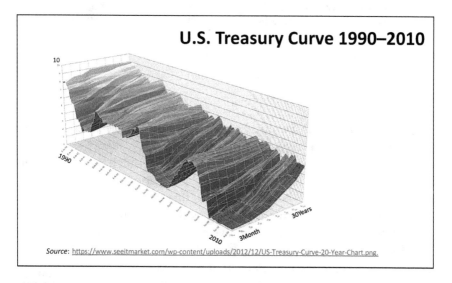

U.S. Treasury Curve 1990–2010

Source: https://www.seeitmarket.com/wp-content/uploads/2012/12/US-Treasury-Curve-20-Year-Chart.png.

During the years 1990–2010, the yield curve for U.S. interest rates changed significantly. Short-term interest rates fell from about 8% in the early 1990s to effectively zero by the end of the 2000s. During this time, long-term interest rates dropped from 9% to 4%.

Most of the time, the yield curve was positive, but during certain periods, it was negative (late 1990s and 2005–2006).

This chart illustrates the frequent movements which occur in the yield curve over time, as well as the corresponding changes in interest rate risk levels.

5.2.3. *Basis risk*

Basis risk

- Basis risk occurs when the shifts in interest rates very between different financial markets or instruments with similar repricing characteristics:
  - Savings account/loan
  - T-bill/bank deposit
  - Bonds of different rankings

Basis risk occurs when the shifts in interest rates vary between different financial markets or instruments with similar repricing characteristics. Let us take for example a savings account and a loan which are identical in the amount of money they pay, their payback period, repayment terms, etc. The only difference between them is that one is an incoming cash flow and the other is outgoing. As long as the difference between credit risk and debit risk remains constant, we may predict the extent of the cash flow. However, an unforeseen change in the gap between these two interest rates may lead to the materialization of a loss.

Another example is the interest rate on a treasury bill (T-bill) compared to that of a bank deposit. Let us suppose the two investments are identical in the amount of money they pay, their payback period, repayment terms, etc. The two will nevertheless differ in pricing, as the T-bill is tradable but the deposit is not. The T-bill investment is revaluated on a daily basis according to changes in the market interest rate, whereas the value of the deposit is much more stable. This can lead to the materialization of losses as a result of basis risk.[3]

A final example is the pricing of two bonds, identical in coupon sum, payment dates, time ranges, etc., differing only in their credit rating. The

---

[3] The tradability of an asset is an indicator of its liquidity risk. As discussed in the chapter on liquidity risk, increased tradability signifies a lower liquidity risk, as the asset may be sold on the market with greater ease. In this example, however, aside from its effect on liquidity, the tradability of the assets also affects their value, which in turn affects the interest rate risk.

higher-rated bond (e.g., AA) will be priced higher than the one with the lower credit rating (say B).

As discussed in the chapter on credit risk, each rating group is assigned a probability of default which changes over time. It is possible for the two bonds to remain in their respective rating groups even if their PD values have changed. As a result, their interest rates may also be subject to change. Unforeseen changes may lead to the materialization of interest rate risk originating in basis risk.

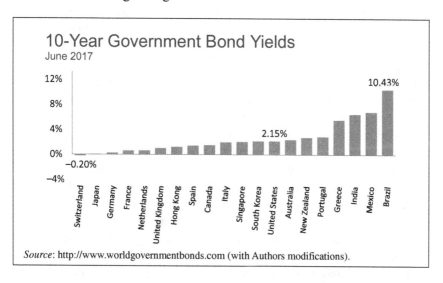

Source: http://www.worldgovernmentbonds.com (with Authors modifications).

Two ten-year government bonds with identical terms, but issued by different governments, may differ significantly in their yields. The different yields reflect the risk premium demanded by investors. An investment in Brazilian government bonds is considered riskier than an investment in U.S. government bonds. Thus, for instance, in June 2017, the yield on a U.S. government bond was 2.15%, whereas the yield for a similar bond issued by the government of Brazil was 10.43%. Changes in the risk premium demanded by investors may lead to a materialization of interest rate risk.

Of particular interest is the case of Switzerland, whose government bonds have a negative interest rate. Many theories which incorporate interest rates in their formulas limit their conclusions exclusively to positive interest rates. These models support a view which has developed over the years, that interest rates cannot fall below 0%. These theories rely on the reasonable assumption that investors will not invest their money in assets which will return less than what they currently have. Furthermore, these theories claim, if interest rates are negative, people will withdraw their deposits and prefer to hold their money in cash. With regard to loans, the theories assert that no bank would agree to grant a loan with a negative interest rate — the bank would rather not grant the loan at all. These theories are, in fact, backed by empirical evidence — throughout history, instances of negative interest rates have been exceedingly rare.

Since the crisis of 2008, interest rates in financial markets have dropped to extremely low levels and occasionally all the way to zero. In some countries, as we have seen, they have even dropped below zero. This phenomenon challenges not only the prevalent theories but also the authorities responsible for determining monetary policy. On the one hand, the negative interest rates of the central banks in Sweden and Switzerland have not caused the public to withdraw their deposits as predicted. On the other hand, the negative interest rates of the central banks for a time horizon of one year have not always been translated into negative credit interest rates, so the reality may not, in fact, stand in contradiction to the theory in this case.

It would seem that public reaction to the negative interest rates in Sweden and Switzerland has so far been rather mild. However, if the trend of decreasing interest rates continues, this may trigger a sudden reaction at some point, where the entire public withdraws its deposits all at once. This type of herd mentality, also referred to as a bank run (discussed in previous chapters), if it occurs not just in a single bank but across the entire banking system, could lead to the financial collapse of the state and even spread to other countries.

Extremely low (or negative) interest rates pose a significant challenge for anyone who deals with monetary matters, particularly for those involved in setting monetary policy or managing interest rate risks.

5.2.4. *Derivatives risk*

Derivatives Risk

- Derivatives risk occurs when a shift in market interest rates results in a change in the timing or value of a cash flow from a financial instrument:
  - Interest rate contracts
  - Interest rate options
  - Option to transition between savings plans

Derivatives risk occurs when a shift in market interest rates results in a change in the timing or value of a cash flow from a financial instrument.

Some asset/liability portfolios contain financial derivatives such as futures contracts, options and swaps. Each type of derivative is priced differently, but all of them are affected by interest rates. Changes in interest rates will therefore naturally affect the pricing of assets and liabilities, even if every other element remains constant.

We distinguish between freestanding derivatives and embedded derivatives. We have discussed various types of freestanding derivatives in the chapter on market risk. Embedded derivatives, by contrast, are a component of, or "embedded" in, another financial asset.

For instance, an option grants the holder the right but does not obligate him or her, to buy, sell or modify in some way the cash flow of financial instruments such as stocks, bonds and currency.

- A freestanding option is an asset or a liability which may be bought, sold, lent, deposited and traded directly at the stock exchange or OTC.
- An embedded option is an integral component of another asset or liability and may not be separated from it.

An example of a freestanding option is a call option on Apple stock traded at the stock exchange.

An example of an embedded option is a bank deposit without a fixed withdrawal date. The depositor has the option to withdraw all or part of the money in the deposit at any time. This option is not freestanding as it is directly linked to the deposit. It may not be traded directly, either.

When managing interest rate risks, one must take into account both freestanding derivatives and embedded derivatives.

As part of the discussion of the interest rate risk embodied in financial derivatives, let us mention some of the financial instruments whose terms of realization are dictated by the interest rates themselves:

- A **cap** is an option which protects against an increase in interest rates. At any change in interest rates, the option writer will pay the difference between the preset interest rate and the market interest rate if the market rate is higher than the preset rate.

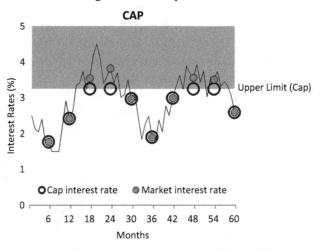

A cap may be viewed as a form of insurance against a rise in interest rates. In the example above, the interest is paid out semi-annually. When the market interest rate is lower than 3.25% (converging circles), the market interest rate is paid. When the interest rate exceeds 3.25%, the upper cap — in this example 3.25% — is paid instead.

- A **floor** is an option which protects against a decrease in interest rates. At any change in interest rates, the option writer will pay the difference between the preset interest rate and the market interest rate, if the market rate is lower than the preset rate.

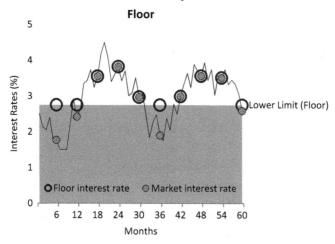

A floor may be viewed as a form of insurance against a drop in interest rates. In the example above, the interest is paid out semi-annually. When the market interest rate is higher than 2.75% (converging circles), the market interest rate is paid. When the interest rate drops below 2.75%, the bottom limit — in this example, 2.75% — is paid instead.

- A **swaption** is a contract between two sides, whose purpose is to exchange the flow of future interest rate payments for some other cash flow. Swaptions typically substitute a fixed interest rate for a variable interest rate in order to reduce the exposure to fluctuations in interest rates.

- A **bond option** is the option to buy or sell a bond before it expires, at a predetermined price. The price of a bond depends directly on the interest rate curve, which therefore dictates the exercise terms of the bond.

5.3. Measurement

Interest Rate Risk Assessment

- **Exposure**
  - By financial instruments
  - By time segments + gap analysis
- **Sensitivity**
  - Duration
  - Rho
- **Loss**
  - VaR, EaR
- **Simulation**
  - Simulation of different interest rate scenarios and their effect on the cash flow
    - Static simulation   Estimate of cash flows in different scenarios
    - Dynamic simulation   Assumptions on the behavior of the financial institution and its clients in response to changes in the interest environment

---

The measurement of interest rate risk is a complex process. Large financial institutions (banks, insurance companies, etc.) employ highly sophisticated technological systems which measure every significant interest rate risk affecting their assets and liabilities. Such systems measure the evolution of the exposure to interest rate risk over time, and some of them may even provide future predictions. These technological systems alert the financial institutions to abnormal exposures which could put their profits or capital at risk.

This book is too narrow in scope to detail every single method which exists for measuring and mitigating interest rate risk. Nevertheless, we shall try to convey the four main principles of interest rate risk assessment.

5.3.1. *Exposure*

Measurement of the value of financial instruments in which interest rates are the primary component which affects pricing. Such instruments include deposits, loans, bonds, actuarial liabilities and interest rate derivatives.

The extent of exposure allows us to measure the damage potential of a failure, regardless of the probability that the damage will be realized.

5.3.1.1. *Exposure according to financial instruments*

This method sorts the various financial instruments into categories, and the total holdings in each category are written down. For example:

Instrument	Sum	Percentage out of portfolio (%)
Bank deposits	50	10
Loans	150	30
Bonds	100	20
Actuarial liabilities	0	0
Derivatives	0	0
Other instruments where interest rate is not a primary component of pricing (cash, stocks, options, real estate, etc.)	200	40
Total	**500**	**100**

In the example above, the exposure to credit (loans + bonds) constitutes 50% of the portfolio, whereas the exposure to deposits is just 10%. An increase in the interest rate will raise the interest payments on loans, reduce the value of the bonds and lower the interest rates on deposits. This portfolio is therefore exposed to an increase in interest rates.

5.3.1.2. *Division by time segments*

When analyzing exposure according to time intervals, we allocate all assets, liabilities and off-balance positions which are sensitive to interest rates by time segments according to the payback period (for fixed interest rates) or the time until they are to be repriced (for variable interest rates). Using the table, we may come up with simple indicators for the sensitivity to interest rate risk of both profits (gap analysis) and market value. The width of the gap for a given time segment (that is, assets minus liabilities), in addition to off-balance-sheet exposures whose repricing or due date occurs during the same time segment, provides an indication of the exposure of the financial entity to repricing risk. By applying sensitive weights to each time segment, we may also use the table of due dates or repricing dates as a measure of the effects of variable interest rates on the market value of the financial entity.

5.3.2. *Sensitivity*

An important question when assessing interest rate risk is as follows: What would be the extent of damage to the present value of a future cash flow from each of the instruments mentioned above, if the interest rate were to change by 1%? In order to answer this question, we may use the **modified duration** of the cash flow. We shall explain modified duration in greater detail in a separate section.

Some risk managers in financial institutions divide assets and liabilities into time intervals according to their modified duration rather than their payback period. This is not an error but a different perspective which grants them a more complete understanding of the interest rate risks they face.

For options which are priced according to the Black–Scholes formula, the sensitivity of the option value to a change in interest rates may be measured using Rho(ρ):

$$\rho = \frac{\partial V}{\partial r}$$

where V is the option value and r is the interest rate.

Out of all the elements which may affect the pricing of an option (real price, exercise price, fluctuation, time to maturity and interest rate), interest rates are often the least significant. Nevertheless, institutions which trade in options must also incorporate the interest rate risk of options into their calculations, and Rho allows them to do this in a relatively simple manner.

5.3.3. *Loss*

In contrast with exposure, which measures the damage potential, and sensitivity, which measures the extent of loss given a specific event, loss is a measure which examines probability as well. The distribution of interest rates over varying time ranges may be estimated, and, using complex statistical calculations, we may identify yield curves where, at a 99% probability, no lower (or higher) yield curves exist. For these yield curves, we may calculate the value at risk (VaR) and earnings at risk (EaR).

This estimate of the loss at risk takes into account the potential damage as well as the probability that it will occur, both in terms of the effect on the expected profits of the portfolio and on its market value.

5.3.4. *Simulation*

This risk assessment method tests various scenarios in which changes in interest rates occur. The simulation may include stress scenarios, what-ifs and Monte Carlo simulations.

We distinguish between a static simulation and a dynamic simulation.

A static simulation allows us to estimate the effects of various interest rate scenarios on cash flow. Using this method, we perform a simulation of the interest rates in various scenarios (stress scenarios, what-if scenarios, Monte Carlo simulations, etc.) and calculate the profits and market value of the portfolio in each scenario. For instance, in a scenario where the interest rate goes up by 3%, all cash flows are calculated according to the increased interest rate and compared to the actual situation in the market.

A dynamic simulation takes into account the behavior of the financial institution and its customers in response to changes in the interest rate environment. For instance, in a scenario where the interest rate goes up by 3%, it is probable that the demand for credit components will shrink and the demand for savings components will expand. These changes must be incorporated into the dynamic simulation. The results are compared to the actual state of the market as well as to the results of the static simulation.

5.3.4.1. *Modified duration*

As we have mentioned above, when we attempt to examine the sensitivity of the current value of future cash flows to a 1% change in interest rates, we may use modified duration.

Modified Duration

Modified duration (*MD*) of cash flow

T	term to maturity
c_t	payment during period t
r	interest rate
B	value of cash flow

$$MD = \frac{\sum_{t=1}^{T} t\, \frac{C_t}{(1+r_t)^t}}{\sum_{t=1}^{T} \frac{C_t}{(1+r_t)^t}} \bigg/ (1+r)$$

Estimate of change to *B* (in percentage) due to changes in *r*:

$$\frac{\Delta B}{B} = -MD\,\Delta r$$

The modified duration of a future cash flow is defined in the following manner:

$$MD = \frac{\sum_{t=1}^{T} t\, \frac{C_t}{(1+r_t)^t}}{\sum_{t=1}^{T} \frac{C_t}{(1+r_t)^t}} \bigg/ (1+r)$$

where *MD* is the modified duration, *T* is the term to maturity, c_t is the payment during period t, *r* is the interest rate and *B* is the value of cash flow.

Modified duration may be used as an estimate of the change to *B* due to changes to *r* (in percentage):

$$\frac{\Delta B}{B} = -MD\Delta r$$

If MD equals 2.5, an increase of 1% in the interest rate will cause the value of the cash flow to drop by 2.5%.

Modified Duration

Calculation of modified duration for a three-year bond. The bond's present value is USD 100, and it pays out a coupon twice a year for an annual rate of 10%. The yield is 12% ($r = 0.12$).

Time (y)	Cash Flow ($)	NPV ($)	Weighted NPV	
0.5	5	4.725	2.362	
1.0	5	4.464	4.464	
1.5	5	4.218	6.328	
2.0	5	3.986	7.972	
2.5	5	3.766	9.416	
3.0	105	74.74	224.21	
Total	130	95.90	254.75	2.657
MD				**2.372**

Let us suppose we have a three-year bond with a present value of USD 100, which pays a 10% coupon semi-annually. Let us suppose that this bond has a yield of 12%. Let us examine the table in the image:

- The first column in the table represents time, t, in years (half a year, one year, a year and a half, etc.).
- The second column represents the cash flow, c_t. As the bond pays a coupon of 10% annually, we will get USD 5 every six months, ending the period with USD 130.
- The third column contains the present value of the coupon, $\frac{C_t}{(1+r_i)^t}$. In our example, this value is USD 95.9 in total.
- The fourth column represents the time-adjusted present value, $t\frac{C_t}{(1+r_i)^t}$. This amounts to 254.75.
- The fifth column contains the ratio of the two sums, 2.657, capitalized so that the modified duration is 2.372.

In this example, the modified duration is 2.372. This means that a growth of 1% in the interest rate will result in a loss of 2.372% for the value of the cash flow.

Let us assume that the interest rate has risen by 1–13%. According to the modified duration, the value of the cash flow ought to go down by

2.37%. And, indeed, the value of the cash flow went down by 2.33%, not far from the value we obtained by calculating the modified duration.

It is important to note that modified duration serves as an effective approximation only when the changes in interest rates are small. For changes greater than 2%, the measurement is considerably less precise, although it may still provide a rough estimate of the sensitivity of the portfolio value to interest rates.

5.3.4.2. *Excel*

In order to calculate modified duration, we use the table which may be seen in the image, employing the following formulas:

	C	D	E	F	G	H
4	12%	Time (y)	Cash Flow ($)	NPV ($)	Weighted NPV	
5		0.5	5	= E5/(1+$C$4)^D5	= D5*F5	
6		1	5	= E6/(1+$C$4)^D6	= D6*F6	
7		1.5	5	= E7/(1+$C$4)^D7	= D7*F7	
8		2	5	= E8/(1+$C$4)^D8	= D8*F8	
9		2.5	5	= E9/(1+$C$4)^D9	= D9*F9	
10		3	105	= E10/(1+$C$4)^D10	= D10*F10	
11						
12		Total	= SUM(E5:E10)	= SUM(F5:F10)	= SUM (G5:G10)	= G12/F12
13						= H12/(1+C4)

5.4. Capital Allocation

Capital Allocation

- Standard approach
  - Term to maturity
  - Duration
- Internal models approach

As with other types of risk, interest rate risk also requires reserve of capital which will act as a financial buffer for the entity in times of crisis. Various supervisory authorities in different countries have different specifications for the manner in which this capital reserve should be calculated and allocated. The recommendations of Basel II present two main approaches for calculating the capital requirement for interest rate risks. One approach is the "standard approach" — this is the simpler approach, and we will describe it in the following. The other is the "internal model approach", which is better adapted to the specific characteristics of each particular financial institution and which we will not expand upon in this book.

The standard approach allows us to use one of the following two methods to calculate the capital allocation required for interest rate risks.

5.4.1. *Term to maturity*

The principle at the heart of this method is the classification of financial assets into categories according to their interest rates and payback period, setting a risk factor for each category according to which the capital must be allocated.

For example, let us examine the following table of risk factors:

Interest rate ≥ 3%	Interest rate < 3%	Risk factor
1–2 years	1–1.9 years	2.5%
Up to 3 years	Up to 2.8 years	3.5%
Up to 4 years	Up to 3.6 years	4.5%

Now, let us suppose we have a three-year bond with a 4% interest rate, and our exposure to this bond is EUR 100,000. The adjusted exposure in this case would be EUR 3,500, and this is also the sum we must allocate to defend against the interest rate risk of this bond.

Assets and liabilities may cancel each other out, and in this way, we may reduce the capital requirement for interest rate risks. However, strict regulations exist which determine the manner in which the weighted exposures may cancel each other out. For this reason, one must comply with the regulations of the specific country in question.

5.4.2. *Modified duration*

If we choose to calculate the capital requirement according to this method, we must base our calculations on the modified duration of the financial instrument. As we have shown earlier, the modified duration may be used to estimate the change in the value of the cash flow of a financial instrument due to changes in interest rates.

The change in interest rates which must be taken into account is determined in advance. Many regulators, in conformance with the recommendations of Basel II, publish tables which match the changes in interest rates to time intervals. For example:

Modified duration	Change in interest rate(%)
1–2 years	2
2.8–3.6 years	1.5
Over 20 years	1.2

For example, if we have an asset, let us suppose a bond, whose modified duration is three years, a 1.5% increase in interest rates will cause a drop of 4.5% in the value of the cash flow.

Let us assume that our exposure to this asset is EUR 100,000. In this case, in order to shield ourselves from the interest rate risk of this bond, we must allocate EUR 4,500.

As with the previous method, assets and liabilities may cancel each other out to reduce the capital requirement. Once again, strict regulations are in place, which dictates the manner in which this may be done. For this reason, one must comply with the regulations of the specific country in question.

5.4.3. *Derivatives*

The capital requirement for exposure to the interest rate risks of financial derivatives must be calculated differently for each type of derivative (futures, swaps, options, etc.).

We shall not elaborate on the various calculation methods in this book. We will, however, stress the fact that when we calculate the capital requirement which must be allocated to interest rate risk, we must not forget to include the derivatives in our calculations.

Chapter 6

Operational Risks

Accompanying presentations: *6. Risk Management — Operational Risk
(Part I)
6. Risk Management — Operational Risk
(Part II)*

6.1.   Operations

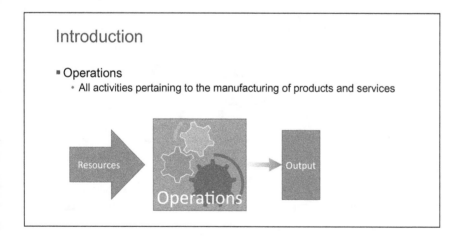

Operations is a general term which encompasses all activities pertaining
to the manufacturing of products and services.

The operations process requires resources such as manpower, machinery, raw materials, human capital and money, bringing them together and converting them into output such as products or services.

For instance, at the end of a proper operations process, we may expect timbers to turn into chairs or tables, or a visit to the doctor to result in an easing of pain.

In many organizations, the operations department is the core of their business activity. For example, in a bread factory, the core business is the production of bread; in an investment house, the core business is the management of investments.

The operations department is of crucial importance when conducting business. For this reason, in most factories and businesses, the responsibility of managing the operations department is assigned to a high-ranking executive person within an organization at the very least. For smaller businesses, the CEO or even the owners themselves are responsible for this role.

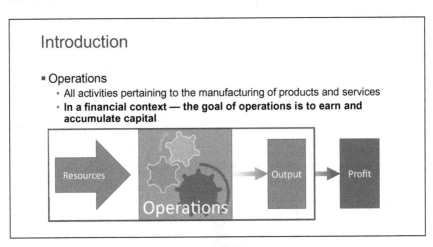

In a financial context, the objective of operations is to earn and accumulate capital by selling the company's product. In this context, the processes of selling the product, creating profits and accumulating capital form part of the range of operating activities of a business, even though they themselves may not be considered part of the operations department.

6.2. Operational Risk

> ## Operational Risk
>
> **Operational risk is the potential loss in profits or capital due to inadequacies or failures of internal processes, people or systems, or due to external events.**
>
> *This definition includes legal risk but excludes strategic and reputational risk.*

Operational risk[1] is the potential loss in profits or capital due to inadequacies or failures of internal processes, people or systems, or due to external events.

The definition of operational risk includes legal risk but excludes strategic risk[2] and reputational risk.[3]

The term "operational risk" is rather misleading! Although the definition of "operational risk" (occasionally also referred to as "operational risks" in the plural) employs the term "operation" — which might be interpreted as risk pertaining exclusively to the operations department as

---

[1] Some interesting facts…

In aviation, medicine, military and a number of other fields, operational risk management has been conducted for many years.

In the financial sector, operational risk is indeed one of the main components of risk management, but it is a very young field when compared to market risks, interest rate risks, insurance risks, etc. Not until the early 2000s, with the implementation of Basel II, did banks begin to apply operational risk management measures, which subsequently spread to other financial sectors as well.

[2] Strategic risk — any action or oversight on behalf of the firm itself which might prevent it from realizing its financial objectives. For further details, see the following chapter on "Additional Risks".

[3] Reputational risk — the risk of loss due to damage to the reputation of a company in the eyes of its clients or suppliers. For further details, see the following chapter on "Additional Risks".

introduced at the beginning of this chapter — the definition is in fact much broader in scope.

In addition to faults in the operations department, operational risk also refers to faults in various other departments such as sales, marketing, human resources, accounting, finance and senior management.

Operational risk might therefore be more adequately termed "activity risk" or "execution risk". Although the term "operational risk" does not accurately describe the actual risks involved, and may indeed be somewhat misleading, we will continue to use this term, as it has become ingrained in the professional language of financial risk management.

6.2.1. *Risk factors*

The definition of a risk is typically founded upon a single risk factor which generates the possibility for a loss in profits or capital. For instance, interest rate risk is the possibility of loss which results from fluctuations in the risk factor of interest rates, liquidity risk is the possibility of loss due to the risk factor of liquidity, credit risk is the possibility of loss due to non-compliance with the terms of credit (risk factor of credit), inflation risk is the risk of loss due to the risk factor of inflation, exchange rate risk is the possibility of loss due to changes in the risk factor of exchange rates, and the list goes on.

Not so with operational risk. The definition of operational risk is based upon no fewer than four(!) risk factors, which differ considerably from each other:

- internal processes,
- people,
- systems,
- external events.

Furthermore, unlike, for example, exchange rate risk, where the exchange rate may only move up or down on a single axis, the "people" factor alone may shift in any direction imaginable and generate a vast array of failures.

Of all the various types of risk, operational risk is the most complex to manage. In the following sections, we shall attempt to explain how operational risk may be managed, beginning with its identification and classification.

6.2.2.   *Identification and classification*

Classification of Operational Risks According to Risk Factor

- People
  - Internal fraud and "deliberate errors"
  - International cybercrime
  - Inappropriate use of confidential customer information
- Systems
  - Hardware or software failure
  - Production line failure

- External events
  - Low customer satisfaction
  - Competition in the market
  - Exposure to suppliers
  - *Force majeure*
- Processes
  - Processing a new employee
  - Shortage of skilled manpower
  - Flawed procedures or organizational structure

Operational risks may be divided into a number of categories. For example, they may be classified according to the risk factor: people, systems, internal processes or external events. Here are some examples of events classified according to risk factor:

- **People**
  Examples:
  o   internal fraud and "deliberate errors",
  o   international cybercrime,
  o   inappropriate use of confidential customer information.
- **Systems**
  Examples:
  o   hardware or software failure,
  o   production line failure.
- **External events**
  Examples:
  o   customer dissatisfaction,
  o   competition in the market,

  o exposure to suppliers,
  o *force majeure.*
- **Processes**
Examples:
  o processing a new employee,
  o shortage of skilled manpower,
  o flawed procedures or organizational structure.

Classification of Operational Risks (Basel II)

- **Embezzlement**: "Internal fraud" committed entirely by an employee or a group of employees, or by external elements with the assistance and collaboration of an employee.

- **Fraud**: "External fraud" committed by a person or group with no involvement of company employees.

- **Employment practices and workplace safety**: Events as which harm the company and are the result of the relationship between employees and employers.

- **Clients, products and business practices**: Failures in the relationship between the company and its clients.

- **Damage to physical assets**: Events which harm the physical capital of the company, including incidents which are the result of human factors as well as those resulting from *force majeure*.

- **Business disruption and systems failures**: Failure of systems or machines.

- **Execution, delivery and process management**: Failure in work processes.

A different system for classifying operational risks may be found in Basel II. According to the Accord, operational risks should be classified according to risk events in the following manner:

- **Embezzlement:** "internal fraud" committed entirely by an employee or a group of employees, or by external elements aided and abetted by an employee. Examples of embezzlement: "deliberate mistakes" such as swapping the name of the asset owner for the name of the employee, an employee stealing customer funds, use of an employee's private bank account for insider trading, etc.
- **Fraud:** "external fraud" committed by a person or group with no involvement of company employees. For examples, bank robbery, identity theft and hacking into company computers.
- **Employment practices and workplace safety:** events which harm the company and are the result of the relationship between employees

and employers. For instance, workers' compensation claims, violations of workplace health and safety laws, labor union activities such as strikes and protests, claims of discrimination, etc.

- **Clients, products and business practices:** failures in the relationship between the company and its clients, such as loss of customer trust, inappropriate usage of confidential client information, inappropriate trade activities using the company account, money laundering and sale of illicit products.
- **Damage to physical assets:** events which damage the physical capital of the company, including incidents which are the result of human factors as well as those resulting from *force majeure*. For example, vandalism, terror attacks, earthquakes, fires and floods.
- **Business disruption and systems failures:** failure of systems or machines. For instance, software or hardware failure, communications malfunctions, failures in the supply of public infrastructure services such as electricity, water or waste disposal.
- **Execution, delivery and process management:** failure of work processes, e.g., incorrectly input data, flawed management of collateral, incomplete legal documents, unauthorized access to customer accounts, flawed performance of a third party (not the customer) and disputes with suppliers.

The classification of risks is an essential part of operational risk management. Classification facilitates the diagnosis and measurement of failures and, of course, is central to identifying the appropriate mitigation.

6.3. Measurement

Measurement

- Exposure
- Expert opinion
- Statistical methods
- Simulation

Much like the estimates of other forms of risk, the measurement of operational risk focuses on the "possibility of incurring a loss in profits or capital" (see definition of operational risk at the start of this chapter). There exist several methods for measuring operational risk, namely exposure, expert opinion and statistical methods. Let us go over these methods in greater detail.

6.3.1. *Exposure*

> ## Measurement — Exposure
>
> - Total scope of business activity
> - Scope of every type of business activity separately

The scope of exposure allows us to estimate the damage potential of a failure, regardless of the probability that the damage will materialize. Unlike all other forms of financial risk, where one cannot suffer losses greater than the value of a portfolio or loan, when it comes to operational risks, the potential losses could exceed the total value of the company!

Let us explain. The exposure of an asset portfolio to market risks, for instance, cannot exceed the value of the portfolio. In an extreme scenario where the investment house loses all of its assets, whose origins are the deposits of its clients, the remaining debt of the investment house will be less than or at most equal to the value of its customers' deposits. While this amount may be exceedingly large, it will never be greater than the value of the portfolio itself.

Not so with exposure to operational risks. If it turns out that the aforementioned investment house has failed to comply with government regulations, it could, in addition to its debt to its customers, face non-compliance fines. Furthermore, the aforementioned investment house could face damage claims by customers. All this can well exceed the value of the portfolio. Apart from the direct exposure to financial loss, the managers of the investment house may also stand trial or even face a prison sentence, thus losing their personal freedom, to which it is difficult to assign a precise financial value. On the day of their release, such managers would struggle to find a new job in their respective fields, constituting a loss of future alternative income, which is very difficult to measure.

Let us give another example to demonstrate the difficulty of measuring exposure to operational risk: a small company which produces chemical fertilizer, whose value does not exceed USD 10 million. Such a company could one day discover that it is responsible for polluting the waters of a nearby creek, after hazardous waste leaked from one of its storage facilities. As a result of this pollution, dozens of people living upstream died of various illnesses. The company faces substantial losses, not only due to regulatory sanctions or fines but also due to losses in legal proceedings against the company, all of which could amount to tens of millions of U.S. Dollars — far exceeding the value of the company itself. If the environmental protection regulations in place are particularly strict, the directors of the company could serve a prison sentence in this example as well.

As part of a proper risk management process, and despite the great difficulty of measuring exposure to operational risk, once we have identified the operational risks, we must proceed to quantify them.[4] The quantification of these risks affects the decision-making process of a company's management. For instance, in large organizations, which periodically quantify hundreds of different operational risks, it is impossible to combat all these risks at once. A significant factor in selecting to concentrate our efforts on one risk at the expense of another is the extent by which the former risk is greater than the latter. For example, having

---

[4]Some interesting facts…

Due to the great difficulty of measuring exposure to operational risk according to the methods we have described for other types of risk management, even veteran risk managers often find themselves at a loss. In their view, since, when measuring exposure to operational risks, "anything goes", it is essentially impossible to truly measure exposure to operational risks. Insurance companies are great admirers of this flawed approach. On the one hand, despite the claim above, it is a fact that insurance companies are, in fact, able to measure the various operational risks and even provide insurance against them (theft, fire, accident, etc.); on the other hand, due to this claim, those same insurance companies can charge any price they want for the insurance they provide. In this context, we shall focus on a number of ideas quantifying operational risks, which may aid in their management.

quantified the potential damages due to the materialization of operational risks, we may first decide to improve the fire monitoring and prevention mechanisms in our large storage facility, and only then proceed to mitigate those risks associated with malfunction in the telephone line of our order fulfillment department.

With regard to measuring the exposure to operational risk, Basel II proposed a simple method for the banking sector. According to this method, the scope of the bank's activity must be calculated — a known value determined by the bank's accountants and typically available to the public — it is equal to the average annual income for the past three years. This value is the bank's exposure to operational risk. The reasoning behind this method is that the exposure of a bank to operational risks grows in accordance with the scope of its activities.

The recommendations brought forth in Basel II facilitated a more precise assessment of operational risks faced by banks by sorting their activities into various subactivities, and then measuring the scope of each subactivity separately. In this way, it is possible to identify differences in the operational risks of two banks whose business activity is of roughly the same scope. Thus, if the bulk of one bank's activity is concentrated in corporate finance, whereas the other primarily deals in retail banking, one bank will be more exposed than the other despite the overall business activity of both being similar in scope.

Although this system, with several adjustments, may be implemented in other market sectors as well, this is rarely done. Non-banking entities tend to adopt alternative approaches to measuring operational risk.

6.3.2. *Expert opinion*

Measurement — Expert Opinion

- How often could an operational risk event materialize?
- What is the expected loss for such an event?
- Verbal assessment

Another method for measuring operational risk is the employment of an expert opinion. Using this approach, an estimate of the loss in profits or capital is given separately for each individual business activity. In order to perform such an assessment, one may seek assistance from external specialists, such as consultant firms. It is also possible to employ internal elements such as the division or section chiefs of the relevant field, who tend to be familiar with the problems and malfunctions which occur throughout the course of their work.

A large number of consulting firms assist various organizations in assessing their operational risks. Each company has developed its own methodology in accordance with its particular field of specialization. There are therefore substantial differences in the way each company collects data, selects the questions which will appear on its risk surveys, analyzes data, implements operational risk management within the organization, etc. However, most of these consulting firms share the following common elements.

In order to consolidate an expert opinion, a periodic survey is used, which attempts to answer two questions:

First, how often could an operational risk event materialize?

And second, what is the projected loss from this event?

Using the answers to these questions, we may assign a separate quantifiable estimate to the exposure to operational risk engendered in each activity. The total sum of all these activities is the value of the exposure to operational risks of the entire organization.

In addition to the answers to these questions, a verbal assessment is often added as well. This verbal report assists in making the numerical estimate more precise and wider in scope in two ways:

First, the verbal assessment allows us to gauge the correlation between the materialization of one risk and the materialization of another. For instance, an incident where unauthorized access to customer accounts is granted, which is classified under "execution, distribution and management processes," is normally assessed separately from an "embezzlement" event. The first incident could result in a loss due to a regulatory fine for non-compliance with the law. The second could result in a loss due to the theft itself.

There is of course a connection between these two incidents, as one may lead to the other. The overall risk assessment must factor in the correspondences between the various risks.

Second, a verbal assessment may aid in analyzing various scenarios. For example, an earthquake incident which threatens buildings in a mountainous region may be analyzed differently from one affecting buildings located in a coastal area. An example of this is a financial institution in Indonesia, which, in the year 2005, reported tens of millions of U.S. Dollars in damages due to the total destruction of several of its branches. This damage was incurred as the result of an earthquake which struck the region in December 2004, whose epicenter was approximately 100 kilometers off the coast of Sumatra. The earthquake triggered a tsunami 15–20 meters high, which washed over the entire coastal region, causing the deaths of thousands of people. The mountainous regions, however, remained virtually unscathed.

When properly done, an expert opinion is a more precise method than an estimate of exposure as a percentage of business activity. It is, however, significantly slower to perform as well as considerably more expensive.

6.3.3. *Statistical methods*

6.3.3.1. *Background*

Measurement — Statistical Methods

- What is the distribution of losses?

Statistical methods are the most advanced and precise of all the measurement approaches in existence. They allow us to portray the distribution of expected operational losses over a certain period of time in the most detailed manner. Statistical methods rely on failure events reported daily throughout the organization by means of the monitoring and reporting arrays which have been put in place. For instance, in a chocolate factory, any malfunction in the packing machine is registered as it occurs; this report is extremely detailed and answers a variety of questions; for instance, for how long was the machine out of service, what caused the malfunction, how much production was lost due to the malfunction, what is the value of the products which were not produced during this time, which parties were involved in the incident, etc. These data may be analyzed periodically according to various cross-sections and statistical considerations, teaching us how the operation of the machine may be improved, what training the employees need or whether the machine should be replaced.

These methods require an allocation of resources to the collection and analysis of data by statisticians and analysts. Many firms therefore tend to outsource the operational risk management process.

Some companies employ external advisors as part of an adequate risk management process.

Others prefer to transfer the risk to an insurance company.

For insurance companies, statistical measurements of operational risks are a routine matter — car insurance, home theft insurance, fire insurance, professional insurance and even insurance against natural disasters such as floods or earthquakes. In addition to their professional expertise in measuring operational risks, insurance companies also know how to set the risk premium required to cover the damages which would be incurred should the risk materialize.

If the solution is so simple — transfer the entire business of dealing with operational risks to the insurance company — why go to all the trouble of managing them yourself?

Companies which transfer the risk mitigation to insurance companies, skipping several crucial steps in the risk management process and mitigating the risk by transferring it to the insurance company, could find themselves particularly vulnerable to risks. The directors of such companies frequently succumb to the mistaken assumption that by transferring the risk to the insurance company, they have "solved" the issue of managing operational risks. This could not be further from the truth:

> First of all, companies which have not properly surveyed their operational risks may end up purchasing two separate insurance policies which cover the same event, thus spending more than the necessary amount on their insurance.
>
> Second, without surveying the risks, these companies may fail to purchase insurance for a risk which threatens them or even discover in the aftermath of an incident that their insurance policy does not cover it.

Third, these companies do not measure the risk and therefore cannot quantify the threat they face. This is similar to a doctor whose diagnosis of a patient amounts to the words "you have a fever!". Naturally, it is not enough to be content with such a general statement — it is important to quantify exactly just how high the fever is. The treatment when the thermometer indicates 38 degrees will be fundamentally different from the treatment when the patient has a fever of 41.5 degrees. The precise body temperature determines the type of treatment required and its urgency. In the first case, we may require nothing more than a simple fever-reducing drug. In the latter event, more drastic measures will be required to cool the body down, including a very cold bath and perhaps even transfer to the hospital. It is essential to quantify the operational risk in order to make the correct decisions regarding its mitigation.

Fourth, those companies which do not conduct full risk management may overlook alternative methods for reducing operational risk (avoiding or reducing risk, accepting its consequences or making a recovery plan). These last methods are very often much better suited to mitigating the various risk scenarios.

Out of all the risk measurement methods available, statistical methods are the most accurate. They are, however, also the most expensive methods.

6.3.3.2. *Distribution of operational losses*

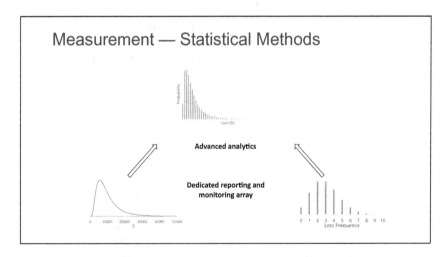

The statistical methods allow us to present the risk of loss in profits or capital as a distribution, where the *x*-axis represents the total expected loss throughout a given period (let us suppose one year) and the *y*-axis reflects the probability of this loss materializing.

The total expected loss consists of two components:

Q — Frequency. How often are losses expected to occur in the coming year?

S — Severity. What is the extent of each loss?

$$\text{Loss} = Q*S$$

In order to calculate the distribution of losses, Loss, one must first know the distributions of frequency, Q, and severity, S.

An appropriate distribution for Q could be the Poisson distribution of a discrete random variable with the parameter 1 representing the rate of events. The higher the value of this parameter, the faster the rate of events. In a similar fashion, the lower its value, the slower the rate.

The function of the density of a Poisson distribution is as follows:

$$P(q,\lambda) = e^{-\lambda}\frac{q}{q!}$$

where λ represents the parameter "rate".

An example of a Poisson distribution

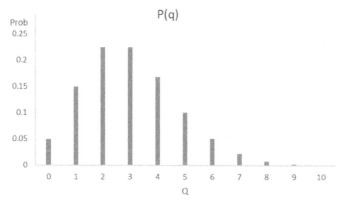

Excel

In order to calculate the Poisson distribution in Excel, we may employ the function = POISSON.DIST() in the following manner:

$Poisson(q, \lambda)$ $q = 2; \lambda = 3$ = POISSON.DIST(2,3,FALSE)

The value of the function in this case is 0.224041808.

The reason for the presence of the word "FALSE" in the function is in order to receive as an answer the density at point 2.

Were we to seek the cumulative density, we would need to type in "TRUE", giving us a value of 0.423190081.

The respective distribution for s could be a log-normal distribution, defined by an average and standard deviation in the following manner:

$$P(s,\mu,\sigma) = \frac{1}{s\sigma\sqrt{2\pi}} e^{-\frac{(\ln(s)-\mu)^2}{2\sigma^2}}$$

where μ, σ are the average and standard deviation respectively of the severity.

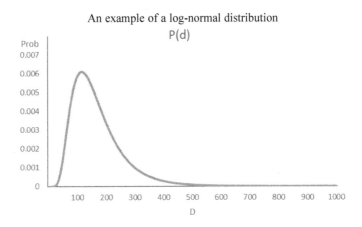

An example of a log-normal distribution

Excel

In order to calculate a log-normal distribution in Excel, we may employ the function = LOGNORM.DIST() in the following manner:

LogNormal(s,μ,σ) $s = 100$; $\mu = 5$; $\sigma = 0.5$ = LOGNORM.
DIST(100,5,0.5,FALSE)

The value of the function in this case is 0.005841646.

The reason for the presence of the word "FALSE" in the function is in order to receive as an answer the density at point 100.

Were we to seek the cumulative density, we would need to type in "TRUE", giving us a value of 0.214863287.

In order to calculate the distribution of the total expected loss, the Monte Carlo method is used, which factors in both of the distributions above in the following manner:

(i) sampling of frequency based on Poisson distribution,
(ii) sampling of severity based on log-normal distribution,
(iii) calculating the total loss as the product of the two components above,
(iv) constructing a distribution for the total expected loss.

Excel
In order to obtain a sampling of the frequency based on a Poisson distribution, we must create a user-defined function in Visual Basic:

```
Function RandomPoisson(Lambda As Integer)

    Dim X As Integer
    Dim P, ExpLambda As Variant

    X = 0
    ExpLambda = Exp(–Lambda)
    P = 1

    Do While P >= ExpLambda
        X = X + 1
        P = P * Rnd()
    Loop

    RandomPoisson = X – 1

End Function
```

The value of Lambda must be an integer (i.e., 1, 2, ...).

The function returns a random number from the Poisson distribution with the value l.

The code earlier is not the best in terms of computational efficiency, but in order to understand the quantification of operational risk, its performance is more than adequate (a sample of ten thousand random variables in Excel should not take an excessive amount of time).

In order to sample the severity out of the log-normal distribution, we may use the following function:

LogNormal.INV(Prob,μ,σ)
Prob = Rand(); $\mu = 5$; $\sigma = 0.5$ = LOGNORM.INV(Rand(),5,0.5)

The function = Rand() is used to sample a number from a uniform distribution between 0 and 1.

The function = LOGNORM.INV returns a value from the log-normal distribution which matches the random probability which has been selected for the function.

The product of these two numbers is a random number from the distribution of the expected loss. Here are two examples of loss distributions:

(1) A loss distribution with the following characteristics:

$$\mu = 5$$
$$\sigma = 0.5$$
$$\lambda = 3$$

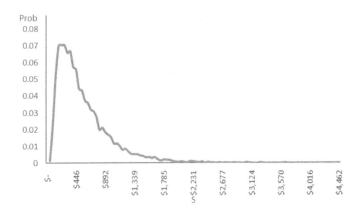

This distribution shows losses up to USD 1,000 for the most part, followed by a long tail with a lower probability of losses up to USD 3,000.

(2) A loss distribution with similar characteristics but a smaller standard deviation:

$$\mu = 5$$
$$\sigma = 0.1$$
$$\lambda = 3$$

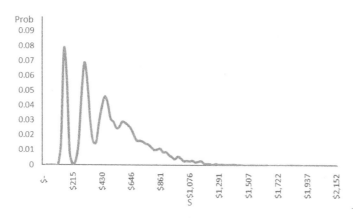

This distribution shows losses up to USD 1,000 for the most part, followed by a long tail with a lower probability of losses up to USD 3,000.

Due to the smaller standard deviation of loss severity, this distribution is considerably more complex. We observe a high probability of relatively small losses (approximately USD 170), a spike at USD 300, yet another spike at USD 400, followed by a gradual decline similar to that seen in the first distribution above.

This form of distribution is more easily seen using a simulation method.

Excel

Pressing the F9 key in Excel usually allows us to calculate the various functions. However, in this case, as we have a user-defined function, Excel does not recalculate it even when we press F9. For Excel to calculate user-defined functions as well, we must simultaneously press CTRL+ALT+SHIFT+F9. This calculation is often rather time consuming.

In order to get Excel to recalculate the function more quickly each time, we may add this code later on and then link it to an object in the worksheet which we will use to run the function. The code is as follows:

```
Sub Simulate()
    Application.CalculateFullRebuild
End Sub
```

6.3.3.3. *Estimating the distribution of operational losses*

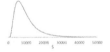

Measurement — Statistical Methods

■ The key lies in correctly estimating the distribution
■ The challenges:
  • Not all events are reported.
  • How should we incorporate a "near-miss" incident?
  • Should an unexpected success be considered an operational failure?
  • Extreme events, which could cause tremendous damage and even drive the company to bankruptcy, will not be found in internal databases.

The statistical methods rely on data gathered throughout the organization. From the data, we may learn about the frequency with which various events occur, as well as the severity of damage from each event.

The challenge lies in correctly estimating the distribution based upon these data. Statisticians and econometricians face a number of issues, the most prominent of which are the following:

• **Not every incident is reported:** This means that the data reveal an incomplete picture of the actual losses. Thus, for instance, employees may have reported three incidents during the last week, but, in practice, seven incidents occurred. This will have an effect on the frequency estimate.

- **"Near-miss" incidents also occur:** Such events do not end in damage or losses but must be reported as well. For example, employees who every now and then trip on the stairs leading to the office and walk away unharmed. In the vast majority of cases, since no injury occurred, such events are not reported. There is usually some hazard involved, such as rickety or slippery steps, which may only be fixed if someone says something.

    When estimating operational risks, such "near-miss" incidents must be incorporated into the loss database even if no damage was caused.

- **Unexpected successes:** In many organizations which conduct operational risk management, unexpected success is also counted as an operational risk incident which must be reported. Let us suppose a dealer has inadvertently purchased additional stocks of NedBank LTD instead of selling them. An hour later, the dealer discovered the error, corrected it and even filed a report of a failure event. During this hour, the value of the bank's stock went up and the mistake returned not a loss but a profit of tens of thousands of U.S. Dollars. The dealer must nevertheless report the details of the incident and file the profit as a loss.

- **Extreme events:** Particularly extreme events which could cause tremendous damage, or even drive the organization to bankruptcy, will not be present in the organization's internal database (for obvious reasons).

    Such extreme events are highly unlikely to occur, but their potential effects are disastrous. On the distribution chart, such events will be situated in the tail of the graph.

Measurement — Statistical Methods

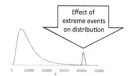

Effect of extreme events on distribution

- Extreme events, which could cause tremendous damage and even drive the company to bankruptcy, may be found in external databases.
- These allow us to more precisely estimate the "tail" of the distribution.

If we rely exclusively on an organization's internal data in order to estimate the distribution of losses, we run the risk of overlooking extreme events which could bring the company to the brink of bankruptcy. An extreme event leading to bankruptcy will naturally no longer be reported in the internal systems of the company, which has effectively ceased to exist at this stage.

In order to add the necessary data on extreme events to our statistical estimates, we must look to external data which describe other, similar companies, which have experienced extreme events or even ceased to exist altogether.

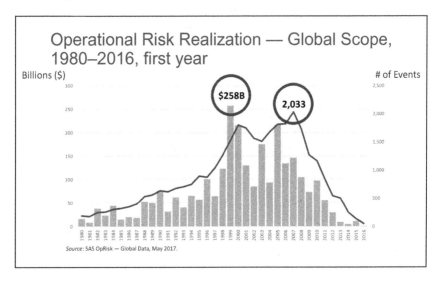

External data on operational risks are provided by various information companies. One of these is the analytics firm SAS, which gathers data on materialized operational risks across the world. Events involving damages in excess of USD 100,000 are added to a large database consisting of tens of thousands of incidents.

The column chart in this image represents the total operational damages incurred every year between 1980 and 2016. Some events unfolded over several years, and the values shown in the chart refer to the year in which the event began. It is evident from the chart that 1999 was the record year during this period for the extent of damage caused by operational risks, amounting to over a quarter of a trillion U.S. Dollars (For the sake of comparison, this is a greater figure than the combined GDP of Qatar and Ethiopia today. And this is of course only a sample of events exceeding USD 100,000).

Many operational failure events ended in 2000 with the global stock market crash known as the dot-com crisis.

The line in the image marks the number of incidents which occurred during each of the years in this time frame. The record year was 2007, which saw more than 2,000 failure events. These events reached their peak in 2008 with the subprime crisis.

One interesting thing we may learn from this image is that there is a gap between the extent of operational damages and the number of incidents. The work plan for the next quarter must take into account both the number of events which occurred and the damage which could be suffered due to the occurrence of just a single, major event. Public organizations will tend to concentrate on dealing with those events which occur more frequently, due to the reputational damage of such events. By contrast, private organizations prefer to dedicate most of their efforts to less common but larger events, which could lead to their collapse.

Creating an estimate of the distribution of losses based on the data requires a wide scope of knowledge and expertise in a variety of areas and is therefore not very widespread among many financial organizations. The statistical and econometrical methods remain, however, the most extensive and precise methods for quantifying operational risk. For medium-sized and larger organizations, this is a relatively minor investment compared to the returns. Apart from the wealth of information obtained, which enables better management of resources, there is also a considerable contribution to the organizational culture and risk management norms of the company, which may prevent future damages or even reduce the severity of damage in the early stages of a failure event.

6.4. Operational Risk Management

We are now at the stage of "monitoring and assessing risk" in the risk management process (see introduction). The next step in the process is the implementation of risk reduction measures. Which risks should we concentrate our efforts on and how must we mitigate each one of them?

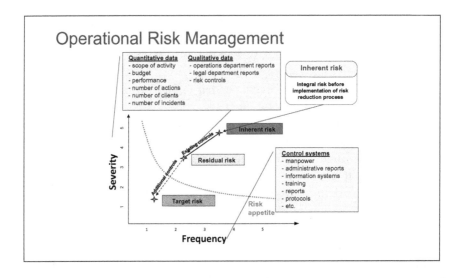

There are several ways to continue the process of operational risk management from here, which must be adapted to each organization individually. However, most of these methods make use of the methodology outlined in the following:

- Draw a coordinate system where the *x*-axis represents frequency (Q) and the *y*-axis represents severity (S). Each axis is divided into five subcategories as follows:
  o very low,
  o low,
  o medium,
  o high,
  o very high.

  This subdivision into five categories is intended to simplify the decision-making process from a visual perspective. The points which represent the risks must be carefully and precisely placed on the chart.
- "Risk appetite" is marked on the coordinate system.

  Risk appetite is the level of risk to which an organization is willing to expose itself before any risk-reduction action has been performed. For instance, in an office building in Spain, a malfunction in the air conditioning system, which occurs once per year for two hours, is a risk the company will tolerate without installing a backup system.

- Conversely, a water outage in the same building, which could disable the fire suppression system, is beyond the limits of the organization's tolerance. In such a case, the risk levels involved are such that the organization will not take the risk and will implement procedures to reduce the exposure to this risk. Risk severity may be inferred from quantitative and qualitative data received from various organizational systems as well as from expert assessments.
- The frequency of incidents may be inferred from a wide array of monitoring systems, e.g., systems for reporting employee work hours, administrative reports, training feedback and reporting protocols.
- On top of the coordinate system, each risk is assigned a point which reflects its inherent risk.

    Inherent risk is the risk assessment before the implementation of risk reduction methods. For instance, the risk of a fire breaking out in a supply warehouse may be low in frequency but catastrophic in severity — it could cause the total destruction of all of the organization's supplies.
- Consequently, the residual risk is determined separately for each risk.

    Residual risk is the risk assessment once risk reduction has been implemented. The residual risk represents the effect of controls on the reduction of the risk. For example, if we install a fire detector in the warehouse, we may detect the fire as soon as it breaks out and call the fire department, thus reducing the severity of the damage and salvaging at least some of the supplies stored in the warehouse.

    The relation between inherent risk and residual risk is expressed thus as follows:

Inherent risk = (residual risk) − (effect of controls)

- Very often, the residual risk still remains too high, beyond our tolerance threshold, i.e., risk appetite. In such cases, a target risk is set, towards which we aspire during the risk reduction process.

    Target risk is the risk level we wish to attain after implementing additional risk reduction measures. For instance, were we to add a fire sprinkler system, it would be activated automatically as soon as the fire detector detected that a fire had broken out. This would allow us to reduce the severity of the damage and save most of the supplies in the warehouse.
- In order to ease the decision-making process, the coordinate system is superimposed on a table referred to as a "heat map".

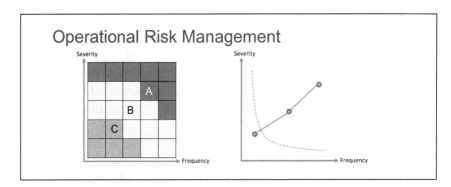

The risks found in the (A) zone demand strategic attention in response to the question of whether there is any justification at all for exposure to them.

Those risks in the (B) zone require risk reduction processes which will mitigate the risk and move it closer towards the (C) zone.

Risks situated in the (C) zone fall within the risk appetite threshold and do not require any additional risk reduction procedure. Nevertheless, they do require regular monitoring in order to ensure that they remain within the threshold over time.

How can we reduce the risk? We may employ the methods introduced in the introduction chapter: avoiding risk, mitigating the risk, transferring the risk to another party, accepting the consequences and planning a recovery. We shall discuss the relationship between the heat map and risk mitigation in the chapter dealing with organizational risk management.

Operational Risk Management

- Creation of loss-reduction methods for operational risk
- Employee training, integration of computer systems, surveys, additional controls
- Conducting RCSA (Risk Control and Self Assessment)
  - Identification of operational risks through surveys filled by senior managers in various lines of business.
- Creating KRIs (Key Risk Indicators)
  - Key indicators for identifying operational risks (employee turnover, number of temporary employees, employer-employee relations, failed transactions, open positions, etc.).

There are a number of widely accepted actions we may take in order to reduce operational risks:

- The analysis of methods to reduce operational risk losses is a process many organizations perform periodically. This process is often overseen by external consulting firms with prior experience in the execution of such processes.
- Employee training, installing computer systems, conducting surveys and setting up various controls form part of the process of reducing operational risks which is conducted by the organization itself within the course of its routine activities.
- Conducting surveys, whose purpose is to identify the epicenters of risk in an organization, are sent out to the employees. Using sophisticated data systems, this process can be carried out continuously with the cooperation of the entire workforce of the organization.
- Establishing risk indicators which alert us to an increase in risk, even if it has not yet materialized. For example, one such indicator is the measurement of employee absenteeism. Information on the absence of employees at the beginning of the work day may point to increased risk in several areas, so if, for instance, on a certain morning 25% of the employees were not present for their shift, malfunctions in the manufacturing line may be expected to increase throughout the day due to the greater workload on the remaining employees. Preparing in advance for such an event could greatly reduce the damages for the remainder of the shift.

The customary steps for reducing operational risks demand honest and truthful reporting by employees. In practice, employees often refrain from reporting risks, malfunctions or failures due to the reaction of their direct supervisor. Very few organizations instruct their junior and intermediate managers on the appropriate response to an unpleasant or inconvenient report. An organizational culture and relationships which encourage reporting are of crucial importance(!) to the proper management of operational risks. On occasion, the report results in accusations and even legal discussions which obstruct a thorough investigation of the incident. In the aviation sector, for instance, severe accidents are investigated in great detail, until the circumstances leading up to the failure can be understood in their entirety. This is the only way to learn which controls have failed and how we may reduce future risks.[5]

---

[5]Some interesting facts…

Many organizations make use of "After Action Review" in order to further the organizational learning process.

An after action review is the process of uncovering an event, phenomenon, failure or error in which the organization was involved, in a manner which facilitates learning drawing conclusions and implementing changes of a practical nature.

An after action review consists of several stages:

1. Defining the focus of the after action review:
This definition typically relies on the event, phenomenon, failure or error which forms the cause for the review. The definition is specific and also sets the boundaries of the review. The trigger for the review is an incident which occurred, without which the review would not have taken place.

2. Gathering facts and findings:
This step is usually conducted in direct connection to the incident. This includes gathering information on the environment in which the incident occurred, the people who were involved in it, technological systems, organizational structure, work processes, etc.

3. Analysis and identification of the factors which caused the incident:
In the analysis stage, the facts and findings are analyzed and an attempt is made to track down the key factors which caused the incident. Many questions arise at this point. The product of this stage is a list of the factors leading up to the incident.

4. Drawing conclusions and implementing changes:
This is often greatly influenced by the personal world view of the after action review. It is therefore essential for them to be impartial, experienced and professional. Reviewers tend to be key figures in the organization who are intimately familiar with its inner workings.

6.5. Capital Allocation

Approaches to Capital Allocation

- Basic Indicator
  - Capital allocation according to the scope of business activity.

- Standard Approach
  - Capital allocation according to the scope of activity in each type of business activity separately.

- Advanced Measurement Approach
  - Capital allocation according to statistical principles, scenarios and expert assessments.

As with other risks, operational risks also require to reserve capital which will serve the financial entity in times of crisis. Different regulators in different countries employ various methods for calculating and allocating this reserve. The recommendations issued in Basel II presented three main approaches for calculating the capital requirement for operational risks.

6.5.1. *Basic indicator approach*

According to the basic indicator approach (BIA), the capital which is to be allocated to operational risk is equal to a fixed percentage of the average positive gross income for the three years prior to the calculation. In the event that one of these years saw a negative gross annual income, or one equal to zero, this year is to be excluded from both the numerator and the denominator of the equation of the capital requirement.

The requirement is calculated on a quarterly basis in the following manner:

$$K = \frac{4}{12 - \sum_{t=1}^{12} I_{\{G_t \leq 0\}}} \sum_{t=1}^{12} I_{\{G_t > 0\}} G_t \times \alpha$$

where K is the capital requirement according to the basic indicator approach, $\sum_{t=1}^{T} I_{\{G_t \leq 0\}}$ is the number of quarters which saw negative income, G_t is the gross income for a given quarter, $I_{\{G_t > 0\}}$ is a function which returns a value of 1 in case of positive income, and 0 otherwise and α is a coefficient. Set to 15% by the Basel Committee.

Multiplication by four converts the quarterly measurements to annual ones.

The value 12 represents the number of quarters in three years.

Examples for the calculation of gross income according to the basic indicator approach is as follows:

o positive gross income of USD 30 million in four out of twelve quarters,
o positive gross income of USD 20 million in four out of twelve quarters,
o negative gross income in four out of twelve quarters.
  • The average annual income is USD 25 million per quarter, or USD 100 million per year.
  • The capital requirement is 15% of the annual income, which in this case amounts to USD 15 million.

6.5.2. *Standardized approach*

According to the standardized approach, a bank's activities are divided into eight lines of business, with each of these assigned a unique coefficient, α:

1.	Corporate finance	18%
2.	Trading and sales	18%
3.	Retail banking	12%
4.	Commercial banking	15%
5.	Payment and settlement	18%
6.	Agency services	15%
7.	Asset management	12%
8.	Retail brokerage	12%

6.5.3. *Advanced measurement approach*

The advanced measurement approach (AMA) relies on statistical analyses, scenarios and expert assessments in order to estimate the distribution of operational risks. Based on this estimate, it is possible to calculate the capital requirement which is to be allocated for operational risk.

6.5.4. *Strengths and weaknesses of the various approaches*

Approaches to Capital Allocation

First two approaches

- Advantages
  - Simple to implement
  - Assume a connection between the scope of activity and the level of risk (albeit fixed and generalized).
- Disadvantages
  - The connection between activity and risk is imprecise and no distinction is made for different organizations.
  - Risk reduction procedures have no effect on the calculation.
  - The development of quantification over the course of time reflects only the development of business activity, rather than the development of the risk.

The first two approaches, the basic indicator approach and the standardized approach, are both fairly simple to implement. Quarterly income is measured as part of routine banking activity, and this measurement allows us to calculate the adequate capital for operational risk management.

This simplicity, however, is a weakness as well as a strength:

1. The correlation between business activity and operational risk is imprecise, i.e., it is difficult to compare different organizations. Let us take two banks with a similar income structure. The first bank conducts operational risk management, has employee training programs, invests in monitoring systems and executes risk reduction plans. The second bank does nothing of the sort.

As both banks share the same income structure, both will have a similar capital requirement. If we compare these two banks based solely on their capital requirement, we might mistakenly conclude that both banks are equally exposed to operational risks.

2. If the second bank decides to initiate active operational risk management procedures and even succeed in substantially reducing its operational risks, it might still find at the end of the year that this hard work has had no effect at all on the capital requirement, which remains no smaller than before.[6] This will have a negative impact on the economic motivation of financial organizations to reduce their operational risks.

3. Over the course of time, business activity grows. This does not necessarily mean that operational risks increase as well at the same amount. It is certainly possible that as business activity has expanded, so too has operational risk management increased significantly. The capital requirement will nonetheless grow due to the growth in business activity, regardless of any risk management measures which have been established during this time.

Approaches to Capital Allocation

Advanced Measurement Approach (AMA)

- **Advantages**
  - Precise measurement of the correlation between activity and risk according to the specific organization in question
  - Risk reduction processes are reflected in the calculation
  - Reflect the development of risks and controls over time
- **Disadvantages**
  - Complexity
  - External regulation is difficult to implement

The advanced measurement approach overcomes the disadvantages of the first two approaches:

---

[6]Banks strive to reduce the capital requirement as much as possible, as this is capital they cannot use to grant loans or, in other words, a wasted source of alternative income.

1. This method allows us to bind business activity with operational risk. It is therefore possible to compare the mitigation of operational risks between multiple organizations.
2. Operational risk reduction procedures are reflected in the statistical estimates. Effective risk reduction corresponds to a lower capital requirement.
3. It is possible to conduct periodic monitoring of the mitigation of operational risk and observe, on the one hand, the effect of the scope of business activity on the growth in risk and, at the same time, how improved controls and work processes result in a reduction of risk.

The disadvantage of this approach is its complex application, which requires human capital, sophisticated technology and substantial expertise. Furthermore, many regulators struggle to effectively monitor the measurement process when the advanced measurement approach is employed and often prefer simpler approaches.

In most countries, risk measurement is conducted according to the standardized approach.

Financial entities which implement the advanced approach have succeeded in lowering their insurance premiums by millions of U.S. Dollars. A European financial organization paid approximately EUR 10 million every year in insurance premiums. Having begun to manage its operational risks according to the advanced approach, it soon discovered that some of the premiums were unnecessarily high. After sustained remapping and remeasuring, it succeeded in reducing its premiums by 20%. In the first year alone, this organization already managed to save EUR 2 million.

6.6. Specific Topics Pertaining to Operational Risks

Operational risks constitute a particularly extensive field, encompassing a wide variety of risks (see the section on identification and classification of risks).

From among these many different risks, we have selected four which we will discuss in detail.

6.6.1. *Compliance*

> ## Compliance
>
> ▪ The risk of legal or regulatory sanctions, financial loss or
>   reputational damage which a company may incur as a result of
>   non-compliance with the law.

Compliance, or rather the risk of non-compliance, is the risk of legal or
regulatory sanctions, financial loss or reputational damage which a company may incur as a result of non-compliance with the law.

> ## Compliance
>
> ▪ Recent years have seen a rise in the compliance risk of
>   financial organizations
> ▪ Greater financial sanctions
> ▪ More class action lawsuits
> ▪ Reputational damage and extensive media coverage of flaws in
>   the compliance of an organization with the law

The topic of compliance has been managed by financial organizations for
many years. However, in recent years, there has been an increase in the
compliance risk of financial organization. This increase in risk occurred
in the wake of substantial increases in the monetary sanctions imposed on
lawbreaking entities. Whereas in the past regulators had limited authority
with regard to monetary sanctions, in recent times, their powers have been
greatly augmented. From the perspective of financial entities, this means
an increase in the severity of the damage they risk incurring from non-
compliance. At the same time, there has been an increase in the number of
class actions against financial organizations. These class actions are occasionally initiated by private individuals who base their claims on violations of the law by the financial organizations.

The issue of compliance has entered public awareness on a large scale, in part due to the extensive media coverage of instances where financial organizations failed to comply with the provisions of the law.

Factors Which Increase Compliance Risk

- Regulatory activism
  - Activism by financial and economic regulators, the justice ministry, courts of law, parliament, etc., as well as expansion of the authorities of supervisory authorities.
- Civil/consumer activism
  - Class actions, organizations, increased involvement of consumers and media.
- Complexity of business activity
  - Market risks, technology, overseas activity.

The causes for the increase in compliance risk are as follows:

- An increase in regulatory activism. Each regulatory authority has grown and its powers expanded. Furthermore, ties between regulators in different countries have grown stronger, with international cooperation an information flowing across the globe. In some cases, international legislation now compels financial organizations in one country to report to a regulator in another and vice versa.
- An increase in public activism. Social networks have resulted in increased awareness of legal violations as well as made it possible to organize lawsuits with greater ease. The influence of consumers on producers and service providers has greatly increased due to the pressure of damage to their reputation.
- Complexity of business activity. Production and service actions which were once simple have become exceedingly complex. Each action now requires very high standards of short timetables, information security, privacy, environmental protection, etc.

Conversely, the response to compliance risk in many organizations has remained superficial:

Common Failings

- Insufficient familiarity with the provisions of the law
- Incorrect interpretation of the law
- Inadequate preparation for changes in regulation
- Overlooked regulatory duties
  - Provisions which reach across multiple fields of expertise
  - Personnel changes in key positions, etc.
- Difficulties in monitoring and supervision
  - Of knowledge centers such as legal advisors, actuaries, investment managers.
  - Of employee non-compliance – financial crime, insubordination to managers, troublesome workplace norms.

- Many organizations are not sufficiently familiar with the provisions of the law. Furthermore, due to regulatory activism, organizations need to keep up to date with new instructions which frequently arise.
- Those organizations which do manage to stay up to date often fail to correctly interpret the law. This leads to an increase in exposure to compliance risk.
- Regulations frequently change, and organizations are often unable to create a compliance array which can adapt to the ever-changing regulatory reality.
- The effect of this is that regulatory duties may be overlooked. This most often affects compliance with instructions which cover multiple fields of specialization, as well as cases where the individual responsible for ensuring compliance has been replaced by another individual insufficiently acquainted with the field.
- Compliance is often managed by senior professionals within the organization. Management and control of compliance are exceedingly difficult, and all too often, these very employees become a risk focus for financial crime.

Management — Who Is in Charge?

- Most large financial institutions appoint a compliance officer
- Occasionally assigned to the risk management department, regulation department or legal department
- Occasionally, compliance risk lacks a clear address

In financial institutions, the responsibility of ensuring compliance falls on the shoulders of the compliance officer. As the position of compliance officer precedes that of operational risk manager chronologically, in many banks, both positions exist concurrently. However, within the context of operational risk management, the organizational hierarchy should be such that the compliance officer is subordinate to the operational risk manager.

In non-banking organizations, compliance is rarely assigned to the risk management department. It is more commonly the responsibility of the department in charge of legal counsel.

All too often, there is no single person or body in charge of compliance risk, and the exposure to this risk is therefore high.

Management — Implementation

- Survey of all laws and guidelines pertaining to the organization.
- Establishment of a system for distributing relevant laws and guidelines to units within the organization.
- Establishment of a dedicated reporting and control array (much like operational risks) for monitoring non-compliance incidents.
- Quantitative assessment of expected damages of non-compliance.

Compliance risk must be managed constantly. First, a survey must be conducted of all the laws and instructions relevant to the organization. These must include guidelines issued by the management of the organization itself for internal use. For instance, a food factory must study and develop familiarity with all laws concerning the food industry, whereas a pharmaceutical plant must specialize in all the regulations pertaining to the manufacturing of pharmaceuticals.

It is not enough to have an individual or group within the organization familiar with all the regulations. There must be a system in place for conveying these regulations, laws and guidelines to every department in the organization to which they are relevant.

At the same time, a system must be established for the monitoring and reporting of non-compliance incidents within the organization.

Finally, a quantitative estimate must be made of the expected damages due to non-compliance.

The definition of operational risk contains legal risk. Compliance risk, or rather the risk of non-compliance, is therefore included within the scope of operational risk.

6.6.2.   *Money laundering and terrorism financing*

Money Laundering and Terrorism Financing

- Money laundering is a financial act whose goal is to convert capital originating from tax evasion or criminal activity, or intended to finance terrorism, into legal money.
- Involves the concealment of the source and destination of the money.
- Considered a criminal offense.
- Many countries have joined the international fight against money laundering.

Money laundering is a financial act whose goal is to convert capital originating from tax evasion or criminal activity, or intended to finance terrorism, into legal money which may be used within the legitimate financial system.

Money laundering involves the concealment of the source and destination of the money, and in many countries, it is considered a criminal offense for which the penalty is a prison sentence.

Due to the global nature of financial activity, prevention of money laundering requires international cooperation. Many countries have joined the fight against money laundering, working in conjunction with each other.

Money Laundering Process

- Three subprocesses, which may occur simultaneously or sequentially:
  - Placement
    - The insertion of money originating from criminal activity into the financial system without reporting it to the authorities (it is possible to split deposit, spread them among several financial institutions, smuggle cash into areas with lax enforcement, etc.).
  - Layering
    - Breaking the link with the illicit source of the capital, converting it into legal tender by constructing many layers which mask its source if inspected.
  - Integration
    - Turning the money into a part of legitimate financial activity.

The process of money laundering comprises three stages, which may either occur sequentially or simultaneously:

- **Placement**

The insertion of money originating from criminal activity into the financial system without reporting it to the authorities (it is possible to split deposit, spread them among several financial institutions, smuggle cash into areas with lax enforcement, etc.).

To counter this stage, international standardization and cooperation are required in order to identify the insertion of money already in the early stages of laundering.

- **Layering**

Breaking the link with the illicit source of the capital, converting it into legal tender by constructing many layers which mask its source if inspected. Lately, new regulatory guidelines have been introduced in many countries which require financial entities to be aware of the source of their customers' funds.

- **Integration**

Turning the money into a part of legitimate financial activity. This is the final stage of the process, following which the funds may be used in any legal activity.

Money Laundering and Terrorism Financing — Who Is in Charge?

- In most large financial institutions — compliance officer.
- Occasionally — risk management department, regulation department or the legal department.

The responsibility for compliance with regulatory guidelines lies in this case with the compliance officer in most large financial institutions. However, in other organizations, we may find that it lies with the risk management department, the regulation department or the legal department.

Money Laundering and Terrorism Financing — Monitoring

- Monitoring of financial activity
- Examples:
  - Obligation to report transactions of USD 10,000 or more into or out of the country
  - Prohibition on dealing with organizations on a "blacklist"
  - Conducting a get to Know Your Customer (KYC) procedure

Regulators monitor money laundering by demanding that any irregular activity be reported. In addition, these regulators publish blacklists of parties with whom trade is prohibited. These are usually known terrorist organizations.

The most complex element required by regulation is the "get to know your client" process of the financial organization, which stipulates that each client responds to a comprehensive list of questions which describe the nature of the financial activity the client intends to conduct as well as the client's sources of funding.

Within the framework of operational risk, money laundering is typically listed under the category "customers, products and business practices" and is therefore the responsibility of the operational risk manager.

6.6.3. *Embezzlement and fraud*

Embezzlement and Fraud

- Fraud is the deliberate misleading of a person or a group of people which causes damage to the party which has been misled.
- Embezzlement is fraud which has been committed by an employee within the organization.
- More incidents of fraud than embezzlement.
- Greater extent of damages from embezzlement than fraud.

Fraud is the deliberate misleading of a person or a group of people which causes damage to the party which has been misled. Embezzlement is fraud which has been committed by an employee within the organization.

On average, the number of fraud incidents is greater than the number of cases of embezzlement. However, the average scope of the latter is significantly larger than that of the former. Embezzlement is harder to detect, as the culprit is a person within the organization, often a veteran employee who is intimately familiar with the organization and its inner workings.

Embezzlement and Fraud — Who is in Charge?

- Embezzlement and fraud — operational risk manager.
- Embezzlement — compliance officer as well (ensures steps are carried out which reduce the risk of embezzlement).

The responsibility for managing fraud and embezzlement risk lies with the operational risk manager. With regard to embezzlement, the compliance officer is also charged with ensuring that regulatory guidelines intended to combat the phenomenon are implemented properly.

Embezzlement and Fraud — Monitoring

- Part of the operational risk management process

Regulation states that the matter of fraud and embezzlement lies within the jurisdiction of operational risk management. It seems, however, that the current efforts to combat this risk are far from satisfactory. The next section on financial crime deals with this in depth.

6.6.4. *Financial crime*

6.6.4.1. *Background*

Financial Crime

- Financial crime — often referred to as "white-collar" crime
  - Fraud, money laundering, internal embezzlement, impersonation, forgery, blackmail, theft, etc.
- The extent of financial crime in financial services companies over the past decade has been very cautiously estimated at USD 100 billion.

Financial crime, often referred to as "white-collar" crime, is a widespread and severe issue all across the world. A recent FBI survey found that in the preceding twelve months, approximately one in every four United States citizens had fallen victim to a financial crime of one sort or another (fraud, money laundering, internal embezzlement, impersonation, forgery, blackmail, theft, etc.).

The extent of financial crime in financial service companies over the past decade has been very cautiously estimated at USD 100 billion. Aside from the catastrophic impact they often have on profit margins, financial crimes in general and internal embezzlement in particular can have a dramatic impact on business organizations and pose a major, sometimes even existential threat to organizations they affect.

Despite the importance assigned to the matter by law enforcement agencies, many crimes either remain undiscovered or are only discovered too late. Thus, business organizations cannot rely upon the police for protection, and, for their own survival, must therefore undertake serious measures to combat financial crime themselves, merely to guarantee their survival.[7]

---

[7]Some interesting facts...
Frank Abagnale committed fraud for the first time when he was just sixteen years old; simple fraud, paying USD 3,400 with a credit card which did not belong to him. The credit card belonged to his father. Next, he forged some checks which he deposited into his own bank account. When the bank demanded the money, Frank opened additional accounts under false identities — a pilot for Pan American World Airways, a professor at Columbia University, a pediatrician and a Harvard lawyer — and won himself a further USD 40,000. By the age of 21, Frank Abagnale had forged checks in 26 different countries for a total of USD 2.5 million. He was caught in France in 1969, faced trial in the United States and sentenced to twelve years in prison. In 1974, he was released on the condition that he assist law enforcement agencies in their efforts to combat financial crime. His autobiography was adapted into a film directed by Steven Spielberg and starring Leonardo DiCaprio and Tom Hanks.

45 years later, in March 2015, it would appear that the lessons have not been learned. Wells Fargo Bank, based in the United States, reported a minor loss of USD 140,000 from a fraud incident involving bouncing checks. A more comprehensive report revealed that a group of ten people had stolen about one million U.S. Dollars from BECU (Boeing Employees' Credit Union) as well as from a number of credit card companies, Banner Bank and several other banks. The group deposited funds in 219 different bank accounts using stolen checks and withdrew money using debit cards before the banks could detect the fraud. The group even managed to recruit additional bank customers who provided them with their account numbers and proceeded to create new debit cards for these accounts using a method called "card cracking". The group had been operating around the state of Washington for five years before its activity was detected.

Over the years, the criminals and their techniques have changed, but the essence of the crime, i.e., forged checks, the victim, i.e., a commercial bank, and even the time elapsed before it was discovered, i.e., five years, all appear to have remained more or less constant.

Must financial entities resign themselves to forged checks and financial crime in general as an inevitable part of doing business? Must they simply accept it as a sort of chronic

6.6.4.2. *Data*

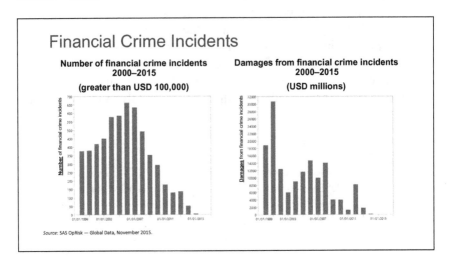

To learn about the distribution of damages in a variety of cross-sections, we turn to the data collected by SAS Institute, a company which conducts analysis of incidents in which operational damages in excess of USD 100,000 were incurred worldwide. The data in the image cover the period between January 2000 and November 2015.

---

illness, known to all, which affects 3–10% of all financial activity, and all they can do is "learn to live with it"?

This would seem to be the case in many financial organizations. More than half of all financial crimes are not discovered through the active efforts of the organization. Rather, they are either reported or uncovered by chance or due to external factors such as police investigations. Many organizations do not even have a department charged with investigating fraud, and those that do often lack the necessary manpower. Those that have the manpower tend to lack the advanced technological systems required to effectively track suspicious activity and process large amounts of investigation material.

The scope of financial crime worldwide, only in financial firms and just in the past decade, is estimated to be well in excess of USD 100 billion. On average, two years elapse from the moment a crime is committed until its discovery, and in some cases, as described above, it may even be more than twice as long. Financial crimes include fraud, money laundering, internal embezzlement, impersonation, forgery, blackmail, theft, unauthorized transactions and violations of privacy.

During the last fifteen years, the number of damage incidents resulting from financial crimes increased until 2006 and has since seen a significant decrease.

On the other hand, the total extent of damages resulting from financial crimes was at its peak at the beginning of the century, decreased in 2003, increased again between 2005 and 2008, and, apart from 2012, has consistently decreased every single year since. This decrease in recent years, in both the extent of damage and the number of incidents, is owed at least in part to the expansion of regulation alongside increased use of technology to track financial crimes by both public and private entities.

There would appear to be a very tenuous correlation between the number of crime incidents and the amount of money involved in those incidents. Equally tenuous is the correlation between the allocation of resources to deal with a small number of large incidents and the allocation of resources to deal with a larger number of smaller incidents. Collection and analysis of data are of the essence if one wishes to set priorities and determine the appropriate course of action in order to reduce financial crime.

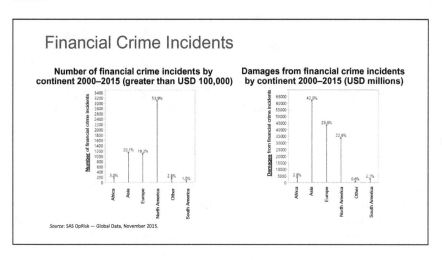

Financial Crime Incidents

Number of financial crime incidents by continent 2000–2015 (greater than USD 100,000)

Damages from financial crime incidents by continent 2000–2015 (USD millions)

Source: SAS OpRisk — Global Data, November 2015.

North America saw the highest number of damage incidents resulting from financial crime, with over half of all reported incidents (53.9%) and more than double the number of reported incidents in Asia (20.1%).

Very few incidents were reported in Africa (3%) and South America (1%). The reason for this is, of course, the obligation to report such incidents in the United States and Canada, alongside greater media coverage which conveys the details of the incident to the public.

The total damages suffered in North America during this time, however, accounts for less than a quarter (22.9%) of all losses reported worldwide and indicates stricter supervision, including among other things technological systems and a corporate culture which assist in detecting financial crime in its early stages. By comparison, almost half (42%) of all losses reported worldwide were incurred in Asia.

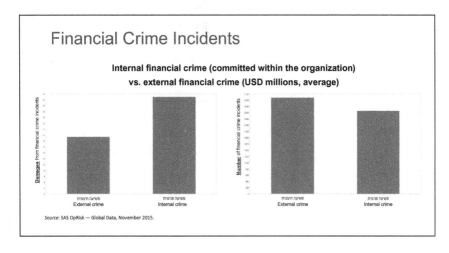

Comparing the prevalence of internal financial crimes (committed within an organization, usually by an employee or a group of employees) and external financial crimes (committed outside the organization) reveals an interesting trend. While the number of external crime incidents is somewhat larger than that of internal crime incidents, the losses caused by internal crimes are almost twice as great as those caused by external crimes. One possible explanation for this finding is that while the potential for committing financial crimes is spread fairly evenly over the population, what distinguishes an outsider from an employee of a given organization is the amount of inside information available to the employee.

Compared to the outsider, therefore, the employee is capable of committing crimes on a much larger scale.

6.6.4.3. *Areas of focus in the fight against financial crime*

The motivations which cause people to commit financial crimes have been extensively researched. A common view is that the main elements causing financial crime represent the three points of what is often referred to as the "fraud triangle":

Pressure: Greed is one of the primary forms of mental pressure which compel people to commit financial crimes. And yet, even those without a fully fledged psychological pathology, people who have simply found themselves in stressful circumstances, may be tempted to commit crimes. Such pressure can result, for instance, from debts accumulated due to ordinary household activity (e.g., mortgages). In some cases, the source of the pressure may be genuine threats or blackmail made by criminals to ensure that an employee aids them in carrying out their scheme.

Rationalization: In order to commit a financial crime, one must formulate a set of rationalizations for the deed. Dissatisfaction with the service provided, anger at the employer's behavior, flawed corporate culture, wrong social attitudes, etc. can all serve as rationalization for committing financial crime.

Opportunity: The pressures which drive an employee to commit fraud and the rationalizations for committing the deed are two important components in the fraud triangle. However, in order for the crime to be carried out in practice, a third element is required, opportunity. Such opportunity, which is more easily identified by employees due to their role within the organization, can arise due to lack of supervision or internal controls which may be flawed, inefficient or even entirely non-existent. Limited or non-existent early-warning systems widen the security breaches within the organization and along with them the opportunities for outside parties to commit fraud.

In order to prevent financial crime, it is necessary to remove just a single component from the fraud triangle (pressure, rationalization, opportunity). It has been found that the most efficient method of combating financial crime is by attacking the element of opportunity. Organizations reduce the opportunities for committing crime by improving supervision and streamlining internal processes, as well as by implementing more accurate, flexible and sophisticated detection systems.

Numerous methods may be employed in the fight against financial crime. Different organizations employ different methods to match activities, the threats they face, the resources at their disposal, the division of responsibilities between the organization and public authorities, etc. Despite the varied approaches taken by different organizations, five primary areas of focus may be identified in which the fight against financial crime is concentrated:

1. **Prevention** of financial crime by various methods.
2. **Detection** of activities suspected of being cases of financial crime.
3. **Investigation** of suspects and suspicious activities.
4. **Mitigation** of the findings of the investigation.
5. **Comprehensive review and analysis** of the entire course of the incident from beginning to end, in order to improve the organization's performance in the other areas of focus as well.

1. Prevention of financial crime

In the modern world, financial crimes are prevented through various controls: preventive controls such as work protocols, segregation of duties, training courses for employees; automated controls performed as business activity is being conducted, which include user permissions, alerts when inputting information (for instance, setting a maximum limit for the sum of money to be entered or producing multiple invoices) and authorization chains; as well as periodic processes such as fraud and embezzlement surveys, internal and external audits and so on. Such mechanisms serve the purpose of deterring potential criminals.

These organizational controls have a crucial role in preventing financial crime. Thus, for instance, much forethought is applied to segregating duties, identifying conflicts, locating loopholes in the various processes, granting new powers in such a manner as to prevent conflicts of interests, establishing mutual supervision and so forth. Having completed this process of in-depth consideration, the organization implements its conclusions and establishes new positions in the workplace accordingly.

Nevertheless, in most organizations, these controls are only checked at very wide intervals, if at all. Few organizations continue to test the efficacy of new controls and fewer still monitor them regularly over a long period of time or pause to consider whether further controls are needed. For example, "segregation of duties" only extends as far as creating new positions and assigning employees to fill them. The danger, naturally, lies in the fact that the very concept of segregation of duties is void of meaning if, over the years, the employees the organization has assigned to these new positions have banded together to form a conspiracy.

2. Detection of suspicious activity

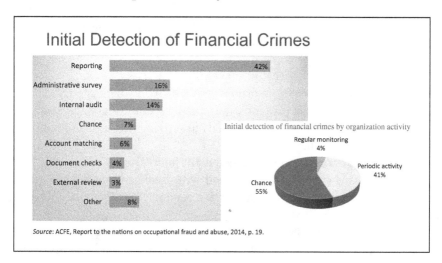

Source: ACFE, Report to the nations on occupational fraud and abuse, 2014, p. 19.

The methods used today to detect suspected criminal activity were examined in an ACFE survey. The survey found that in 42% of cases, the crime was detected when someone reported it, 16% of crimes were discovered through management surveys, 14% through internal audits and 7% due to an error committed by the perpetrator.

Classifying the findings of the survey according to the actions performed by the various organizations to uncover the crimes, we discover that more than half (55%) of all crimes are not discovered through active monitoring by the organization (instead, they are either reported — 42%, discovered by chance — 7%, through an external review — 3% or as a result of an investigation conducted by the police or some other external authority — 3% included in the category "Other"). Furthermore, 41% are not discovered through regular, everyday monitoring (alternative detection methods include the following: 16% — periodic activity such as management surveys; 14% — internal monitoring processes; 6% — account matching; 4% — document checks; 1% — other periodic activities, included in the category "Other").

Just 4%(!) of all financial crimes are discovered as the result of regular monitoring by the organization; this usually occurs when the IT division detects an abuse of user permissions on one of the organization's computers (4%, included in "Other").

Given the scope of the damages caused by financial crime, and the existential threat it poses to the organization, these are dramatic findings — organizations are simply not doing enough to detect financial crimes!

3. Investigation of suspects and suspicious activity

The investigation of suspected crimes is conducted by dedicated units and divisions whose purpose is to look into financial crime alerts. A "successful" investigation is one which succeeds in proving that a financial crime has indeed been committed.

Some investigations are conducted by internal elements within the organization, and others are outsourced with funding from the organization. In other cases, the investigations are conducted by the police when a formal complaint is filed.

Many organizations report that only 20–30% of investigations funded by the organization are concluded successfully. 70–80% of investigations lead nowhere. Such investigations harm the organization both directly and indirectly, the former since the organization has wasted money on an irrelevant investigation, and the latter for needlessly harassing a client and damaging that client's reputation.

The low success rate of investigations may be attributed to two causes. First, many financial crime alerts turn out to be false alarms. Second, inefficiently conducted investigations may not be able to find proof of a crime even if one has indeed been committed.

Although investigators may be skilled and professional, they often lack the means to conduct a proper investigation, namely systems which allow information to be managed and shared with other investigators or with the legal department, basic data analysis technologies, or mechanisms for automatic detection of correlation between multiple entities under investigation. This creates a reality in which incriminating evidence is inefficiently documented, and insufficient manpower is allocated to investigations, which yield nothing but frustration.

4. Treating the findings of an investigation

The manner in which the findings of an investigation are treated is usually determined by the type of financial crime and by the organization's policy regarding such crimes. Depending on the type of crime, organizations may not always have discretion in determining how to react. For example, in cases of money laundering, forgery or felony offenses, regulated organizations are legally obligated to report the crime to the authorities. In extreme cases, the organization may choose to file a lawsuit and even involve the police or other public enforcement agencies. In other cases, the organization may content itself merely with issuing a warning or administrative fine or logging the case in the employee's personnel record. An organization may also fire an employee who has committed fraud, stop working with a dishonest supplier or even deny a criminal the organization's services.

However, one of the most common reactions among organizations is one of no response at all. Though this may occasionally be a reasonable course of action, this complete absence of any response is often the result of negligence or an excessive workload.

5. Review and analysis

The review and analysis of all the data pertaining to the crime-fighting process generally rely upon the organizations' information systems. When countering fraud, massive amounts of data are reviewed, sorted in various ways and examined for correlations with various other datasets. This must all be performed on a very tight schedule (sometimes in the handful of seconds it takes for a transaction to be completed).

The data are analyzed using sophisticated analytical tools which require large amounts of processing power. Some information systems simply cannot cope with the sheer volume of information, neither in terms of large-scale data processing ability nor in terms of the rate at which the data are processed. These system limitations in both software and hardware tend to be neglected by business entities.

Different organizations allocate resources in varying ways to each one of the five areas of focus. It would appear, however, that improvements are in order in every single area. Furthermore, understanding the correlation between the various areas of focus can ensure a much more efficient use of the resources allocated to fighting financial crime.

6.6.4.4.　*The challenges of detecting financial crimes*

The first challenge in combating financial crime is determining whether an action has been committed by an honest client or a criminal, a loyal employee or a fraudster. Those performing financial transactions, clients and employees alike, may be placed in one of the following three categories:

1. **The innocent:** This is the main category, to which the majority of people belong, and toward which the organization's product or service and customer experience are oriented. This is also the primary group which shows up at the workplace in order to earn an honest living.
2. **The criminals:** This group ought to be small and insignificant, but in some organizations, it can be fairly sizable and even well organized. In other organizations, the group may be small but influential and could even drive the entire organization to bankruptcy (the Israeli Trade Bank, the Madoff Ponzi scheme, the collapse of Amaranth Advisors LLC, etc.).
3. **The intermediate group:** This category includes generally honest people who might however consider errors and loopholes (for instance, in the terms of an insurance policy) to be an opportunity to commit fraud or some other financial crime.

Those who belong to the first group are the clients we would like to serve well and the employees we would like to provide with a proactive work environment. The second group are people we would rather avoid taking on as customers or employees. Those in the third group must be correctly assigned to one of the first two categories. Any organization which seeks to preserve its reputation over a long period of time will sooner or later have to become highly skilled at classifying its clients.

The challenge of distinguishing these categories extends not only to people but also to deals, accounts, computer addresses, companies and other entities which must be similarly classified.

The second challenge is proving that a financial crime has in fact been committed. Taking fraud as an example: Although this might seem so fundamental that it need not even be mentioned, one must first define precisely what fraud is. Though there might appear to be a clear-cut dichotomy — guilty or not guilty — reality turns out to be somewhat more complex. In many cases, a person who has purchased a product and wishes to return it may request a refund. However, when it comes to non-expendable products (such as computers), a person may purchase a product, use it for a certain purpose and subsequently return it and receive a full refund. How many times must this pattern repeat itself for us to decide that this is fraudulent behavior? What if the buyer only requests a refund from each business once but repeats this with multiple businesses? How does one track down such a person?

A person may be eligible for compensation due to the imprecise wording of the terms of an insurance policy. Is a customer who has taken advantage of such a loophole to be considered a criminal? Is the answer to this question different for an insurance company which tends to pay the full amount in compensation and another which tries to avoid it as often as possible?

In many cases, an incident will only be considered a case of fraud if the client who committed the fraud is found guilty from a legal perspective. What happens if a client is acquitted due to insufficient evidence? Will the affected business remove that client from its blacklist? How should a company deal with an employee who is currently on trial for fraud, given the presumption of innocence? What if this trial drags on for several years?

Overcoming the challenge of obtaining proof of a crime motivates organizations to deal with financial crimes. On the other hand, repeated failures may cause the organization to abandon the fight altogether, accept financial crime as a fact of life and effectively finance it by raising the prices of products and services for honest customers.

The third challenge is the investigation of the suspected crime. The purpose of the investigation is to confirm or refute the suspicion. A successful investigation is one where legally admissible evidence can be found for what had until that point been merely a probable crime. This is a very complex process, both operationally and legally, particularly when the findings are to be used to convict a criminal and must therefore be admissible as evidence in court. This area of focus is so critical that many organizations have formed dedicated investigation units. The size of such units can range from a handful of investigators up to dozens or even hundreds of professionals. These investigators go out into the field, take pictures, collect documents and testimonies and gather further crucial information, with the goal of bringing the investigation to a success. The challenge lies in granting these investigators the advanced technology necessary to automatically cross-reference information, share information efficiently and incorporate the lessons learned from the investigation so that future investigations may be conducted in a more efficient manner.

In practice, an investigation is often treated as an isolated event, and the knowledge gained stored in such a way that it cannot be retrieved through data systems and used to assist in subsequent investigations.

The fourth challenge lies in determining how to respond to the findings of an investigation. Supposing it has been proven beyond all doubt that an employee has committed a crime, what would be the best way to handle the situation? Should it be noted in the employee's personnel file? Should the employee be suspended? Fired? Prosecuted? Or perhaps all of the above combined? Does it depend on the timing? Perhaps the best reaction would be to do nothing at all? How does one deal with a large number of cases simultaneously?

As far as pursuing legal action, even if the organization has managed to gather all the necessary incriminating evidence, this is no guarantee of a conviction. The entire legal process may take years, in various different courthouses, involve huge arrays of lawyers, require professional opinions, further inquiries, unexpected expenses and more, and after all this, the defendant may still be fully acquitted. Occasionally, the litigation is expected to last so long that it negates the value of winning the case to such an extent that organizations may prefer to forgo the process altogether.

If an organization decides to fire an employee, this employee may decide to sue the employer, sometimes with success.

Evidently, proper handling of a definite incident of financial crime is a highly complex process, so much so that organizations often prefer to avoid it altogether.

The fifth challenge pertains to the conclusion of the previous stages. Once an investigation has been concluded, its results must be examined, a review should be conducted and the tracking methods and investigation process re-evaluated. The results may reflect four possible outcomes; two are considered "proper": classifying an innocuous incident as innocuous or a criminal incident as criminal; and two are considered "improper": classifying an innocuous incident as criminal or a criminal incident as innocuous.

The proper outcomes are used to analyze and streamline the process of detection and investigation. The improper outcomes are used to re-examine the flaws in the process and rectify them.

The ability to classify a person as belonging to the correct category is extremely important to ensuring optimal management. The dilemma is in comparing the cost of a financial crime to the cost of looking into every single innocent individual and determining which is more cost-effective. This cost is not necessarily a monetary one but may instead be expressed in reputational damage.

The sixth challenge is both the last challenge and the first, namely attempting to reduce the number of financial crime incidents in the organization and the extent of the damage they cause. Two fundamentally different approaches to policy exist in this context. The first approach classifies every individual as belonging to the "innocent" group until proven guilty. The second approach is to classify every individual as belonging to the "criminal" category until proven otherwise. The presumption of innocence in court is an example of the former; airport security checks are an example of the latter. Determining the correct approach relies upon an in-depth analysis which takes into account the extent of damage predicted, the probability of its occurrence, the costs of implementing the approach and so forth.

6.6.4.5. *Responding to the challenges*

The past decade has seen several new additions to the arsenal in the fight against fraud. Sophisticated analytical solutions are implemented in technological systems, which allow tracking of suspicious events and entities. Investigation management systems support the fight by processing evidence, sharing information between investigations, analyzing data, uncovering new evidence and more. These systems even raise indications and alerts which permit swift identification of a financial crime (even at the very moment of its occurrence) and prevention of future crimes.

These new tools for detecting and investigating financial crime must meet a very stringent set of demands:

- **Definitions:** As financial crime can be rather complex to define, the identification of suspicious events must allow for multiple definitions. Improperly filled forms can on the one hand be an indication of fraud but may also be nothing more than a genuine error. The ability to distinguish between such cases is crucial, as each one is handled in a different manner, often by separate divisions within the organization. In the first case, further investigation is indeed required, but the second case should be dealt with by the immediate manager. New tools must allow for analysis which takes such multiple definitions into account.
- **Timely alerts:** Receiving warning in time is of great importance in reducing damages and tracking the criminal. On occasion, payment arrangements (such as 90 days end of month) mean that invoice scams may be discovered only three months after the deed. Cross-referencing data, network analysis and other forms of sophisticated analysis often help significantly reduce the elapsed time between the moment a crime is committed and the moment of its discovery. New tracking instruments must enable early discovery and ideally allow us to detect the crime as it is being committed.
- **Precise identification:** Imprecise alerts create a needlessly high workload — the complex investigation of an innocent customer requires the allocation of resources which could be better employed elsewhere and also serves to antagonize the customer. On the other hand, failing to give timely warning of a crime could have even more dire consequences for the organization. Tools which increase the odds of

successful identification and reduce the number of false alarms have become a central requirement in the struggle against financial crime.

- **Streamlined response:** Responding to various incidents in an appropriate and timely manner is important for proper business conduct in general and combating financial crime in particular. Optimization of the response usually focuses on the human element to the exclusion of all else, when, in fact, better integration of technologies and improved human–machine interface give a significant boost to the ability of financial entities to meet the markets' requirements, which grow ever more demanding as competition and regulation increase.

    An organization which successfully classifies its clients so that it only does business with honest citizens can create a "green lane" for them and speed up processes. Such streamlining has become a necessity — an organization which refuses to do so will soon discover that it can no longer keep up with the competition. New tools must be operationally flexible in order to rapidly adapt to changing market dynamics and regulations, and to streamline work processes. This is the direction in which the field of customer credit approval is headed, for example.

- **Maximizing the odds of a successful investigation:** Proper management, storage and sharing of investigation material increase the likelihood that an incident will be dealt with appropriately and even increase the odds of a successful lawsuit (if it has been decided that this is the best course of action). The successful handling of financial crime incidents is a basic requirement. The tools used to manage the investigation and respond to the crime have to serve the management processes in every respect and thus allow for shorter timetables, lower costs and even reduced risk of further financial crime incidents.

- **Privacy:** Precise identification of high-risk activity, and in particular preventive identification of such activity, requires large amounts of data in order to establish connections, e.g., between employees and clients. According to the traditional model, all the information is placed at the disposal of a special team at the early stages of an investigation. The use of automated systems which enable access to data only when there is a high probability of criminal activity greatly reduces the exposure of the investigation team to employee data. Many financial organizations have successfully bridged this gap and are capable of identifying probable criminal activity without compromising the privacy of their employees.

Technological progress in recent years has enabled great advances in the capacity for rapid analysis of large amounts of data. The ability to perform high-performance analysis and rapid data processing allows financial crime detection systems to take advantage of all the data at the organization's disposal in order to issue alerts in real time.

Advanced technology has made it possible for organizations to implement a strategy of bi-faceted defense. On the one hand, financial crime may be picked out of the massive database, the proverbial "needle in a haystack"; on the other hand, existing data may provide new profiles and behavioral patterns which can assist in tracking down financial crime. These actions now require no more than the push of a button, and they are completed within a reasonable time frame, with no need to rely on the IT department for their completion.

The various detection and investigation methods include several technological components, including the following.

6.6.4.5.1.   Business rules

Business rules are the simplest and most widespread identification technique used by organizations. Business rules are a method to compress the knowledge and experience of the best financial crime investigators by coding it at three levels:

1. What turns an event (e.g., a financial transaction) into a potential risk?
2. Why is an entity (e.g., an employee or an address) considered dangerous?
3. What are the risks attached to a network of entities?

In this way, a suspected embezzlement alarm will be triggered if, for instance, an employee logs into a large account and performs a change of address, issues a new credit card and withdraws large amounts of cash.

6.6.4.5.2. Anomaly identification

Anomaly identification is an effective method for determining the risk focus of a certain entity in relation to its surroundings. Anomalies are usually identified by grouping sets of data together using various statistical tools and algorithms and examining abnormal values. A series of unusually large orders from a group of suppliers may trigger a procurement fraud alert.

6.6.4.5.3. Advanced analytics

Advanced analytical techniques include sophisticated prediction algorithms, such as decision trees, neural networks, regression, survival analysis, time series and smoothing and approximation techniques, among others. These methods enable the construction of behavioral models and more accurate predictions which reduce the number of false alarms and increase the likelihood of identifying genuine crimes. For example, performing credit card transactions at multiple businesses, in excess of a certain statistical value which varies according to environmental conditions, will trigger a warning for stolen credit card information and even block the credit card to protect the client's money.

6.6.4.5.4. Text mining

Text mining has become an increasingly significant capability with the growth of social media. Various text mining abilities are used to analyze unstructured data alongside the analysis of structured data, which allows for improved risk assessment. Text mining capabilities include the following:

- Text structure analysis
  o parts of speech,
  o noun categories,
  o identification of multiple-word terms.
- Text filtering
  o identifying the base components of relevant terms,
  o identifying spelling errors,
  o recognizing synonyms.

254 Lecture Notes in Risk Management

- Areas of interest
  o giving weight to terms and frequencies and filtering out irrelevant terms,
  o common e-mail terminology,
  o grouping of terms into categories,
  o identifying key topics and phrases (such as terms related to trade confirmations).
- Automatic extraction of entities based on tagging of parts of speech and identification of patterns.
- Identification of correlations between categories, terms and entities.
- Automatic discovery of facts and events (who does what and when)
- Analysis of sentiment (extraction of expressions of opinion from text).
- Creation of dynamic ontologies in document repositories (use of advanced linguistic analysis to create a hierarchy of relationships between semantic terms).

The results of text mining can form a component in business rules — a certain sentence structure which has previously been identified as high risk; they may also serve as explanatory variables in advanced analytics — a certain number of occurrences of a word in a given text, alongside other statistical variables, may raise suspicion of criminal activity. A certain spelling mistake may, for instance, allow us to track down a doctor who has been helping patients obtain prescription drugs for recreational purposes.

6.6.4.5.5. Data warehouse searches

Data warehouse searching is the ability to automatically compare a certain entity to the various databases, both within the organization and without. The data in these databases contain a history of fraud events and of entities with links to financial crime. This search approach guarantees that an event will not be repeated a second time. In Israel, for example, searches in the database periodically published by the Money Laundering and Terror Financing Prohibition Authority form part of the ongoing crime-fighting activity to which many organizations are committed.

6.6.4.5.6.   Network analysis

Using varied analytical methods, one may arrange and classify data as distinct entities and identify the complete array of connections between them. These entities may be employees, groups of employees, customers, types of customers, companies, branches, addresses, etc. Using various techniques, it is possible to construct an interwoven web of connections which reflects the network activity between the entities. Methods based on network analysis automatically make connections between the various entities and are capable of mapping subnetworks within the larger network. This is done by combining the organization's internal data with the data provided by a third party. These methods make it possible to track the development of a network over time and obtain a complete picture of the activity within the organization. It is then a simple matter to analyze all the details of a single transaction, namely, who were the clients and employees involved and at what stages they were involved, which other transactions were related to this transaction, what guarantees were given and by whom, which other transactions were performed in close proximity, which accounts were involved, etc.

The network image provides two things.

First, experience shows that the number of financial crime alerts has risen and the proportion of false alarms has declined. Second, the ability to visualize a network aids in investigating alerts more efficiently.

There exists also a hybrid approach which combines all the methods above, through which every event and entity in an organization is automatically given a risk ranking. This approach identifies suspicious events and prioritizes the response to these events based on the risk ranking. This results in a significant reduction in false alarms.

Alongside the automated tools, financial institutions are searching for new ways to review their data swiftly and easily while expanding into areas of risk which had not been perceived as such in the past. In this manner, a constant feedback loop is created for the automated detection methods, and the system is updated with further insights and risks which were revealed during the review. The ability to review cases and produce insights which may then quickly and efficiently be integrated into the automated systems is essential to fighting fraud and embezzlement, as criminals constantly learn from experience and update their methods as well.

6.6.4.6. Conclusion

The fight against financial crime is not only the preserve of the authorities. It affects business organizations at every level. Businesses may collapse entirely in the aftermath of a crime; such is the extent of financial losses incurred, whether from external fraud or internal embezzlement. The responsibility for the stability of the organization lies with its senior management, which is committed to developing the internal processes and control systems used by the organization in order to prevent criminal activity.

Furthermore, customers would rather turn to companies which are committed to protecting them from financial crime, which conduct audits and investigations and actively watch over the property, privacy, money and personal security of the customers. Companies which neglect the fight against financial crime will eventually find themselves unable to compete or attract honest customers.

Alongside the prevention of financial crimes using existing methods, new technologies must be introduced which can accurately predict the next crime before it causes irreversible damage to the organization. Most organizations have at their disposal vast databases which, combined with new, advanced analytical techniques and tracking and investigation methods, can be immensely valuable in countering financial crime. Any organization which does not act to integrate advanced technological crime-fighting systems will be perceived by existing clients as irresponsible, and the influx of new clients, at least of the desirable sort, will dwindle until it disappears completely.

The obvious effect of implementing sophisticated technological solutions to detect financial crime would be a reduction in the damages caused by criminal activity, less costly investigations and the establishment of proper deterrence against crime. Such efforts, along with the appropriate public relations campaign, can greatly improve the reputation of a business entity. Companies which seek to grow and expand will have to take into account the fact that their clients are becoming increasingly aware of this sensitive topic.

Chapter 7

Additional Risks

Accompanying presentation: 7. Risk Management — Additional Risks

7.1. Background

Risks are often categorized into several families, mainly market risks, credit risks, liquidity risks, interest rate risks and operational risks. There are, however, additional risks which are not included in any of the major families, such as strategic risk, reputational risk and others.

Risk managers, consultants and risk management consulting firms hold long and detailed lists of potential risks to which a financial company could be exposed. These lists are employed in risk management, risk surveys, consulting work, etc.

In this chapter, we shall introduce some of these additional risks which financial organizations face. These risks are named after the risk factor which causes them.

7.1.1. *Financial irregularities risk*

Financial Irregularities Risk

- Poses a threat to the company
- Poses a threat to shareholders

- 2002 Sarbanes–Oxley Act (SOX)
  - Increased personal liability of CEOs and CFOs
  - Expanded the authorities of securities regulators
  - Accountants are tasked exclusively with accounting
  - Inspection companies must be periodically replaced
  - Managers must return bonuses in case of inaccurate financial statements
  - Etc.

"Financial irregularities" is a general term for disruptions in the financial reports of individuals, private or public companies, non-profit organizations, etc. Financial reports reflect the financial status of the entity and allow its owners to manage, track, monitor, analyze and plan its future activity. A good financial report is a faithful reflection of the financial status of the entity. A bad report does not reflect the true status of the organization, creating a risk which could lead to its collapse.

When a company is adequately managed, financial irregularities are located and rectified promptly. The management of the company is familiar with its financial status and quickly spots any inaccuracies and irregularities in its financial reports. In the proper course of affairs, the management will demand a revised report which faithfully reflects the financial status of the company. Such reports are used to manage, track and plan future activity. Many tax rates are set according to these reports.

There have been many instances over the years where businesses went bankrupt due to financial irregularities. These include Tyco, Peregrine Systems, Worldcom, Enron and many more. These companies published fabricated financial balances as part of a deliberate accounting scam, with the full knowledge and involvement of the company's management. According to the balances they presented, the companies were performing well, but these balances bore no relation to reality whatsoever. In practice, the companies were bleeding money, and the public, which had based its investment decisions on the false balances, lost its money once the companies collapsed.

The best-known such instance is that of Enron. In the aftermath of Enron's collapse, U.S. Senator Paul Sarbanes and Representative Michael G. Oxley drafted the Sarbanes–Oxley Act, which stipulated that key officials in the company must declare that their company's financial reports accurately reflect the status of the company.

The mitigation of financial irregularities is a regulatory mandate known as **SOX** (after Senator Sarbanes and Representative Oxley). SOX compels company officials to add their signatures to financial reports, to confirm that these reports are true to the financial reality of the company. This is a very simple idea, but it makes an enormous difference. CEOs who know that they are personally responsible for any financial irregularities conduct themselves differently from those whose liability has not been defined by any law.

Although financial irregularity risk is a form of operational risk, in most companies, SOX is mitigated separately, typically by the accounting department.

7.1.2. *Strategic risk*

Strategic Risk

- Actions or oversights made by the company itself, which could prevent it from achieving its financial goals.

Strategic risks are actions or oversights made by the company itself, which could prevent it from achieving its financial goals. For instance, a strategic decision to begin marketing a certain product in another country which results in a significant drop in profits, or a change in the investment policy of a financial institution which greatly increases its exposure to various risks.

By definition, strategic risk is not part of the family of operational risks but rather an independent risk in its own class.

7.1.3. *Reputational risk*

Reputational Risk

- The risk of loss due to damage to the good name of a company and loss of trust in the company in the eyes of its clients or suppliers.

The risk of loss due to damage to the good name of a company and loss of trust in the company in the eyes of its clients or suppliers. For example, negative publicity regarding inappropriate reply by an airline to one of its passengers based on ethnicity could trigger cancelations of existing bookings and a drop in new ones.

In recent years, as the saying that "there is no such thing as negative publicity" has grown in popularity, the issue of reputational risk has become particularly interesting, and even more so its measurement. While accounting reports do contain a section on the value of reputation, there is virtually no mention of any sort of estimate of reputational risk.

Technological advances have made it possible to implement reputational risk measures which test the ratio of "positive" to "negative" statements on social media, and their effects on the profits and capital of a company. These technological means allow us to quickly locate hotspots of negative publicity. However, the measurement of reputational risk remains a challenge, as such methods only monitor those populations which make use of such platforms, and furthermore struggle to differentiate between factual statements and those based on nothing more than rumor.

Reputation is a slippery concept. Very often, a statement which would be considered negative in one culture may turn out to be positive in another. Thus, an exposed scandal involving the senior management of a company could actually end up advancing sales; conversely, an innocent marketing campaign could lead to a consumer boycott.

The search for better measures of reputational risk must continue, particularly given recent leaps in the rate at which information spreads and the ability to build (and destroy) reputation with extraordinary speed.

Reputational risk, by definition, is also an independent form of risk rather than a subset of operational risks.

7.1.4. *Sector risk*

> ### Sector Risk
>
> ▪ Sector risk reflects the fluctuations in supply and demand of the sector in which a company operates.

Sector risk reflects the fluctuations in supply and demand of the sector in which a company operates. For example, a hotel chain will have much greater exposure to fluctuations in the tourism industry than a food chain which is exposed to fluctuations in the agricultural sector.

For instance, expected growth during the upcoming tourist season requires preparation by accommodation providers. This means not only more rooms but also an expansion of the entire hosting array — additional housekeepers, waiters, cooks, receptionists, etc. More food must be ordered in advance, as well as cleaning supplies, gifts and activities for guests, and so forth. This could all be followed by a particularly disappointing tourist season, leaving hotels with excess supply and financial losses.

7.1.5. *Project risks*

> ### Project Risk
>
> ▪ A project is a temporary effort to create a new product or service
> ▪ A failed project will cause losses to both profits and capital

A project is a temporary effort to create a new product or service. A failed project will cause losses to both profits and capital. Many organizations conduct at least one project if not more, in order to ensure their continued survival in an ever-changing business environment. As this is a temporary effort with high levels of uncertainty, its risks differ from those involved in the routine activities of the organization.

The risks of a project depend on its nature and duration, the amount of resources dedicated to it and many other factors. In the project planning state, a chapter is dedicated to risk management. In this chapter, the expected risks are defined, reporting and monitoring processes are planned and time is allocated to the management of incidents and responses.

In many startup companies, which are often built around one leading project, project risks may be the primary form of risks faced by the company.

7.1.6. *Regulatory risk*

Regulatory Risk

- With the increasing severity of punitive measures, changes in regulation pose an ever-growing threat to businesses.

With the increasing severity of punitive measures, changes in regulation pose an ever-growing threat to businesses. Regulation, in and of itself, aids in reducing risks. When the "rules of the game" are known to all, the scope of uncertainty shrinks considerably, ensuring that business activity is conducted properly.

Occasionally, due to political pressure, international accords, key events, etc., the regulation is updated and additional rules and guidelines are added.

For instance, a regulatory change which sets new standards for cosmetics products could completely disrupt the profitability of the company which manufactures the product. Ensuring that the product conforms to the new standards can entail substantial unforeseen expenses. Furthermore, the company will have to add a sticker or label to each new product to demonstrate its conformance to the new standards. The company will therefore have to purchase a suitable sticker machine or even modify its production lines to allow the label to be added to each individual product. The company will have to absorb all these additional costs simply due to the change in legislation.

7.1.7. *Cyber risks*

Cyber Risks

- Risks present in cyberspace which threaten to disrupt the activity of an organization.

Risks present in cyberspace which threaten to disrupt the activity of an organization. "Cyberspace" is the realm formed by the activity of computer networks and people. The term is often associated with the Internet, but its definition is much wider in scope.

Cyber threats include unauthorized use of identities, disruption of the activity of other cyber users, disabling of services, damage to systems, theft of digital assets, insertion of malicious code, system penetration, exposure of confidential information and much more.

The importance of cyber risks in the world of risk management is growing by the day. This is due to the growing use of cyberspace in every aspect of life and the corresponding growth in the potential damages of such a threat.

Cyber risks are so significant that regulators in many countries have dedicated specific guidelines and instructions to them. While many risk managers consider cyber risks to be a separate family of risks, the risk factors are people, systems and processes which are associated with operational risks and therefore belong to this family of risks.

When dealing with organization-wide risk management, we must clearly define the responsibility for managing cyber risks in order to ensure that they receive the proper mitigation.

7.1.8. *Country risk*

Country Risk

- The risk of a government failing to repay its obligations

The risk of a government failing to repay its obligations.

Country risk belongs to the credit risk family. Governments often raise money by issuing bonds. Anyone who purchases these bonds is exposed to credit risk in the event that the state is unable to return the principal and the promised interest.

As with credit risks, country risk is measured according to credit ratings. Various rating firms rate countries according to their economic history, levels of debt, growth prediction and economic conduct.

Country risk has an effect on the credit rating of all companies based in that country. If a country has a rating of A, this means that any company based in that, regardless of quality, cannot receive an international rating higher than A. For example, a highly stable company wishing to issue bonds in the local stock exchange can receive a rating of AAA, the highest rating possible within the country itself. However, should this company seek to issue bonds abroad, its rating would be no higher than A, as it belongs to a country with this credit rating.

7.1.9. *Environmental risks*

Environmental Risks

- A threat to the interrelationship between humankind and the environment, both natural and artificial.

An environmental risk is a threat to the interrelationship between humankind and the environment, both natural and artificial.

Until the 19th century, the global population would double once every few centuries. During the 20th century alone, the population tripled in size, and by 2017, it had reached 7.4 billion people, with continued growth expected. This population growth has, among other things, accelerated the exploitation of natural resources, produced higher levels of waste and pollution, reduced the natural habitats of plants and animals and created light, noise and radiation hazards.

In recent decades, more and more evidence indicates that the delicate balance between man and the environment has been broken.

From a theoretical standpoint, the materialization of environmental risks would cause every person on earth to breathe air of a lower quality, live among mountains of waste, be unable to enjoy the wonders of nature or even die a slow death as the result of oil leaks, gases, genetically engineered bacteria, radiation, etc. Although environmental protection organizations and populations living in the vicinity of a polluting factory occasionally voice their protest and attempt to improve the situation, most people on earth, especially financial businesses, remain disinterested in environmental risks. Some even go as far as denying the very existence of environmental risks, claiming that this theory is intended to serve certain political interests, perhaps.

From a practical standpoint, in the context of risk management, environmental protection is increasingly gaining traction as a moral value in and of itself. Changes in dietary habits stemming from an ideology of environmental preservation are becoming ever more commonplace. The intolerance of consumers towards factories which generate excessive pollution is growing constantly, even leading on occasion to a consumer boycott. The successes of environmental protection organizations in preserving nature, coupled with cultural changes, have resulted in a process of legislation and increased regulation. There are more and more instances of senior managers convicted and sent to prison for crimes against the environment.

In a sense, environmental risks have effectively merged into strategic risks (disregard for the environment could cause a drop in the demand for products or services) and compliance risks (which lead to legislation-based punitive measures).

Environmental risks are not only the business of a select few individuals who are particularly concerned about the matter. It has become a widespread phenomenon with roots in science and hard data, and its effect on the involvement and responsibility of managers towards the environment cannot be overstated. Many organizations manage environmental risks very seriously, and they have become an integral part of the risk management process.

7.2. Insurance Risks

7.2.1. *Background*

Insurance Risks – Background

Insurance
- The means by which the uncertainty of an individual is converted into the risk of a group.

Insurance is the means by which the uncertainty of an individual is converted into the risk of a group. In the introduction of this book, we presented an example where a driver could personally reduce the risks of an accident by driving cautiously and only when traffic is light. And yet, lacking sufficient information regarding the cautiousness of other drivers, or the times at which wild drivers are active, the driver is in a position of uncertainty, where not every accident scenario is known and information about the other drivers on the road is lacking.

The insurance company, meanwhile, gathers information on all drivers and analyzes it in such a way that it can then calculate the probability that our driver will be involved in an accident. The insurance company also knows how to calculate the cost of the risk and set an appropriate insurance premium.

From the perspective of the insurance company, then, an accident is not a case of uncertainty but one of risk.

Insurance Risks – Background

Categories of insurance risks
- General insurance
  - Property insurance, personal accident insurance, travel insurance, professional liability insurance, etc.
  - Uncertain insurance event
- Health insurance
  - Uncertain insurance event
- Life insurance
  - The insurance event is certain, its timing unknown
  - Benefits relatives

We usually distinguish three categories of insurance:

- **General insurance:** Property insurance, personal accident insurance, travel insurance, professional liability insurance, etc. are all part of the general insurance category.

  General insurance covers an uncertain event. On the one hand, we could experience a long, quiet period with no insurance events; on the other hand, we could experience a period with numerous accidents and substantial damages.
- **Health insurance:** Health insurance covers medical events such as hospitalization, long-term care, medical expenses, etc.

  The insurance event in health insurance is also uncertain. On the one hand, we could experience a long, quiet period with no insurance events; on the other hand, we could experience a lengthy period of hospitalization.
- **Life insurance:** Life insurance guarantees payment to the family or other beneficiaries of an individual in the event of the death of that individual.

  Life insurance differs from general insurance and health insurance in two fundamental ways:
  o The insurance event is certain. The timing is unknown.
  o The insured (who does not benefit from the insurance payout) differs from the beneficiary (e.g., a relative).

Insurance Risks – Background

Basic terminology

- Insurance premium
  - The cost of the insurance, paid by the insured to the insurance company in exchange for the insurance company's commitment to the insurance policy.
- Policy
  - A document signed by the insured which serves as proof of the existence of the insurance contract.
- Sum insured
  - Life insurance: a maximum sum determined in advance, which the insurer will pay the beneficiary once the insurance event occurs.
  - General insurance: the estimated value of the insured property.

Let us go over a number of fundamental terms and concepts in insurance:

- **Insurance premium:** The cost of the insurance paid by the insured to the insurance company in exchange for the insurance company's commitment to the insurance policy.
- **Policy:** A document signed by the insured which serves as proof of the existence of the insurance contract.
- **Sum insured:** Life insurance: A maximum sum determined in advance, which the insurer will pay the beneficiary once the insurance event occurs.
- **General insurance:** The estimated value of the insured property.

Insurance Risks – Background

Basic terminology
- Insurance broker
  - A person who serves as an intermediary between the insurer and the insured.
- Actuary
  - An expert who specializes in calculating the probability of the costs of future risks.

- **Insurance broker:** A person who serves as an intermediary between the insurer and the insured.
- **Actuary:** An expert who specializes in calculating the probability of the costs of future risks.

7.2.2. *Insurance risks*

Insurance risks are the risks associated with the insurance company. Nevertheless, risk managers in financial companies should also take an interest in them:

> ## Insurance Risks
>
> ▪ Risk to the insurer
>   ∙ Pricing risk
>   ∙ Underwriting risk
>   ∙ Calamity risk
>   ∙ Investment risk
>   ∙ Longevity risk

7.2.2.1. *Pricing risk*

Pricing risk is the exposure to loss as a result of a relative increase in the sum which is to be paid out to the insured, compared to the insurance premium charged. The role of the actuary is to ensure that the risk is priced in accordance with the sum which the insurer expects to pay.

7.2.2.2. *Underwriting risk*

Underwriting risk is the exposure to losses due to a mismatch between the policy and the risks it covers. Should the terms of the contract be ill suited to certain situations, or if they are overly vague, the insurance company could end up paying much greater sums than it intended to pay as part of the policy.

7.2.2.3. *Calamity risk*

A calamity is a catastrophic event such as an earthquake, a violent storm, disease, etc., which exposes the insurance company to a marked increase in expenses due to insurance payouts. The risk stems from the timing, i.e., the simultaneous payout of the sum insured to large numbers of insured parties. Such events could lead to the materialization of liquidity risk for the insurance company if it has not conducted adequate preparations for such a calamity in advance (typically by means of reinsurance, i.e., international insurance companies which provide insurance for other insurance companies).

7.2.2.4. *Investment risk*

Insurance companies invest the insurance premiums they receive in an attempt to maximize their profits. Should market risks materialize for the investments of the insurance company, it could find itself facing increased exposure to liquidity risk should the extent of insurance claims exceed the payment capacity of the insurance company.

7.2.2.5. *Longevity risk*

While longevity is generally viewed as a positive occurrence, for insurance companies, longevity increases the sums they must pay out in comparison with the payout for individuals with a shorter life expectancy.

Chapter 8

Enterprise Risk Management

Accompanying presentation: 8. Risk Management — Enterprise Risk Management

8.1. Introduction

In the previous chapters, we discussed each of the various types of risk on its own. Business organizations deal with multiple risks at the same time, and they must prioritize the different risks, analyze the correspondences between them, identify new risks, respond to all the threats to which they are exposed, etc.

Enterprise Risk Management (ERM) is a technique employed by businesses and public organizations alike in order to cope with the many different risks they face.

We shall open this chapter with the case study of a hedge fund called Amaranth Advisors LLC. This fund dealt exclusively in investments, and one might have expected it to be exposed to just one type of risk: market risk. However, as we shall see further in the following, the fund was in fact exposed to a much wider array of risks:

Amaranth Advisors LLC

- U.S.-based hedge fund
- Established in 2000
- Investment policy — arbitrage on convertible bonds

Amaranth Advisors LLC was founded in 2000 in the United States with the purpose of profiting from arbitrage.

In arbitrage, traders take advantage of the differences in the price of an asset between one market and another. For example, Apple stock is traded in various stock exchanges, such as NASDAQ, Vienna and Frankfurt. In theory, the price of an Apple share ought to be identical in all of these. In practice, however, the share price is indeed similar across the different stock exchanges but not identical. It is therefore possible to purchase Apple stock for a lower price at one exchange and sell it at another where the share price is slightly higher, making a profit from the difference in prices (minus transaction fees and exchange rates).

Arbitrage is not risk free. It engenders operational risks such as incorrect identification of assets, lack of synchronization between the various actions, human and system errors and many more. Such an investment also exposes the investor to credit risk should the other party fail to meet its obligations. By contrast, market risks in arbitrage are very low compared to the risk of a direct investment in the assets themselves.

The investment policy of the hedge fund was based on convertible bonds. Its exposure to market risks was minimal.

Amaranth Advisors LLC

- The fund decided to change its investment policy and adopt a "multiple strategy" approach.
- In practice, the fund invested most of its money in futures contracts on gas.
- The new policy was successful and the fund saw high yields, along with an increase in risk.

Not long after its founding, the hedge fund's management decided to modify its investment policy. It expanded the existing arbitrage policy and adopted a "multiple strategy" approach in its place.

It is generally beneficial for a business organization to update and refresh its policies. New opportunities and trends in the market, introduction of advanced technologies, etc. motivate firms to re-examine their policies, update them and even replace them altogether when necessary.

This is precisely what Amaranth Advisors LLC did — it adopted a more general policy which allowed its managers to invest funds in a range of assets, with differing risk levels, using different methods, etc.

The fund's modified policy was immensely successful, yielding substantial profits. In practice, however, the hedge fund concentrated most of its investments in futures contracts on gas and speculation on future gas prices. The increase in profits was therefore accompanied by an increasingly concentrated investment portfolio and higher market risks.

When faced with high present revenues, two related human tendencies often emerge:

(1) first, to dismiss the importance of the risks,
(2) second, to dedicate ever greater sums of money to the successful investment.

Amaranth Advisors LLC

- The chief trader in the energy sector was convinced that the prices of natural gas prices in March would be higher than those in April.
- The demand for the contracts raised their price, increasing the fund's profits "on paper".
- He borrowed money to increase the yield, leveraging it at a rate of 1:8.

Indeed, the chief energy sector trader at Amaranth Advisors succumbed to the first tendency and dismissed the future market risks posed by the new policy. He was convinced that the prices of gas contracts in March would be higher than those in April. He continued to purchase these contracts, all the while completely disregarding the possibility that gas prices might in fact go down.

Due to the demand for the bond created by Amaranth Advisors LLC, its market price soared, causing the fund's profits to grow on paper regardless of the true value of its holdings (which was dependent on the supply and demand for the gas itself).

The second tendency, to increase the investment sum, drove the trader to borrow additional funds in order to increase his investments, to match the rising price of the bonds. The increase in borrowings caused Amaranth Advisors LLC to leverage the investment at eight times its value.

It is worth noting that a leveraged investment, *in and of itself*, poses neither a "high risk" nor a "low risk". Thus, for example, if the extent of the leveraged investment comprised just 1% out of the total asset portfolio, even if the entire investment were lost, the portfolio would suffer an overall loss of just 1%. If a proper risk-reward management process of the entire portfolio has been conducted and the full extent of the consequences has been taken into account, allocating part of an asset portfolio to a risky investment channel may turn out to be a worthwhile investment decision compared to alternative investment avenues.

By contrast, leveraging the greater part of an investment portfolio to the extent done by Amaranth Advisors LLC can have disastrous consequences.

Amaranth Advisors LLC could have enjoyed continued profits had the weather not changed.

Amaranth Advisors LLC

- In 2006, warm temperatures and low demand for gas eroded contract prices.
- In September 2006, prices plummeted and the fund was forced to provide collateral.
- In order to avoid insolvency, the fund had to "liquidate" its contracts.

2006 was a warm and pleasant year, and the demand for heating gas dropped sharply. Alongside the fall in demand, gas prices correspondingly went down as well, as did the price of futures contracts on gas.

The trade rules of most stock exchanges stipulate that collateral must be allocated as an integral part of securities trading, as well as that of certain other types of trades, including futures trading. When the profit margin of a trade grows, the collateral may be reduced. However, when profits go down, the asset holders must increase their collateral. With the fall in bond prices, Amaranth Advisors LLC began losing money. The hedge fund had to increase its collateral allocation, and its obligations kept growing and growing.

The lenders who had extended credit to the fund until that point were no longer willing to tolerate the growing risk, leaving the fund with no means of obtaining additional loans. Having failed to raise the funds needed for the collateral, it was forced to sell its contracts, which led to a further drop in prices and snowballing losses for the hedge fund.

Amaranth Advisors LLC

- Selling the contracts caused the fund's assets to fall from USD 9 billion to USD 3 billion.
- In October 2006, the fund announced that it would cease all operations.

The contract sales caused the value of the fund's assets to plummet from USD 9 billion to USD 3 billion. In the wake of this USD 6 billion loss, the fund announced that it would cease operations.

Amaranth Advisors LLC

Financial damages
- Direct loss of USD 6 billion
- Fined USD 291 million by FERC for market manipulation

As a loss grows and turns into a crisis, yet another human tendency arises: to seek atonement.

> This is a volatile mental state combining feelings of guilt, failure and shame due to the losses incurred, alongside full confidence and hope that past success can be reproduced if only one sticks to the rules which have been followed. In order to recreate the success and bring about the desired atonement, we repeat past actions without ensuring that they continue to be relevant in the current situation. This is clearly not an organized process involving thorough consideration of the best way to fix the unbearable situation in which we have found ourselves. Such actions, therefore, often serve only to exacerbate the crisis.

In an attempt to rescue the fund from its grim prospects, the chief trader attempted to influence bond prices by continuing to purchase bonds.[1]

The Federal Energy Regulatory Commission inspected the fund's purchases and discovered that an attempt had been made to influence the market price of futures contracts. The regulator classified this activity as "market manipulation" and fined the fund for a sum of USD 291 million.

Thus, in addition to its enormous losses of USD 6 billion, the fund now owed almost USD 300 million to the regulator.

Amaranth Advisors LLC

Exposure
- Strategic risk
  - The fund modified its strategy without examining the risks involved
- Market risk
- Incorrect analysis of market risks
- Exposure to a single asset

---

[1] Some interesting facts…

Traders are well acquainted with this phenomenon, which can occur even to the very best of them. When the first signs of such an atonement process are detected, the trader is instructed to cease trading and take a day off. Only then is the trader allowed to go back to trading. From the perspective of management, this is not a punitive measure but one of risk reduction.

This is, of course, a simplified telling of the events. Nevertheless, from a risk management perspective, the failures in this example teach us of the various risks to which the hedge fund was exposed:

- **Strategic risk:** In the beginning, the investment policy of the fund concentrated on convertible bonds. The adoption of a "multiple strategy" approach presented a strategic risk which did not receive adequate mitigation. The policy change was accompanied by a superficial examination of the risks involved, without adequate risk reduction measures or controls. Raising the awareness that even a "minor" change in policy must be managed as a strategic risk can go a long way to reduce exposure to this type of risk.
- **Market risk:** An investment in futures contracts involves a substantial increase in market risk. Shifts in gas prices eventually brought about the collapse of the fund. Although the tools for market risk management were available at the time, insufficient use was made of them. Very often, simple market risk management tools (exposure, standard deviation, etc.) can call attention to the scope of exposure and lead to its quick reduction.
- **Concentration:** The fund was exposed to a single asset worth USD 9 billion, which constituted most of its holdings. Although the new policy was nominally one of "multiple strategies", it made little effort to diversify its investments.

  Monitoring concentration statistics on a monthly basis is a simple tool which can greatly reduce a firm's risk of going bankrupt.
- **Operational risk**

Amaranth Advisors LLC

Exposure
- The crisis broke out with the materialization of market risk, but its origins lay elsewhere.
- Operational risk
  - The company failed to map and survey its risks in the operational process of conducting an investment
  - Absence of minimal controls
    - Chain of approval, separation of duties, monitoring liquidity risk and other risks
  - Absence of risk measures and monitoring and warning systems
- Compliance risk

Although the crisis broke out due to the materialization of market risk, its origins lie elsewhere. Had the fund conducted operational risk management, it would have had to map various work processes, including the process of making investments. Such mapping would have revealed, for instance, that all investment decisions were concentrated in the hands of just a single individual within the fund. Furthermore, it would have drawn attention to the fact that the very same individual also served as an "investment committee" which decides upon the investment structure of the fund, as well as executing those investments himself and serving as a market risk manager monitoring himself.

Had just one of these three duties been separated and transferred to another employee, thus requiring the approval of at least two people for every investment decision, the operational risk of the fund would have been significantly lower.

Systems which monitor and measure risk levels and raise the alarm when predetermined risk levels are exceeded would have been of great assistance in reducing risk. The very fact that operational risk management was being conducted would have compelled the fund managers to tackle other forms of risk management as well.

- **Compliance risk:** During the fund's attempts to increase its profits, it violated a number of laws and regulations. Appointing a compliance officer could have prevented this from happening.
- **Enterprise Risk Management**

Amaranth Advisors LLC

- ERM
  - Enterprise Risk Management — viewing risks from a general perspective
  - Fund management lacked basic risk management training
  - Lack of risk integration
  - Inadequate reporting procedures

The enterprise risk management (ERM) method would have forced the management to conduct an organized risk management process and provided a general perspective of the risks.

Although the concept of ERM was still in its infancy in those days, basic instruction in risk management could have initiated an internal process of enterprise risk management (even though it might have been named differently).

Such a process would have allowed the fund to integrate the risks and establish effective reporting procedures, which would have provided advanced warning of the shifts in risk levels (particularly that of market risk).

8.2. Enterprise Risk Management

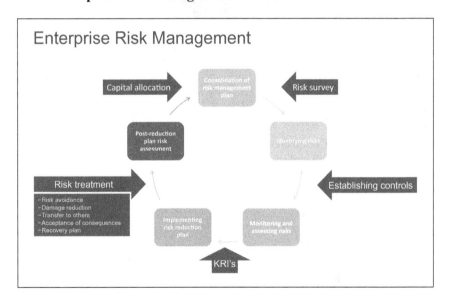

ERM is based on the risk management process outlined in the introduction chapter. As a brief reminder, we shall mention again that this process includes risk identification, assessment and reduction, renewed post-reduction risk assessment and allocation of capital accordingly. How does one implement this process from an organizational standpoint?

8.2.1. *COSO*

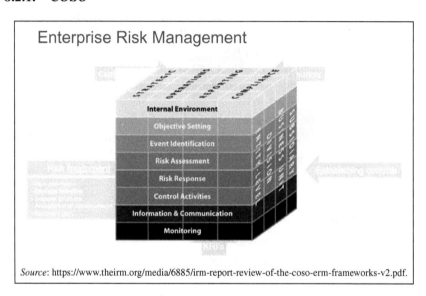

Enterprise Risk Management

Source: https://www.theirm.org/media/6885/irm-report-review-of-the-coso-erm-frameworks-v2.pdf.

Different organizations, consulting firms and risk managements adopt different approaches to enterprise risk management (for example, see the Casualty Actuarial Society — CAS, as well as the RIMS Risk Maturity Model — RMM for enterprise risk management).

One frequently employed method based on the risk management approach is called Committee of Sponsoring Organizations of the Treadway Commission (COSO). For the sake of simplicity, COSO uses a box each face of which represents a different area the organization must manage.

Committee of Sponsoring Organizations of the Treadway Commission (COSO)

- Joint initiative by five U.S. private sector organizations which proposed several key areas of focus for senior management officials at firms and for government organizations:
  - Organizational governance
  - Business ethics
  - Internal control
  - Enterprise risk management
  - Fraud
  - Financial reporting

Institute of Management Accountants (IMA)
American Accounting Association (AAA)
American Institute of Certified Public Accountants (AICPA)
Institute of Internal Auditors (IIA)
Financial Executives International (FEI)

The COSO approach was developed by five organizations in the private sector in the United States,[2] which came together to widen their managerial thought process. This new framework is intended both for the senior management levels of firms and for government institutions, and deals with a number of aspects:

- organizational control,
- business ethics,
- internal controls,
- enterprise risk management,
- fraud,
- financial reporting.

COSO Methodology

- General framework for managing risks and opportunities in order to attain organizational goals:
  - Policy setting
  - Organizational structure and responsibilities of management
  - Methodology and work processes
- Management method based on a risk management approach

This method is unique for combining a risk management perspective with opportunities for attaining organizational goals, including the following:

- policy setting,
- organizational structure and responsibilities of management,
- methodology and work processes.

---

[2]The institutes are as follows:
- Institute of Management Accountants (IMA)
- American Accounting Association (AAA)
- American Institute of Certified Public Accountants (AICPA)
- Institute of Internal Auditors (IIA)
- Financial Executives International (FEI)

8.2.1.1.   *Objectives*

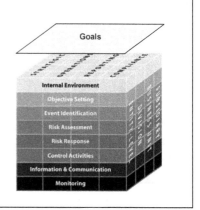

COSO Methodology

Goals
- Strategic
- Operations
- Reporting
- Compliance

The upper face of the COSO box deals with organizational goals:

The **strategic goal** deals with the "what" of the company. Examples of strategic goals are penetrating the Indian market within three years, doubling the current market share in France, developing a new niche in cosmetics or a complementary accessory for running shoes, etc.

The **operational goals** are derived from the strategic goal and meant to support it. Operational goals are increasing sales by 15%, reducing the number of employees by 10%, etc.

Contradicting operational risks can naturally lead to failures. For instance, a goal of increasing sales by 15% and one of reducing the marketing budget by 20% might contradict each other, hence the advantage in viewing all operational goals from a wider organizational perspective.

Reporting with no goal can turn out to be pointless and unhelpful. Defining the purpose of reports — what should be reported, how, why and when, and to whom the report should be sent — can contribute greatly to the overall management of the organization.

Compliance goals are organizational decision which defines which regulations and instructions issued by external entities must be followed, as well as the internal rules and protocols according to which the organization should operate. For example, a company which specializes in managing stock market investments may be expected to view the rules and regulations of the national security regulator as compliance goals. By contrast, it will be indifferent to rules which deal with construction quality. As for internal rules, some organizations issue thick books which detail the protocols and guidelines the organization must follow.

8.2.1.2. *Organizational structure*

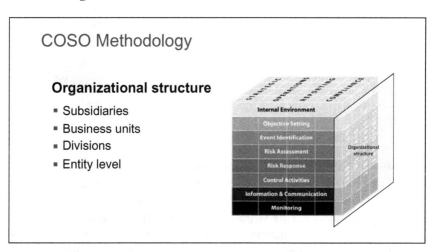

Organizational structure is a management tool which allows the company to meet its goals. An organization whose operational goal is increasing sales will struggle to achieve this goal if its organizational structure lacks a sales unit.

The organizational structure includes **business units** organized in **divisions**, each of which has specific duties, responsibilities and authorities.

When characterizing organizational structure **at the entity level**, the roles of management and its structure are defined as well. Larger organizations often employ a managerial staff in order to operate the entire organization. In order for the organization to operate in an optimal fashion, the responsibilities and authorities of each staff position are defined as well.

8.2.1.3.   *Elements of enterprise risk management*

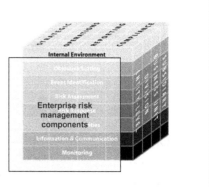

COSO Methodology

Enterprise risk management components
- Internal environment
- Objective setting
- Event identification
- Risk assessment
- Risk response
- Control activities
- Information and communication
- Monitoring

The **internal environment** element refers to organizational culture, ethical values and risk management philosophy, including risk appetite.

Objectives are defined in order to allow managers at various levels to identify potential events which could affect their results. Appropriate goal definition for each management entity in the organization supports the wider organizational goals and remains within the bounds of the organization's risk appetite.

In order to identify internal and external events which affect the goals of each unit, it is important to define, in the best way possible in advance, the risk events and opportunities which could threaten or support organizational goals.

The strategies for **risk assessment**, risk measurement, probability assessment and risk management methodology must be defined for every component on the organizational structure face of the box.

Risk response methods — avoidance, reduction, transfer, acceptance and recovery — must be adapted to the various risk assessments. The risk must be managed in a manner which allows the organization to operate without exceeding the levels of risk it is willing to tolerate.

Control activities are a more detailed assessment of the risks and the ways in which they may be mitigated. This element defines the technological systems which support detection and identification of risks and even calculation of estimates, as well as the work processes for carrying out risk mitigation methods. For instance, reducing risk through employee training requires an array which ensures that every employee, including newly hired employees, receives proper training.

Information sharing and communication within the organization, in such a way that guarantees that relevant information reaches the relevant people in time, is a process which requires careful planning. Effective intra-organization communication must occur at every level of management in order to prevent faults and failures which occur due to inadequate information sharing.

ERM is not a single, momentary action but rather a continuous process requiring constant **monitoring**, adaptation and modification. This is typically done through routine management activity which repeats the initial sequence of actions and streamlines it.

8.2.2. *Risk mitigation decision-making model*

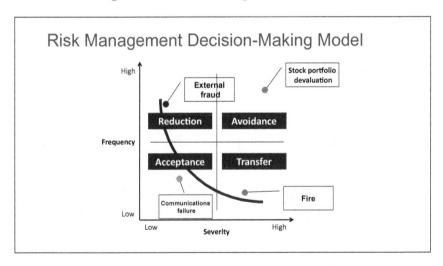

The process of enterprise risk management begins with a mapping of all the risks which have been identified. Each risk is assigned a point on a coordinate system, where the *x*-axis measures the severity of damage and the *y*-axis measures the frequency of the materialization of the risk (e.g., number of failures per year). This mapping should be as detailed as possible, so, for instance, a "fire risk" will be broken down into "fire in the equipment warehouse", "fire in the supply warehouse", "fire in the office building" and so forth.

Large organizations maintain a risk map filled with hundreds of points on the coordinate system.

In this example, we have selected four risks:

- **Low severity and high frequency**

External fraud is an example of a low-severity, high-frequency risk. The severity is low as external fraud tends to involve small sums of money. Instances of external fraud such as theft and forgery occur with a relatively high frequency compared to other types of events.

- **Low severity and low frequency**

Information and Communications Technology (ICT) failures are an example of a low-severity, low-frequency risk. The quality of the technology, the reliability of the infrastructure, maintenance and speed of recovery have turned digital communications into a very reliable instrument, and therefore, in large organizations, such failures occur with low frequency.

Furthermore, even when a failure does occur, the damage is usually quite minor and recovery is quick.

- **High severity and low frequency**

A fire is an example of an event which causes substantial damage (high severity) but occurs infrequently.

- **High severity and high frequency**

A drop in the value of a stock portfolio is an example of an event with high severity as well as high frequency. Due to the constant changes in share prices, an investment in a portfolio composed of stocks may be expected to return a substantial yield in the long term but also significant losses in the short term, which can occur quite often.

The mapping is first performed *before* the risk reduction process is carried out. It provides a visual representation of all the risks faced by an organization and can serve to simplify the decision-making process with regard to risk mitigation. Let us explain:

For high-severity, high-frequency failure events, the best mitigation is typically avoidance. In the example above, a reliable pension fund will most likely choose not to invest in stocks, preferring instead other types of securities with lower levels of risk (and correspondingly lower yields). It thus avoids the risk posed by an investment in a stock portfolio.

High-severity, low-frequency failure events are most often mitigated by the approach of risk transfer. In the example above, the risk is transferred by purchasing an insurance policy which guarantees compensation in the event of a fire.

Low-severity, high-frequency failure events are usually assigned a risk reduction plan. In the case of fraud, this involves increased monitoring of every transaction, integration of technological systems which limit the opportunities for fraud and conducting employee training sessions more often.

Low-severity, low-frequency failure events may not require any risk reduction measures at all. When comparing the cost of the risk reduction measures to the potential damages from such a failure event, we may find out that it is best to simply accept the consequences. For instance, one might purchase flight cancellation insurance, but if the price of a plane ticket is just USD 50, simply absorbing the loss in the event that the flight is canceled might be the better course of action.

How much should we invest in risk-reduction processes? The answer to this question depends on the risk appetite of the organization in question. Using the mapping technique described above, it is easy to set the risk appetite threshold, which is represented by the line going down from left to right. To the left of this line are risks which fall within the limits of the organization's risk appetite. To its right are those risks which exceed the risk appetite of the organization.

Risk reduction measures should cause points on the chart to shift to the left of the risk appetite limit.

In cases where the mitigation is risk avoidance, once the risk has been reduced, the point disappears from the chart.

Where the selected mitigation is risk transfer, the frequency remains as before as we have done nothing to reduce it. However, as with the fire example above, its severity will go down due to the insurance payments.

If we have chosen to reduce the risk, both its severity and its frequency may be expected to go down. In the example above, the new monitoring systems will detect cases of fraud in less time, shortening their duration and preventing the damage from accumulating over time. In addition, the very existence of monitoring systems often deters criminals from committing the crime in the first place. A burglar would rather break into a house with no monitoring systems than a house where a sophisticated alarm system has been installed.

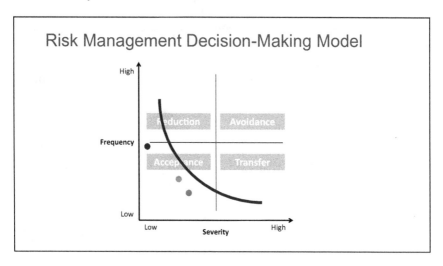

Having carried out risk reduction measures, we redraw the risk map. Most of the dots representing the different risks should now be found to the left of the risk appetite line.

With time, monitoring systems may erode and new risks may form. Many organizations therefore constantly perform a reassessment of risks.

ERM

- Entity-level perspective of risks
- Examination of strategic decisions taking risks into account
- Adaptation of work processes and risk management methodologies to strategic objectives
- Measurement and assessment of risks
- Continuous monitoring and control
- In-depth familiarity with regulation

ERM requires an entity-level view of risks and an examination of strategic decisions from the perspective of risk management. The advantage of the ERM process is that it adapts work processes and risk management methods to match the strategic goals of the organization, all the while measuring and assessing risks. This process compels the organization to perform periodic monitoring and dedicate significant efforts to dealing with regulation.

ERM

- Late for an important meeting? Company car? 1% chance of getting caught by a police officer?

Personal risk management ≠ Enterprise risk management

Personal risk management	Enterprise risk management
99% chance of not getting a ticket	Organization employing 1,000 people
Decision: drive faster to make it in time	Ten traffic tickets every day

---

Personal risk management and enterprise risk management are two different things. Let us explain:

Suppose I am running late for a very important meeting. I'm driving a company vehicle. In order to reach the meeting in time, I can drive over the speed limit. There is a 1% probability that I will be stopped by the police. In other words, I have a 99% probability of making it in time without being caught.

When the decision is personal, most people prefer not to be late for their meeting and drive above the speed limit. An individual would consider a probability of 99% to be a high likelihood of committing the traffic violation without being caught.

In an organization employing 1,000 people, this decision could mean an average of ten traffic tickets every day. In order to reduce the risk, many organizations require that their employees undergo driving instruction or even employ harsh punitive measures, e.g., suspending the violating employee's right to drive a company car for a certain period of time.

Although they both seem to refer to the same risk, the risk management decisions of individuals or small businesses are very different from those of large organizations. Risk managers in large organizations operate differently from their counterparts in smaller organizations.

ERM

- **Regulation**
  - Professional permit (doctor, electrician, investment consultant, etc.).
  - Business permit (adequate environmental conditions and prevention of hazards and nuisances; elimination of safety risks and security measures against break-ins; etc.).

- **Risk management**
  - Overlap in risk treatment ("You're the third person asking me exactly the same thing..." — frustrated employee).
  - Untreated risks ("How could this not be covered by our insurance?!" — frustrated CEO).

Another example demonstrating the differences between personal risk management and enterprise risk management is as follows.

In order to be allowed to work as a medical doctor, one requires a license. Electricians, investment advisors, taxi drivers and many others are also required to hold a license. Each of these professionals conducts personal risk management according to their profession.

An entrepreneur who has decided to bring together several doctors and open a clinic requires a business permit. In order to obtain this permit, the entrepreneur must guarantee adequate environmental conditions and eliminate any hazards or nuisances, prevent dangers to the public well-being and provide protection against burglary, ensure the safety of all the people in the clinic and its vicinity, etc. The transition from profession to business puts the entrepreneur up against a much wider array of organizational risks.

As mentioned above, one way to deal with these risks is by employing ERM. Enterprise risk management allows us to avoid two phenomena which are particularly widespread among organizations:

- **Overlap in risk mitigation:** Different people within the organization are responsible for managing the risks which fall under their area of expertise. Such positions include the risk manager, compliance officer, chief controller, SOX officer and accounting officer. Managers and employees are often required to send the same reports to each of these officials. In most cases, they report the same things but in different ways and using different systems. This is, of course, a waste of time which causes both managers and employees to believe that the organization dedicates more resources to monitoring and reports than it does to production.

ERM greatly reduces such overlap and streamlines the risk mitigation process.

- **Non-mitigated risks:** Without the overall organizational perspective, various risks tend to be overlooked and remain untreated. All too often, when a risk materializes, an organization discovers that it had previously been identified but received no mitigation.

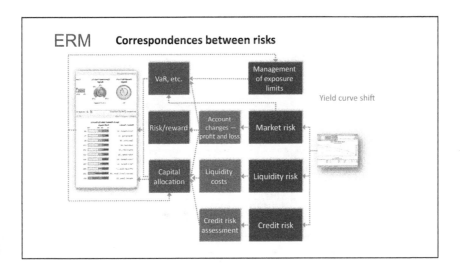

The different risks are often interrelated. Let us suppose, for instance, that there has been a shift in the market yield curve. Such a shift affects the various risk measures pertaining to market risk, liquidity risk, credit risk, etc. These changes in risk measures affect the capital, profits and losses of the organization, which consequently affect additional risk measures such as VaR and capital allocation, which are bound by the organization's risk appetite. Many times, due to the shift in risk measures, the risk appetite changes as well. When market risks go down, organizations tend to increase their risk appetite; conversely, when market risks go up, organizations typically reduce their risk appetite.

As part of the ERM process, it is important to map the effects of different risks on each other. For example, an increase in the liquidity risk of an organization could damage its credit rating. A lower credit rating limits the organization's ability to raise capital at low cost, thus further increasing the liquidity risk. Quantifying the risk and identifying the values which will experience an accelerated growth in risks can only be done with a wide perspective, taking the operations of the entire organization into account.

8.2.3. *Lines of defense*

ERM

- Risk management protocol comprising three lines of defense
- Risk management at different levels of authority in three lines

	Function	Subordination	
First line	Business lines	Business line manager subordinate directly to CEO	The management of the unit taking the risks carries full responsibility for risk management and for implementing an adequate control environment for its activity (four-eyes principle, dedicated control mechanisms).
Second line	Risk management	CEO	Assists management in promoting an integrated, entity-level risk perspective, planning and developing the risk management work framework and setting the work methodology, challenging business line risk management in order to guarantee its integrity and effectiveness.
Third line	Internal control	Board of directors	Examines (typically in retrospect) the integrity and efficacy of risk management procedures in accordance with the organization's objectives and identifies faults in internal controls.

Enterprise risk management is conducted at various levels of authority, arranged in three lines of defense.

The first line is the management of the division undertaking the risk. The management of this division is also responsible for ensuring that the environment is suitable for employing the necessary controls. For instance, in a division responsible for granting credit, the management is expected to set clear protocols for granting (or denying) credit. At the moment of execution, at least two separate officials are required to sign off on the credit transaction. The purpose of this is to reduce human error as much as possible.

At **the second line** stands the organization's risk manager and his or her subordinates. The role of the risk manager is to promote a pan-organizational view of all the risks, plan and develop the working framework for managing risks and guarantee the integrity and effectiveness of the organization's risk management.

The third line is made up of internal controls which retrospectively inspect the propriety and efficiency of the risk management procedures with regard to the organization's goals. It is often these internal controls which detect incidents of internal embezzlement. This detection, however, typically occurs only long after the act.

ERM

Role	Essence
Management and board of directors	Risk/reward decision-making, implementation of organizational culture
CEO	Execution of decisions, risk/reward decision-making, implementation of organizational culture
Deputy CEOs	Comprehensive risk management, each in his or her own field
Risk manager	Control of risk management in all fields, integration at entity level, measurement and assessment according to fields, implementation of culture and employee training, accompanying risk reduction processes, reporting
Junior managers	Risk management and prevention of failures while performing work processes, alerts, reports
Risk controllers	Control of work processes, alerts, reports
Employees	Performing their jobs within an organizational culture of risk management, alerts, reports
External elements (clients, regulators, journalists, etc.)	Opportunity to learn from letters of thanks, complaints, reviews, etc.

The role of the organization's management and board of directors is to make decisions pertaining to risks and rewards. It is at this level that the risk appetite of the organization is determined and risk management methodologies are approved. Another essential role filled by management is establishing and permeating a culture of risk management throughout the organization.

The CEO is responsible for executing the decisions of the organization's managers and shaping its culture. The CEO, as a key figure in the organization, has tremendous influence on its culture of learning from past mistakes and managing risks.

Deputy CEOs are the first line of defense in risk management, each in his or her area of expertise.

The risk manager serves as the second line of defense in risk management and must monitor the risk management processes in the different divisions, integrate them at the enterprise level, measure and quantify risk according to areas and at the enterprise level, establish a culture of risk management, ensure that employees receive adequate training, accompany risk reduction processes and, of course, ensure that reports are written and reach their destinations.

Junior managers are responsible for managing risks and preventing failure during the execution of work processes. They must call attention to dangers and failures and send reports to the relevant people.

The role of the risk controller is to monitor work processes and notify of events as they occur.

The remaining employees perform their duties within an organizational culture of risk management, and they must also send notice whenever an incident occurs so that the risk may be mitigated appropriately.

External elements such as clients who file complaints every now and then, audits by regulators or investigative journalists looking into incidents at different organizations form part of the routine activity of the organization. Such elements can serve as a useful source of information on malfunctions, faults and risks which have been spotted by others outside the organization.

8.2.4. *Reporting*

A reporting culture forms the basis for adequate risk management. Employees often fail to report malfunctions as their managers may respond to the report in an inappropriate manner. Managers often refrain from reporting failures which fall under their responsibility out of fear of punishment. Reporting is essential to risk management. We discussed this topic in detail in the chapter on operational risks and would strongly recommend reviewing the section on reporting in that chapter.

8.2.5. *Risk management systems*

Risk Management Systems

- Tracking and assessment systems
  - Suspected fraud detection, credit risk rating, EGRC
- Financial systems
  - Actuator calculations, capital adequacy
- Control systems
  - Attendance clocks, measurement of temperature and humidity, power consumption
- Reporting systems
  - BI systems, Visual Analytics

Almost all organizations rely on technological systems to achieve their goals. Some of these systems are dedicated to financial risk management, such as follows:

- Enterprise Governance, Risk and Compliance (EGRC) systems are used to manage operational risks and compliance risks.
- Antimony laundry systems are used to comply with regulation pertaining to money laundering and terror funding.
- Anti-fraud platforms track financial crimes.
- Systems rate and manage credit risks.
- Systems manage market risks, send out alerts and calculate the required capital allocation.
- The solvency family includes various systems which perform calculations of risk and capital allocation as well as actuary calculations.

And there are a variety of other systems many organizations employ as part of their enterprise risk management.

Many organizations also employ control systems such as employee clocks and systems which measure temperature, humidity, power consumption and load on computer systems.

Alongside these systems, many organizations also use internal reporting systems which may also assist in risk management.

Without such technological systems, it would be virtually impossible to conduct professional risk management while conducting real-time tracking of the development of organizational weaknesses. Large companies dedicate substantial resources to improving their technological environment as well as their risk management processes.

8.2.6. *Cyber risks*

Risk Management Systems

Cyber risks
- Cyber systems are among the largest producers of organizational big data.
- A protection system produces more data in one year than an organization's clients will generate over their entire lifetime.
- Other than thwarted attacks and failed hacking attempts, the systems provide information on the activity of permission holders who access the system (clients and employees).

Cyberspace, a realm which did not even exist until just a few decades ago, is a new risk which now threatens organizations both large and small, and even states. The human presence in cyberspace has grown exponentially due to the many advantages it offers. Alongside the increase in use, risks have grown as well. Many defense systems have been and continue to be developed in order to cope with these cyber risks. These systems generate vast quantities of data which risk managers can use to their advantage.

Risk Management Systems

Cyber
- In the context of risk management, we may learn about:
  - *De facto* and *de jure* work processes
  - Mapping out bottlenecks
  - Pressure buildups
  - Relevance of controls KRIs

These systems can provide information on the gaps between actual work processes and those which were supposed to be in place. Using various measures, we may map out bottlenecks and backlogs (e.g., by the number of e-mails which reach an employee/department). We can examine the relevance of the various controls (for example, according to the duration for which they are active). Finally, it is also possible to derive key risk indicators from the data provided by the systems (such as an increase in the number of cyber-attacks on the organization).

8.3. Conclusion

Some Final Points

- Integration of organizational culture
  - Reporting, reporting, reporting
- Information systems
  - Data, data, data
- Organizational opportunities
  - We can do more

We began by managing each risk separately and then proceeded to discuss enterprise risk management. Were we to concentrate on the essential points without which modern risk management could not exist, we would choose the following three:

- **Reporting:** Without reporting incidents and sharing information, the organization would have to deal with the same failures every day with no possibility of learning from them. As risk managers, it is crucial to ensure that reports are made in the appropriate manner, sent to the relevant people, analyzed, mitigated and reexamined. The manner in which the report is handled is what allows us to conduct professional risk management.
- **Information systems:** The scope of the information and calculations necessary to generate practical knowledge applicable to risk management requires suitable technological systems. Proper gathering and processing of data and its transferal between different computer

systems, storage and presentation are all crucial components of professional risk management.

- **Organizational opportunity:** Risk management should allow the organization to do more. When risks become opportunities and organizations encounter fewer failures and more successes, it becomes clear that the resources spent on information systems, reporting and risk management in general have paid off!

Bibliography

Association of Certified Fraud Examiners. (2014). Report to the Nations on Occupational Fraud and Abuse (p. 19).

Bank for International Settlements. (2011). Statistical Annex.

Basel Committee on Banking Supervision. (2005). An Explanatory Note on the Basel II IRB Risk Weight Functions.

Basel Committee on Banking Supervision. (2013). Basel III: The Liquidity Coverage Ratio and Liquidity Risk Monitoring Tools.

Basel Committee on Banking Supervision. (2014). Basel III: The Net Stable Funding Ratio.

Crockford, G. N. (1982). The bibliography and history of risk management: Some preliminary observations. *The Geneva Papers on Risk and Insurance, 7*, 169–179.

Dionne, G. (2013). Risk management: History, definition and critique. *Risk Management and Insurance Review, 16*(2), 147–166.

ECB. (2009, February). Working Paper Series No. 1008.

Harrington, S., & Niehaus, G. R. (2003). *Risk Management and Insurance.* Chicago, IL: Irwin/McGraw Hill.

Hasbrouck, J., & Schwartz, R. A. (1998). Liquidity and execution costs in equity market. *Journal of Portfolio Management, 14*(3), 10–16.

Hecht, Y. (2010). Presentation at the Adif Conference.

Hull, J. C. (2014). *Risk Management and Financial Institutions* (4th ed.). John Wiley & Sons.

International Swaps and Derivatives Association (ISDA). (n.d.). www.isda.org.

IRM. (2017). Review of the COSO ERM Frameworks.

MarketAxess. (n.d.). www.marketaxess.com.

Mehr, R. I., & Hedges, B. A. (1963). *Risk Management in the Business Enterprise.* Homewood, Illinois: Irwin.

Merton, R. C. (1974). On the pricing of corporate debt: The risk structure of interest rates. *Journal of Finance, 29*(2), 449–470.

Microsoft. (n.d.). SmartArt.

Moody's. (n.d.). www.moodys.com.

Mugerman, Y., Hecht, Y., & Wiener, Z. (2019). On the failure of mutual fund industry regulation. *Emerging Markets Review, 38*, 51–72. https://doi.org/10.1016/j.ememar.2018.11.010.

Mugerman, Y., Tzur, J., & Jacobi, A. (2018). Mortgage loans and bank risk taking: Finding the risk "Sweet Spot". *The Quarterly Journal of Finance, 8*(4), 1–29. https://doi.org/10.1142/S2010139218400086.

SAS Institute Inc. (n.d.). OpRisk Global Data.

SAS Institute Inc. (n.d.). SAS Enterprise Miner™ API Reference for Python.

Standard & Poor's Ratings Services. (2010). *2009 Annual Global Corporate Default Study and Rating Transitions*. New York, NY: McGraw Hill Financial.

Standard & Poor's Ratings Services. (2015). *2014 Annual Global Corporate Default Study and Rating Transitions*. New York, NY: McGraw Hill Financial.

TradeStation. (n.d.). www.tradestation.com.

Williams, A., & Heins, M. H. (1964). *Risk Management and Insurance*. New York, NY: McGraw Hill.

Williams, A., & Heins, M. H. (1995). *Risk Management and Insurance*. New York, NY: McGraw Hill.

Williamson, S. D. (2008). Illiquidity constraints. In S. N. Durlauf & L. E. Blume (Eds.), *The New Palgrave Dictionary of Economics* (2nd ed.). Basingstoke, UK: Palgrave Macmillan.

World Bank. (n.d.). World Bank Open Data. https://data.worldbank.org.

World Government Bonds. (n.d.). www.worldgovernmentbonds.com.

Yahoo Finance. (n.d.). Apple Inc. (AAPL) options chain.

ZeroHedge. (2012). www.zerohedge.com.

Index

CPSIA information can be obtained
at www.ICGtesting.com
Printed in the USA
BVHW052354120723
667151BV00002B/43

9 789811 271946